DAILY LIFE SERIES NO. 8

DAILY LIFE IN
EIGHTEENTH CENTURY ITALY

Frontispiece : The Marcus Aurelius Gate (Rome)
by Robert Herbert, 1733-1808.

MAURICE VAUSSARD

TRANSLATED BY MICHAEL HERON

DAILY LIFE
IN EIGHTEENTH
CENTURY ITALY

THE MACMILLAN COMPANY

NEW YORK

1963

Translated from the French
LA VIE QUOTIDIENNE EN ITALIE AU XVIIIᵉ SIECLE
(*Hachette, Paris, 1959*)

PRINTED IN GREAT BRITAIN

in 11/12 pt. *Juliana Roman type*

BY BLACKFRIARS PRESS LTD, LEICESTER

FOREWORD

The first thing a study of everyday life in eighteenth-century Italy has to take into account is the basic fact of the country's division into several medium- or small-sized States. Unlike France (even before her centralization), England or Spain, Italy was still only a 'geographical expression', to quote Metternich's phrase. Admittedly, customs and habits of thought throughout Italy had more common features than differences, but variations in governments and traditions created considerable divergences in social status, legislation and economic development, both in the oligarchical republics, such as Venice, Genoa and Lucca, and in the Papal State and the Kingdom of Naples. Even within one and the same circle, such as the ecclesiastical world, unity of thought was more apparent than real; this emerged more and more clearly with the approach of the Revolution and when Italy felt its repercussions.

In fact, perhaps even more than the preceding centuries, the eighteenth was an epoch of contrasts. Everyday life was inevitably influenced as a result. Art alone evinced the tendencies common to all artists in the great variety of temperaments of musicians, sculptors and architects. So our task must be to beware of rash generalizations, at the risk of offending those readers in a hurry to reach conclusions, or those proferring surface impressions, as noted by foreign observers, to the deeper realities, and to specify the dates and places to which our observations refer. We make our advance apologies for anything which may make the narrative more discursive.

FOREWORD

CONTENTS

ILLUSTRATIONS

INTRODUCTION

Perhaps the eighteenth century in Italy was not dominated as in France by events of such capital importance as the Revolution and the movements in the world of ideas which prepared it, nor was it one of the most glorious in literature and the arts, with the exception of music, but the most recent historians of Italy are unanimous that it was the age that saw the development of the minds which during the next century effected the independence and unity of their country, with all the resultant profound transformations. That is enough to indicate the eminent part it plays in the general history of Europe.

At Rome, on the political and religious plane, two pontificates especially stood out among other less illustrious and more ephemeral ones. First, that of Benedict XIV (1740-1758), a highly cultivated Pope, anxious to pacify the quarrels over dogma which were then troubling the Church; tolerant enough to have earned Voltaire's homage and yet adamant against any exaggerated concession to Illuminism. Then Pius VI (1775-1799), a luxury-loving pontiff, but also a builder and organizer to whom the Vatican owes a great part of its existing brilliance; inflexible about anything to do with dogma and discipline; greatly attached to the prerogatives of the Holy See, which he hated to see questioned by a number of Catholic States where enlightened despotism and pretensions to enact legislation even in ecclesiastical matters existed; very dignified at the time of the ignored lessons he gave to Emperor Joseph II, still more moving when he had to bow in his painful old age to the territorial ambitions of Bonaparte. Between these two great Popes, the Pontifical court of Clement XIV (1769-1774) is remembered in history as the one which granted those Western European monarchies which had formed a united front for the purpose of the suppression of the Society of Jesus and the dispersal of its members, a measure which, although not actually revoked, was already modified in practice by Pius VI.

At the foot of the Alps, the Kingdom of Savoy, enlarged by Montferrat, Sardinia and rich well-watered lands on both banks of the Po between Sesia and the Ticino, as the result of the Wars of Succession in Spain and Poland, pursued its slow ascent towards a pre-eminent position in the peninsula. In the middle

13

of the eighteenth century it was still only a small State of some three million inhabitants but well governed by energetic able kings, Victor-Amadeus II and then Charles-Emmanuel III (1730-1773). This very ancient dynasty, its nobility and the people which served it were unique in Italy in preserving lively military traditions which had just made themselves felt once again in the campaigns waged at the beginning of the century. There were no great fortunes there, but poverty was equally rare, except in Sardinia whose recent acquisition (1720) had prevented its rational development. This had been entirely neglected by the Spanish State which had hitherto owned it. The alliances of the House of Savoy with the court of France were continuous from the sixteenth century onwards. In the seventeenth century, as we know, the two daughters of King Victor-Amadeus III married the two brothers of Louis XVI. The French language was on an equal footing with Italian in Turin, just as Savoy was equally geographically and ethnically French soil before she became so politically in 1860.

While this small State was growing, the Republic of Venice, with a smaller population, at the other end of the Po valley, was suffering a decline. The loss of her possessions in the Eastern Mediterranean, the growing importance of new maritime routes, the stagnation of her industries, the neutrality which the absence of an effective armed force had imposed on her in the rivalries of the great powers for more than a century, only left her supremacy in the field of art, elegance and printing, while waiting for Goldoni to ensure European fame for her with his comedies. Together with Naples, she also remained the capital of music and bel canto. But they were small mercies which did not spare her the loss of her independence at the end of the century.

Once it became an Austrian possession, Milan, owing to its central position, its wealth and its intellectual and manufacturing activities, preserved an importance out of all proportion to its small territorial extent. A policy of severe restrictions on ecclesiastical privileges, limitations on religious teaching (or other) orders, and taking over property in mortmain was pursued there by the representatives of Maria-Theresa and Joseph II, who encouraged similar measures in the other Italian States. The

Rome: the Piazza di Spagna and Trinita de'Monti   Photo: Mansell
Rome: the Trevi Fountain   Photo: Mansell

3 Turin: Palazzo Madama (1718),

Photo: Mansell

Venice: S. Maria de la Salute and the Grand Canal by
Canaletto, 1697-1768

Photo: Hachette

University of Pavia, a home of Febronianism[1] and that second, more political than mystical Jansenism which was spreading throughout a large part of Europe at the time from Paris and Utrecht, was the centre of the reformist views which were being propagated simultaneously in Tuscany, where the elder brother of Joseph II, the Archduke Peter Leopold, reigned as from 1765.

But even before that, ever since that once glorious family the Medici became extinct with the death of Giovanni Gaston de'Medici (1737) in an atmosphere of bigotry and corruption, a new spirit reigned at Florence which had become a Hapsburg possession by the Treaty of Vienna (1738). The so-called Regency period during the habitual absence of the nominal sovereign, François of Lorraine, husband of Maria-Theresa, gave the effective power to the Tuscan statesmen who produced a large number of wise government directives, especially in the economic field. They were the initiators, before Turgot's reforms, of allowing the free circulation of grain throughout the Grand Duchy, extended by Leopold himself in 1775 to the free importation of foreign cereals. Thus the perpetual threat of a bread shortage, and the selfish speculations resulting from it, came to an end. An era of agricultural progress began for Tuscany, whose marshy zones in the Maremma were also drained at the same time. Peter Leopold also established the equality of all citizens as regards taxation and he was the first sovereign to abolish capital punishment and torture in his State. He raised the standard of studies in the Universities of Pisa and Siena by selecting first-rate teachers and planned great reforms for improving the recruitment of the clergy, especially by an examination held before priests were appointed and by the suppression of parasitical clerics, but he was unable to overcome the hostility of the majority of the Tuscan bishops to these measures and finally had to give them up.

Between Milan and Tuscany, the Duchy of Parma formed a curious pocket of French influence under a great-grandson of Louis XIV, son of Philip V of Spain and Elizabeth Farnese, the Infante don Philip. An enterprising minister, absolutely devoted to the dynasty, Guillaume du Tillot, Marquis de Felino, who managed to win the confidence alike of the young sovereign, Philip V, his father, and Louis XV, his father-in-law, received practically *carte-blanche* from them to ensure an enviable prosperity for this little State by successful reforms. To it flocked French artists, tradesmen, craftsmen and servants of both sexes. Many of them started families and remained there even after the Revolution. But du Tillot experienced a major setback in the education which he arranged for the heir to the throne, the infant Don Fernando, to receive at the hands of the Abbé de Condillac. This propagator of the 'sensualism', which was so popular in Italian literary circles, was unable either to instil his pupil with the philosophical spirit or to keep him on the paths his father had followed. Influenced by a coalition of malcontents, he brutally dismissed du Tillot (1771) as soon as he became head of the Duchy and replaced French influence in the State by Austrian.

In the neighbouring Duchy of Modena, where the d'Este family reigned, a French princess, daughter of the Regent, had also been introduced by marriage at the beginning of the century, but, frivolous and self-infatuated, she spent more time providing material for scandalous gossip by her squabbles with her hide-bound father-in-law than serving the interests of her new country. No outstanding event highlighted Modena's drab provincial existence during the eighteenth century, except perhaps the building of a small Versailles in the charming ducal residence of Rivalta and the brilliant receptions given there to all the European notabilities passing through the State. The young duchess did not even succeed in keeping her husband within the French alliance. The second half of the century saw him enter the service of Austria as governor and Captain General of Lombardy.

The Republic of Genoa, like Venice, declined at this epoch. Unable to control the revolts of its Corsican subjects, the island came under French domination in 1768, a voluntary cession incidentally, which represented one of the rare diplomatic successes of the Versailles Government in the eighteenth century and did not harm Genoa's good relations with her great neighbour. But her trade, suffering the successful competition of new fleets, no longer had the multiple outlets of the past; her aristocracy no longer included any outstanding personalities and she slipped back into the torpor of ceremonious traditions. She had difficulty in defending her shallow territory along the shores of her gulf against ambitious Piedmont's desire for an outlet to the sea and this made it easy to foretell that she would collapse one day.

There does not seem to be much point in covering Neapolitan life in the eighteenth century in detail since the recent excellent book by Réné Bouvier and André Laffargue will satisfy the curiosity of the most demanding reader. The Kingdom of Naples, with its two sections, one on the mainland and the other in Sicily, was by far the biggest State in Italy at that time, with five million inhabitants, but for a long time it was possibly also the worst administered, the most routine-bound and negligent. The beneficial reign of Charles III and the reforming zeal of his minister Tanucci had successful but short-lived results, for on his return to Spain to succeed to his father, Philip V, Charles III left behind him a feeble and incapable heir, Ferdinand IV, whom his wife Maria-Caroline of Austria, by her intrigues, her frivolity and soon her misconduct, finally made hateful to his best subjects and despised by the whole of Europe. Beneath a brilliant exterior and in spite of the merit of a galaxy of eminent men, whom the vengeances that followed the revolution of 1799 were to wipe out, Naples definitively jeopardized her destiny in the course of the eighteenth century.

B

Part I

THE BACKGROUND

CHAPTER I

THE TOWNS

W ITH THE exception of Naples, no Italian town of the eighteenth century could pass for a very large town from the point of view of population. Even Rome had no more than 150,000 inhabitants before the pontificate of Pius VI.[1] The ring of seven hills enclosed quite as many gardens, vines, ruins and even fields as built-up areas. Animals cropped the grass in the Forum, hence its name of *Campo Vaccino*. In 1739 President de Brosses noted that one-third of Rome was inhabited. The ancient merchant republics, in economic decline, were less populated than at the epoch of their splendour. Venice, which had some 150,000 inhabitants at the apogee of the Renaissance (1586), had only 137,000 two centuries later. From 1701 to 1795, Florence's population only increased from 70,000 to 81,000 and Genoa's from 39,000 to 77,000 between 1682 and 1788. Milan's giddy ascent in the nineteenth and twentieth centuries had hardly begun in the eighteenth, although prosperous industries were developing there. Starting with 120,000 souls at the end of the sixteenth century, depopulated by the plague of 1630, which carried off 85,000 people, the Lombard metropolis had only reached the figure of 130,000 inhabitants in 1790.

Turin doubled its population figures between 1702 and 1791, but still without reaching the 100,000 mark. The small capitals of the duchies, such as Parma and Modena, barely exceeded 30,000; Leghorn, principal port of Tuscany, 40,000; Reggio, 18,000. Illustrious cities such as Pavia, Cremona, Brescia, Ferrara, Vicenza and Lucca were on either side of the 25,000 mark. This explains the surprise felt by travellers, especially from France, at the lack of animation in a fair number of Italian towns which they described as 'poorly populated' (Comte de Caylus).

However, the majority of these towns had a glorious past. Some of them had been or still were the capitals of 'Seigniories', States involved in the whole of Europe's history. The majority possessed wonderful artistic treasures, churches and palaces of a size and richness comparable to the most magnificent edifices of

Paris, Vienna, Prague or Madrid. So we should not judge them solely by the size of their populations.

There even existed in Italy very small towns which contained, for example, opera-houses whose equivalent would only be found in the biggest cities of other countries. Thus the Farnese Theatre, built for the Duke of Parma in the seventeenth century with such skill by J. B. Aleotti, a pupil of Palladio, on the model of the Olympic Theatre at Vicenza, that from its fourteen rows of antique tiers, the two storeys of colonnaded boxes which spread out in a half-oval above, and the enormous 'gods', 4,500 people could see and hear the performance perfectly without the actors having to raise their voices.[2] Or again the communal theatre of Bologna, a masterpiece of classicism, built between 1756 and 1763 by Antonio Bibiena and, on a more modest scale, the theatres which Arthur Young was so astonished to find in 1787 in the environs of Milan, at Lodi, a town of 15,000 souls, and Codogno with only 8,000.

As regards outward appearances, the eighteenth century added little to the physiognomy of the majority of Italian capitals, except Venice. The Middle Ages and the Rennaissance laid their definitive mark on Florence, her baroque churches (San Firenze, San Gaetano) are unimportant, and only the vast Capponi Palace, in the street of the same name, retains our attention as a lay monument of the epoch.[3] At Rome, Genoa and in the Kingdom of Naples, baroque won the day in religious architecture and the princely dwellings of the second half of the sixteenth century: the cycle of these grandiose constructions had almost finished when the eighteenth century began. For the sumptuous galas given in the aristocratic or royal palaces the main additions were some wonderful flights of steps: such as, in Genoa, that of the Durazzo-Pallavicini Palace, by Andrea Tagliafico; at Bologna, that of the Aldrovandi Palace, built in 1748; in the Madame Palace at Turin, the monumental double staircase which occupies the whole breadth of the western façade, commissioned in 1718 from Filippo Juvara by the widow of Charles-Emmanuel II, to reach the new apartments built on to the old mediaeval citadel; while at Rome, Francesco de Sanctis erected in the foreigners' quarter the staircase of the Trinity of the Mounts (1722-1724) with its exquisite perspectives.

As for Milan, with her ancient and glorious past, we find there wonderful examples of every style: old Roman basilicas, the severe Gothic of the Piazza dei Mercanti, the marmorean upsurge of its Cathedral, multiple creations of Bramante's genius, and the ornamental richness of the façades and courtyards of its Litto and Marino Palaces; but the end of the eighteenth century gave it its distinctive character. Without lingering in the charm of rococo, already sensing the use to which Napoleon would put it, it seems as if its architects were to some degree ahead of their time. Pier-Marini, especially in the Belgiojoso Palace and La Scala, from 1776 to 1778, showed himself to be the rival of Gabriel in the most elegant neo-classicism, the sobriety of which Simone Cantoni was to emphasize even more in the Serbelloni Palace.

Venice, like Florence, already possessed its essential characteristics at the end of the Renaissance, but its artists still did much to animate the last century of Italian splendour. On the Grand Canal, Baldassare Longhena, at the end of the seventeenth century, built the Pesaro and Rezzonico Palaces, both finished in the eighteenth century by Giorgio Massari. Massari was architect also of the Grassi Palace, while Tiepolo embellished the Labia Palace with glorious frescoes in which his pictorial virtuosity evoked the story of Anthony and Cleopatra in a typically Venetian setting.

Today these white marble palaces are public historical monuments giving us a convenient view of the background to the private life of the great lords of the eighteenth century, especially the Rezzonico Palace, now owned by the town and wholly furnished in the baroque style. The first storey or *piano nobile* was wholly given over to a series of vast halls extending along the three main façades of the building making it possible to receive the greater part of the Venetian nobility simultaneously. In the eighteenth century it numbered from 4,500 to 6,000 people; but we should deduct from this the young girls who were never seen in society before their marriage, and the majority of young men, as well as nobles with no fortune or *barnabotti*. There remained the heads of families, who shared between them all the magistrates, and their wives. In 1714 there were 1,731 nobles entitled to take part in the Grand Council. Owing to the extinction of numerous families, this figure was reduced to 962 in 1769, but there were always members who were ill or absent; actual attendance was in the neighbourhood of 900 and in fact 600 of them in patrician dress, with 120 of their wives glittering with jewellery, were received in the Rezzonico Palace on the occasion of the arrival in Venice of the Emperor Joseph II in 1769.

The Pesaro Palace (now the Museum of Modern Art) was even vaster. The second storey of these enormous buildings contained small family apartments for parents and children and some domestic rooms; their ceiling height was considerably less. The Grassi Palace, with simpler lines, had a large atrium in the middle of the ground floor, around which rose staircases leading to the first storey and the galleries which overlooked this atrium. Today it houses numerous conferences. The same dimensions recur in the Roman, Genoese and Neapolitan palaces.

These splendours, closely akin to those which had been built in the Renaissance, give an aspect of unrivalled brilliance to certain of the main thoroughfares of the Italian capitals. The most sumptuous in its originality was certainly the Grand Canal, but the Via Balbi at Genoa, the Corso at Rome, the Via Toledo at Naples and squares such as the Piazza San Carlo at Turin, or the Piazza Navona at Rome, were not far behind it in beauty.

However, it was not the brilliance of Italian towns in the eighteenth century which struck travellers from the north, but rather the mixure of magnificence and filth, the low standard of the inns, especially outside the very big centres, and the narrowness and bad surfacing of its streets, which had no pavements. Father Labat, a Dominican,[4] charmed around 1715 by the delightful nature of the Piazza del Popolo, which is the first thing newcomers see on entering Rome by the Via Flaminia, admired the fan-like arrangement of these three long streets called then as they still are today Ripetta, Corso and Babuino, and noted that they contained parts 'which were remarkable for their size and ornaments, but that they were badly paved and extremely dirty, while the fine houses were interspersed with others which were ugly, low and jerrybuilt'. He forgot to point out that on the piazza itself, where goats fed freely, as they did in the Forum, there were one-storey slum buildings to the right and left, inhabited by washerwomen, in the same way as in the streets between the Corso and the Via Babuno, the quarter of models and women of easy virtue. The cemetery for courtesans, incidentally, was situated at the foot of what is today the Villa Borghese. In the Via di Ripetta there were only the humble homes of sailors, coal, wine and wood merchants.

The road system was deplorable. Dust accumulated in the streets in summer and turned into mud as soon as it rained. A few carts, each loaded with a large barrel full of water, did circulate towards the evening in some of the main thoroughfares but they were never seen elsewhere. The barrel was pierced underneath and from the hole emerged 'a leather tube', which a man walking behind swung from side to side to sprinkle the ground. 'They do not know what sweeping means,' Father Labat goes on, 'they leave it to Providence. Heavy rain showers act as brooms in Rome.'

Milan used less primitive but scarcely more effective methods of cleaning. The cleansing of canals, the spraying the streets and the removal of household rubbish were (inefficiently) carried out by prisoners tied to carts in groups of six, with another acting as driver.

At the beginning of the century, Comte de Caylus — admittedly a difficult man to satisfy and one whose artistic judgments in particular are frequently dubious[5]—never stopped decrying the appearance and the paving of the small and even the large cities. Alexandria was 'large, very badly built and very dirty'; he felt the same about Pavia, whose 'irregularity' he also deplored, while at Spoleto and Ancona, built on slopes, he complained of having to walk up and down hill. He said Padua 'is large, it has a very poverty-stricken appearance; it is badly built, its houses lack any trace of beauty and it is extraordinarily badly paved'. He admits that at Ferrara 'the streets are beautiful and well aligned, but that as a whole it is wretched and under-populated'.[6] Even Genoa and Milan found no favour in his eyes. He felt that there was no justification for qualifying the great Ligurian city as 'superb'; as for Milan, 'this town, for all its size, is very badly built, has irregular streets and is extraordinarily badly paved'. It is obvious that he hardly varies his epithets. The southern provinces as far as Calabria inspired him to make even more contemptuous remarks. However, we know that Italy conquered him to such an extent that he gave up an army career for archaeology and letters.

Towards the end of the century, Goethe made similar observations during his travels through Italy. Even at Venice, he remarked on the lack of a public cleansing service worthy of the name. Rubbish was pushed into corners and from time to time large flat-bottomed boats, manned by the people from the neighbouring islands who needed manure, stopped here and there to take the filth away. 'But there is no regularity or strictness about these arrangements and the filthy state of the town is all the more unpardonable because it is so well situated for cleanliness, as much so as any town in Holland. All the streets are paved and even the most remote quarters have a surfacing of bricks set on edge.'

The Olympian traveller was even more shocked to see broad porticoes and majestic colonnades soiled with filth throughout the country, but especially in the south: 'they are made for the people to relieve themselves whenever they feel the urge'. In an inn at Torbole he noted the absence of 'conveniences'; the valet of whom he made anxious inquiries pointed to the courtyard. But whereabouts? *Da per tutto, dove vuole*, was the answer.' At Naples Grosley noted that 'the courtyards of palaces and hotels, the porches of private houses, the staircases and their landings served alike as receptacles for the needs of passers-by; even people in carriages often got out to mix with the pedestrians for the same purpose, each citizen taking the same liberty in other peoples' houses as he would have done in his own'.

The dark nights encouraged this sordid behaviour. Even in the large towns the lighting at night consisted solely of lamps and candles illuminating religious images—although it is true that there were plenty of them. At Florence, in the month of March 1790 alone, a sum was earmarked for the erection of twenty larger lamps. If anyone had to go out, he took with him a bull's eye lantern. To be sure, the quality never went out except in their coaches, preceded and followed by runners carrying lights if needs be, mainly in Naples and Sicily. Even in Caltagirone, an inland Sicilian town, inaccessible to coaches because of the steep slopes leading to it, the nobility used their own carriages for the shortest visits, but at Florence and further north there was less ceremony. In 1728 Montesquieu noted that the men there went on foot and only women used large carriages. There is no town, he added, where the inhabitants live less luxuriously; 'with a dark lantern at night and an umbrella in the rain, one is fully equipped'.

The narrowness of the streets in the old quarters of the big towns made carriage traffic difficult. But turn-outs used to gather towards evening in some of the more favoured thoroughfares, the Corso at Rome, the Marina de Chiaia at Naples (on Sundays, Tuesdays and Thursdays from the end of June to September 8th), at Palermo, the Marina again, or the Cassaro—it was called a Cassariata—and traversed them from one end to the other at least twice. In this way women could enjoy being admired, as they formerly were in Paris in the Avenue des Acacias or the Avenue du Bois-de-Boulogne. On some days at Naples the carriages parked on the promenade of La Mergellina, and the seigniors arrived by sea, with musicians, in richly decorated feluccas, to serenade the ladies from afar. This parking was a ritual at Turin and provided an excuse for the effort of leaving home. People went to take the air in their carriages in a spot away from the town or its immediate environs and stopped there: gallant gentlemen stood by the doors and chatted with the ladies. It seems as if this was a memory of a time when it might have been inconvenient to receive such visits at home. Later they were admissible, but the custom of such apparently random visits persisted in Piedmont.

The steep slopes of the terrain at Genoa, built like an amphitheatre, forced the nobility to use sedan chairs rather than carriages.

The low population density of the majority of towns gave life an intimate aspect, even further emphasized by the fact that many minor trades were carried on in the street, especially most of those to do with food. Potatoes, aubergines and chestnuts were cooked in the open air; fish was fried and offal, meat and chickens sold outdoors. The large numbers of street-stalls attracted clients all the more because the shops were not normally fitted with windows and only bore wooden or iron signs without the proprietor's name. The cardinal's red hat and the priest's black bandeau indicated hatters at Rome (and elsewhere); a pair of scissors indicated a tailor; a brass shaving plate, a barber's; a snake, a chemist; a bleeding arm or foot, a leech; a Turk smoking a pipe, a tobacconist; a barrel, a restaurant; a cock, eagle, bear or sun, an inn named accordingly, a trumpet, a posting station, etc. Rome had some of its own special signs: a Swiss in the Papal Guard meant a lace merchant; while a barber announced without reticence, 'Here we castrate the singers in the papal chapels'.

At Rome again, the various trade guilds were grouped in a single quarter or even in a single street which still bears their names. They are numerous in that part of the ancient city contained in the bend of the Tiber between the Cavour bridge and the Tiberina island: e.g. the streets of the Cappellari (hatters) and Guibbonari (second-hand dealers) on both sides of the Campo dei Fiori; the Falegnami (cabinet-makers) and Funari (rope sellers) between Via Arenula and the Piazza Campitelli; the Pettinari (*pettine*—comb) running the length of the Spada Palace, and the Catinari (nail-smiths) behind Sant'Andrea della Valle. The Coronari had their street and square opposite the Castello Sant' Angelo. Watchmakers were concentrated in the Piazza Capranica, goldsmiths and jewellers in the via Pellegrino, behind the Chancellor's Palace, braziers in the Piazza Navona, rag-and-bone men at Monte Giordano, cardboard makers, transcribers and booksellers from the Statue of Pasquino to the Chiesa Nuova, poultry sellers between the Piazza della Cancellaria and the Piazza della Valle. In the fruit, vegetable and cereal market, which was held every Wednesday in the Piazza Navona, a sort of flea-market was also held among the stands of the charlatans and street-singers.

In many of the medium-sized towns, and even the small capitals, everyone was known, at least within his own social class. The arrival of a distinguished foreigner caused a sensation and he was immediately received in all the best houses. The quarters were usually named after the patron saint of a neighbouring church—there were 110 churches in Turin in the middle of the eighteenth century, 260 at Milan and 81 parishes at Rome, not counting the monasteries and oratories. Private letters were addressed with little more than the saints' name in addition to the addressee's, e.g. 'In Borgo Spesso past the alley of Saint

Jacopo, first door on the left in the Saint Andrea section'. It was not the custom to number the houses and the majority of the streets had no visible names.

Montesquieu was most annoyed by the State authorities' detailed knowledge of the activities, behaviour and exact resources of all their subjects. 'I wouldn't be a subject of one of these petty princes for anything in the world!' he wrote of the King of Sardinia. 'They know everything you do; they always have their eye on you; they know your income down to the last sou; find ways of making you spend it if you are wealthy; send you agents who make you put money into meadows which you have invested in vines. It's much better to be a nobody in the States of one of the great rulers.'

And again: 'The tiniest details about families are known, down to the marriages in the big villages and interest is taken in them'. But these narrow territorial delimitations, coupled with a much more intimate contact than is usual even between rigorously separated social classes, had their good side. At Venice, where the marriage of a nobleman with a plebeian would never have been authorized, the people had a deep affection for the aristocracy and gave them faithful constant service.

Eighteenth-century Italy had her own rather special way of dividing up the hours of the day. The day began half an hour after sunset, when the Ave Maria (Angelus) sounded. The time of midday and midnight varied therefore with the seasons and the latitude. When the night lasted ten hours and the day fourteen, convention had it that sunrise was at 10 o'clock and that it was noon at 5 p.m., i.e. seven hours later, and midnight twelve hours later (7 plus 5), i.e. at 5 a.m. according to our way of counting. Strictly speaking, midday and midnight should have changed only a few minutes every day. But to make life easier the variation was limited to half an hour a fortnight increasing from February 1st to May 15th and stabilized in June and July, when midnight was fixed at 3 a.m.; while from August 1st to November 15th the day decreased by half an hour a fortnight and was fixed in December and January, when midnight was at 7 p.m., only two hours after the Ave Maria was rung, which took place at 4.51 p.m. in Venice on December 31st.

Meals were served—and have continued to be served—later

than in England; during the hot noonday hours the shops at Rome and elsewhere were closed and covered with awnings. Everyone stayed at home, usually to sleep. 'At that time the only people one sees in the streets are dogs, madmen or Frenchmen,' Father Labat remarked.

CHAPTER II
THE COUNTRY

ESSENTIALLY an agricultural country, Italy has always charmed visitors by the care given to cultivating the soil, even with the slow painful methods used before the machine age. Only a few abandoned zones made arid by deforestation and consequently unhealthy, such as the Roman *campagna*, or lying fallow owing to the indifference of the owners to a more rational development of their properties, as in the Sicilian *latifundia*, might have disappointed the foreign visitor. Even the transmontane travellers, who were only too willing to criticize anything they disliked in the towns, greatly admired the sights they saw in the countryside, especially in the north, which was richer and traditionally better worked. Quite apart from the results achieved by human efforts, they were enchanted by the beauties of nature.

An enquiry made in 1704 from one end of the Papal States to the other showed the general satisfaction of the farmers. The provinces of Macerata, Benevento, Spoleto and Faenza replied that there was hardly an acre of uncultivated land between them. The parish of Viterbo estimated that 'agronomy was thriving'.

Passing through the same countries ten years later, Comte de Caylus wrote that the fertile and pleasant plain in which Foligno lies 'reminded him of the vale of Tempe'. The fields 'full of vines and trees' and with many streams running through them were a perpetual delight to the eye. The road from Passignano to Spoleto seemed 'equally magnificent' to him and he was full of admiration for the country around Pavia.

President de Brosses in his turn praised the attraction of the rich and fertile Milanese countryside, which was well planted with handsome trees and skilfully irrigated. 'I am not surprised,' he observed, 'that such a beautiful country should have given rise to such frequent quarrels over its ownership.'

He reverted to the same subject as he approached Venice. 'It may well be that the landscape between Vicenza and Padua alone is worth the voyage to Italy, especially for the beauty of its vines, which are all trained on trees. They cover all the branches and then as they hang down meet other vine shoots dangling from a neighbouring tree and entwine, so that from one tree to another there are festoons laden with leaves and fruit. . . . There is no more beautiful or better decorated opera scenery than a countryside like this.'

Later he never tired of admiring the rich cereal fields of Campania and the Terra di Lavoro.

Grosley, who published his *Observations about Italy and the Italians* in 1764 under the name of two Swedish gentlemen, estimated that Lodigiano was 'possibly the most fertile canton in Europe'. All this rich pastural zone was already producing butter and cheeses whose reputation is still well known throughout Europe.

On the eve of the Revolution, Arthur Young, travelling as a disciple of the Physiocrats, and as gentleman farmer anxious to compare his own experiences with foreign ones, brought to the observation of the Italian countryside a competence which certainly no one before him had carried so far. Oblivious to the charm of Turin, as soon as he reached Asti he was delighted by the appearance of the crops and vineyards. Like the President de Brosses, he felt that the beauty of the outskirts of Vicenza surpassed everything he had seen in Italy, in spite of the deplorable state of the Venetian roads. He estimated that the irrigation system which ensured the rich yields of the corn fields, rice fields and grassland of eastern Piedmont (Vercelli) and Milan, 'was possibly the most important in the world and certainly the first one attempted in Europe since the fall of the Roman Empire'. An assertion which he supported by recalling initiative taken in this field by various landowners in the Milanese countryside from 1037 to the end of the fifteenth century, when Leonardo da Vinci united the canals supplying Milan with water.

Goethe, crossing Tuscany at the same epoch, watched the farmers around Arezzo ploughing with a wheel-less plough and a rigid share which required exhausting efforts on the part of the man pushing it behind the oxen. He remarked that only a little very light manure was laid by hand and that yet the results were excellent. 'It would be impossible to see better kept fields; not even a clod is left, everything seems to have been passed through a sieve. The wheat crop is all one could wish for. Every

5   *Above* : Piaz
Navona by
Canaletto
1697-1768
Photo: Giraudo

Left : Syracu
the Cathedra
Photo: Manse

second year they sow broad beans for the horses, which are never given any oats here. They also sow lucerne. It is already a wonderful green and will be harvested in March.' On arrival in Sicily, he was not sparing with his praise of the 'extremely beautiful . . . superb . . . incomparable' corn which he saw there and which was harvested in some regions from May 20th onwards. There was not a single weed in the enormous fields. One of these species of corn, sown from January 1st onwards, ripened in three months. It needed little rain but great heat and so was perfectly suited to the Sicilian climate. Barley, sown in November, could be cut at the beginning of June, earlier near the coast and later in the mountains.

Flax was ripe from April onwards. Melons planted in March were ready to eat in June. At the end of April he saw almond trees laden with nuts and fig trees whose already fertilized figs would be ripe by mid-June. He was astonished by all this.

However, the peasants who gave the Italian countryside this luxuriant appearance lived very poorly. Throughout southern Italy—and this situation was not to improve until the present day—they were crowded without the least comfort, without furniture, almost without water, undernourished, poorly clad and completely illiterate in large villages sometimes equal in size to towns, but situated several miles from the fields which they had to cultivate.

In the mountainous regions of Apulia, Lucania and Calabria they were completely isolated. The country was quite devoid of reliable well-kept roads, and the rivers, which were often in flood, had no bridges. There was no question of a school system.

Undoubtedly the worst conditions were found in Sardinia, where the enormous domains of certain Spanish grandees were even more abandoned than those of the Sicilian barons.[1] The water there was so brackish or salty that the Marquis de Saint-Remy, who was viceroy there on two occasions, used to have his own water sent from Pisa, so Montesquieu tells us. Sometimes one could travel twenty miles without seeing a tree or a house. Left to themselves, the peasants never did anything which their fathers had not done before them, not even cutting the grass to feed cattle in the winter because it was not the custom. They

C

lived in huts where the only outlet for the smoke was a hole in the roof.

Life was less wretched the further north one went. In Tuscany, a region where métayage* was practised, the domains of the clergy and the nobility were also large, but the owners spent a part of the year on their properties and the *métairies* (*fattorie*) of reasonable size were well distributed throughout the countryside and introduced a lively element. At the beginning of the nineteenth century the Tuscan aristocracy showed a very keen interest in agronomy, both theoretical and practical.

The vast plains of the Po valley were not particularly favourable to peasant ownership (although it became widely prevalent in the next century); the digging of irrigation channels, the upkeep of rice fields needed considerable capital. *Métayage* was practised there, depending on the zones, simultaneously with farming proper, especially in Emilia and Veneto, but the *métayers* there lacked resources.

They could not procure cattle nor pay their taxes in cash. At the end of the century Arthur Young attributed this poverty to the inadequate size of the farms. 'The supporters of small-scale farming,' he wrote, 'should come here to learn how they are inevitably ruined in the end.' Only the big properties in the Milan district, devoted to rice growing and pasturage, seemed to be really prosperous.

In Piedmont, especially its mountainous districts, and in the Lombardy mountains, the small rural property on the other hand was already highly developed (and has remained so). The land there is fertile and the peasants, Montesquieu remarked, were sometimes as rich as their masters, which was not saying much. We know that this country supplied Italy's best soldiers at the period, one could almost say the only ones. Their state of mind was rather like that of the Swiss militia, but attachment to cantonal liberty was replaced in their case by monarchical loyalty. The Revolution found few recruits here.

In both the smiling and the abandoned countrysides the nobility mainly owned 'villas'. There were hardly any castles in Italy except in the Alpine valleys for the defence of passes and

* A system by which a farmer pays a fixed proportion of the crops, instead of money rent. Translator's note.

cols—for example in the Valle d'Aosta—but they were often more or less in ruins. Undoubtedly the wonderful Medici villas at Careggi and Cafaggiolo, built in the fifteenth century, with their few windows covered with iron grilles and their thick walls crowned with austere corbelling, recall the period of civil wars. Some families still lived in vast residences dating from remote epochs, such as the counts of Collalto in Venetia, the barons Ricasoli at Brolio, near Siena, the Odescalchi at Ladispoli in the outskirts of Rome. But the Roman princes and the rich Venetian merchants set the fashion in the sixteenth and seventeenth centuries by building in the midst of lovely gardens full of statues and terraced with broad flights of steps with numerous fountains and rockeries, the famous villas of Frascati, Genzano and Castelgandolfo or those at Venice lining the Brenta Canal, a country extension of the Grand Canal, which were praised by every visitor to Italy in the Settecento.[2]

Here again the eighteenth century added little to the creations of the preceding age. However we must mention the magnificent Villa Albani (now Torlonia) built for the luxury-loving cardinal Alexander Albani by Carlo Marchionni in 1757 in a baroque style already steeped in classicism, with its arcaded ground floor, its two storeys with Corinthian pilasters and its vast gardens on the French model. But in this case we can scarcely talk of the country, for this residence is situated at the gates of Rome. Cernobbio's Villa d'Este dates from the sixteenth century but includes eighteenth-century decorations in its gardens, particularly the rococo flight of steps. At Stra, the Villa Pisani, built in 1740 by the Procurator of San Marco, Alvise Pisani, was enriched in 1762 by a Tiepolo ceiling in its magnificent ballroom. The villas of the Foscari, the Contarini, the Erizzo and the Farsetti on the Brenta were very nearly as attractive.

CHAPTER III

FURNITURE AND COSTUME

THE VAST size of the Italian palaces needed both good taste and fortune if the interior decoration and furniture were to match the splendour of the façades. Some patrician families managed to achieve this, especially in Venice, but their success was far from general. Between the floor tiled with marble and the ceilings coffered with gold, or frescoed, or decorated with sculptured figures and draperies, the baroque style lavished chandeliers of Murano glass, mirrors, decorative paintings framed in stucco or heavy wood, ebony statues of allegorical figures, couches, consoles and spacious lacquered or gilded armchairs, generally with rather over-elaborate shapes.[1] There was no denying the impression of wealth they produced and there were some real treasures in these palaces, but the general effect was strangely lacking in intimacy and not always in the best of taste.

At this point one must be allowed to challenge the opinion of Signor Pompeo Molmenti—it is hard to decide whether to attribute it to a curious lack of knowledge or an excess of national pride—when he maintains that the Louis XV furniture made by French cabinet makers is inferior to that produced in Italy at the same epoch, if not in Tuscany and further south, at least in Milan, Genoa, and especially Venice. To him Brustolon and his pupils seem once again to have established Italian supremacy in artistic matters. 'No one could deny that the Venetian pieces in carved wood are so pure of line and slender, so new and charming that nothing can compare with them', writes this usually more cautious historian.[2] Anyone who has been able to compare the furniture in the Louvre, at Versailles or in the auctions of the Galerie Charpentier with that for example in the Rezzonico Palace or the Correr Museum, rich in furniture by Brustolon, would soon demolish such an untenable preference, unless the rococo which flourished in the eighteenth-century Venice—at the same time as at the other end of the peninsula, at Lecca—is considered as one of the high points of art.

We do not feel impelled to share the regrets of President de Brosses and many visitors to Italy in the eighteenth century that the love of luxury and outward show common among the Italians made the rich men who could do so devote their revenues to building vast residences rather than lavishing them on banquets whose memory was soon forgotten. If the gourmets were discomfited, posterity can be grateful to the aristocracy of the peninsula. However, it is true that it was almost impossible to furnish these enormous buildings. The waggish Burgundy magistrate wrote of the Borghese Palace:

'All these great apartments, which are so vast and so superb, are only there for foreigners: the masters of the house cannot live in them, since they contain neither lavatories, comfort nor adequate furniture; and there is hardly any of the latter even in the upper storey apartments which are inhabited. . . . The sole decoration in the rooms consists of pictures with which the four walls are covered from top to bottom in such profusion and with so little space between them that to tell the truth they are often more tiring than attractive to the eye. On top of this they spend hardly anything on frames, the majority of them being old, black and shabby, and for all the tremendous number they crowd in they have to mix a fair quantity of mediocre works with the beautiful ones.'

What he says here about the Borghese Palace could equally be applied to the Doria-Pamphili Palace; at Genoa to the two Brignole-Sale (*Bianco* and *Rosso*) Palaces; quite recently at Florence to the Corsini Palace, and a quantity of others unknown to the public. These collections abounded in canvases of the Bolognese school, by Annibale Carracci, Guercino, Albani, Guido Reni, Bernardo Strozzi, Sassoferrato and their rivals, as well as works by Sustermans and productions by minor Dutch, Flemish and Venetian painters. The way they are crowded together is tiring to the eye and distracts the attention which two or three masterpieces deserve.

Although paintings filled many Italian palaces, they contained nothing by way of protection against cold weather, which can happen, after all, even in a southern country. Tapestries were rare, carpets were very seldom used and shutters and heating non-existent. Although there were generally fireplaces in the north, they disappeared the further south one travelled. Montesquieu remarked on this at Florence in 1728. He was told that a fire was unhealthy, but he assumed that a desire to save money had a good deal to do with the established custom. To warm their hands, people used *scaldini*, small earthenware pots full of charcoal and fitted with a handle. Permanent stoves (*foconi*), also burning charcoal were found in a few places. At Rome they were not lit in the sacristies and the antechambers of bishops or even cardinals until after 25th November. In the middle of the century nearly all the windows were fitted with glass, but sixty years earlier they were very often lacking in modest houses.

At the time of Montesquieu's journey, Father Labat was struck at Tivoli by the poverty of the furniture in the houses of merchants who passed for rich men.

'I would have been very angry if I had had to give fifty écus for all their furniture,' he wrote. 'A few old arm chairs, a few bad pictures, a mirror the size of your hand, together with some tables and badly made chests; that makes up the inventory.'

Plates and dishes were of clay and earthenware; they were coarse and clumsily made. And he estimated that in the whole town there were 'less kitchen utensils than in one mediocre hostelry on the way from Paris to Orléans'. Even in Roman middle-class circles, which were a little wealthier, the furniture was heavy and dark, the chairs uncomfortable, armchairs unknown and the general effect austere, cold and formal. Only orange and lemon trees, and flowers in window boxes when the house had a terrace, added a note of gaiety to this austerity.

French visitors to Sicily made similar remarks at the end of the century. Roland, the future Girondist minister, who made a trip to the large island in 1776 and described it in his letters to his fiancé, found that none of the lower classes had beds, but only a few rush or reed mats on which those who possessed them spread out one or more overcoats if it was necessary. They went to bed fully dressed and 'their toilet takes about as much time as a dog's: they shake themselves and there they are on their feet . . .'.

The nobles and middle classes in the small towns were scarcely any better off. They had plenty of space in their dwellings but their curtainless beds were of the model tried by Goethe: miserable mattresses spread on planks supported by trestles. In addition they had a few leather or cane chairs and worthless tables. At Licata, Roland saw one of these beds in the games and conversation room of his hosts' house, with clothes thrown over the tables. Walls and ceiling were coated with plain distemper which time had turned brown. Sometimes small mirrors with large frames of dyed wood crowded with baroque decoration were hung too high to be used. If there was any gilding, dust and cobwebs covered it. Even in Catania, Roland found a desire for luxury associated with slovenliness and discomfort; 'Bedrooms with a bed covered with silk, gilded panelling, windows and ceilings of reeds through which the tiles and the daylight could be seen'. Even in the palaces, with walls hung with damask, the only seats were hard straight-backed chairs of the type on which valets slept in the antechambers when they had no pallets on which to lie.

Eighteenth-century Italian furniture, then, offers one example of the extraordinary contrasts, far exceeding the variety of social stations, which we mentioned in the Foreword as one of the characteristic features of the epoch.

The costume of the patrician is particularly worthy of interest in the oligarchical republics of Venice and Genoa, where all the public offices were concentrated in their hands. The memory of the Roman Senate undoubtedly guided their thoughts, closely associated with a sincerely professed religion when the Christian faith remained active and with the habits of economy which created the wealthy houses. All that had fallen into disuse in the eighteenth century, but it still inspired the sumptuary laws which were gradually transgressed even by the men who had promulgated them and their wives. However, traces have lingered on to the present day, for example, in the very simple decoration of Venetian gondolas which are uniformly painted and upholstered in black.

The main item of male dress for Venetian noblemen was the *veste patrizia*, a sort of Roman Toga assumed at the age of twenty as the insignia of their dignity. It consisted of an ample cassock falling to the feet, with very full sleeves, made on woollen cloth and lined with fine furs in winter, of silk in summer, and coloured black, violet, red or cream according to rank and employment. The senators and procurators of San Marco wore *veste* of purple damask, embroidered with broad rich leaf-work, and stoles of cream velvet. The other patricians had to be satisfied with plain undecorated colours, mainly violet, as a sign of equality. It is the costume which we see on the important personages portrayed particularly by Titian, Tintoretto and Paul Veronese. Their headgear was round and brimless.

But the young people wanted to introduce innovations. As early as 1668 a member of the Grand Council attended it in a *tabarro*, the large round cloak with a turned-back collar which became the fashion for both sexes in the eighteenth century and constantly appears in the pictures of Guardi and Longhi, generally accompanied for women by a *mantellina* covering the shoulders and bust. But the Council of Ten was on the watch and took swift action. In 1704 it threatened any noble who appeared in public without a *veste* with five years' imprisonment and a fine of 1,000 ducats.

It was already too late; this decree was never applied, in spite of reports by secret agents who denounced nobles seen about town in the *tabarro*.

The toga was no longer worn except in the Ducal Palace and remained there in vestiaries appropriated under the Procurator-ships, as the more modest lawyer's robe does today in the law courts.

Paris and London fashions, both in dress and hair styles, invaded the peninsula. At first the wig was forbidden. But even in 1668 Count Scipione de Collalto, returning from a Paris embassy, appeared in the Piazza San Marco in a large wig. The traditionalists fought a stubborn battle against the new custom. Antonio Correr founded an association of 250 patricians who swore never to wear a wig; when he died in 1757 he was the only one who had remained faithful to his vow.

In 1688 the Council of Ten had strictly prohibited the wearing of a wig with the toga—which implies a tacit tolerance in other circumstances. In fact, as early as 1702 an album of Venetian sketches shows the highest magistrates, including the doge, wearing wigs. Wigs even appeared on the portal of churches (on the façade of Santa Maria Zobenigo, built in 1678, five members of the Barbaro family can be seen, three of them with wigs) on the funerary monument of the Doge Pesaro, which dates from

1699, and elsewhere. In 1701 the custom was more or less general.

The French style of dress also crossed the Alps under the name of *velada*. From the beginning of the eighteenth century nobles and middle classes adopted this elegant garment, open wide across the chest with large side pockets and false back pockets. Modifications in the cut were slow and of minor importance. Coat tails, at first cut straight across in front, became rounded and very close fitting towards the middle of the century. Then from about 1765 to the fall of the Republic, especially in ceremonial costumes, coat tails were gathered from the waist downwards and formed a sort of fan of deep pleats, before becoming smaller and disappearing towards 1790 under the English influence of the frock coat and the dress coat.

Coat tails were supposed to be some distance from the body. Certain Venetian dandies fitted them with whale bone or pieces of gilded leather called *cuor d'oro*. The borders of the *velada* were embroidered in front. The tailors best acquainted with the Paris fashions brightened up this embroidery with imitation precious stones of cut glass. They used buttons of gold, silver, burnished steel and polychrome porcelain decorated with flowers and various emblems. Gold braid and tassels completed the costume.

Underneath the *velada* was worn the long waistcoat or *camisiola* of gold and silver brocade or flowered silk, which was sometimes laced up behind with cords also made of silk.[3] The short breeches were made of *casimir* or *nankin*. Lace frills were attached to the shirt of embroidered linen. And the grey, beige or scarlet *tabarro* covered the whole, accompanied for men by a large fur muff in which they kept their cards and money. Morning dress for nobles was a black deeply pleated *tabarro* with a very broad collar.

The development of women's dress and behaviour was perhaps even more marked at Venice. Before the eighteenth century startling colours and make-up were the signs of a courtesan. Noble and middle-class ladies only dressed in black and hardly ever left their houses except to go to church. If they had to go out in a gondola, two old serving maids accompanied them.[4] In 1766 the astronomer Jérôme de Lalande still praised them for not wearing any rouge (he had already made a similar observation at Turin). He noted that they often had their hair tied with a simple ribbon and went bare-headed to the theatre even 'in the best boxes'. He thought that they were less under the influence of the French fashion than in other Italian capitals, for the Senate and the *Magistrato alle Pompe*—a sort of official arbiter of what was and what was not allowed in sumptuary matters—opposed the entry of fashion magazines into the territory of the Republic. But Lalande was wrong about this. Even without magazines to teach them, the milliners (*crestaie*) and dress-makers exhibited in the windows of the Merceria a large dummy (*piavola de Franza*) dressed in the London and Paris fashion, which the Venetian ladies gazed at with passionate curiosity.[5] And the decrees made in 1707, 1709 and 1732, forbidding women (except young girls) to wear garments of other colours than black under penalty of a fine of 250 ducats, were violated with impunity, as the decrees about men's dress had been. The decree of 1732 also prohibited trimmings of lace, fringes, embroidery, printing and all gathered or stiff ornaments on the cloaks—the *tabarrini* and *mantelletti*. Only the *falbala* were allowed.

To tell the truth, these finicky provisions serve rather as evidence of what had already become accepted usage. At the beginning of the century the *andrienne* appeared. It was named after the costume worn in 1703 at the Comédie Française by the actress Mimi Dancourt in Baron's adaptation of Terence's play *l'Andrienne* (The Woman of Andros). Revealed to the well-dressed women of Venice in 1721 by the new Duchess of Modena, Charlotte-Aglae of Orleans, daughter of the Regent, the *andrienne* remained in fashion until the fall of the Most Serene Republic. As in France, it was held out below the waist by hoops and was generally attached to the skirt and the low-cut bodice. The borders of skirts were embroidered or pleated, the dress included a train of only about eight inches, but long frills of lace hanging down from the cuff (*cascate*) formed a ruinously expensive trimming.

The wig had a less immediate success with ladies of quality than with their husbands. In the seventeenth century they were attached to a hair style which was already architectural but still natural, set off with ribbons, lace, flowers and jewellery. Nevertheless the *tupe*[6] of false hair finally experienced such a vogue, even among the lower classes, that in 1797 there were 852 wig makers, including 534 foreigners,[7] in Venice. The hair they worked with was imported, mainly from Parma and Tuscany, but also from Belgium, the favourite colour, a pale blonde, corresponding to a natural tint which was very common among young Flemish peasant girls.

The first form of feminine wig comprised a row of curls around the forehead and a long tress falling to the shoulder. As in France, the size and height of these head-dresses went on increasing as the end of the century approached. A multitude of pins of all shapes in gold or silver filigree were inserted into it. Scaffoldings like these could nevertheless only be worn without a hat. The graceful three-cornered hat, identical for men and women, which during carnival and masked balls went so well with the *bauta*, that strictly Venetian black veil, covering the head, framing the face and surrounding the shoulders, called for an almost flat hair style. Also in use at Venice, but at Bologna and in Emilia as well, where Lalande mentioned it in 1765, was the *zenda* (or *zendaletto*), a long band of very fine black silk, sometimes bordered with lace and fitted with a light framework of iron wire so that it would not disturb the *tupe*: it replaced hats and fichus and was tied at the waist allowing only the face or a part of it to be seen for reasons often connected with coquetry rather than modesty.

As a cloak, the *tabarrino*, usually white, embroidered with gold and silver, which came to knee level, had become popular with all the patricians in the middle of the century, with a small fur muff and often a fur tie around the neck. The famous picture by Guardi, the *Ridotto*, shows excellent examples of these Venetian fashions.

Hand in hand with this rich finery went a whole gamut of precious trinkets: lorgnettes, snuff-boxes, bottles for smelling salts, boxes for beauty spots and for men *smaniglie* or *polsetto*: an oval gold plaque attached to a black ribbon tied round the wrist.

To tell the truth the practical tolerance of the high authorities of the Republic *vis-à-vis* this display of luxury is explained not only by the difficulty of reacting against fashions which were gaining ground all over Europe, but also by the patricians' need, at a time when traffic was growing from country to country and when a multitude of important personages was flocking to Venice, to receive them at home, since there were still no genuine comfortably appointed hotels even in the big towns, as we shall see in the next chapter. In order to welcome Joseph II, Gustav III of Sweden, the Prince of Wurtemburg and a large suite, and later members of the Russian Imperial family travelling under the name of 'Counts of the North', the Venetian aristocracy showed themselves as sumptuous as the kings of the great powers. They made it a point of honour to dazzle them.

Elsewhere, official regulations were generally better respected, luxury was less widespread, although the cut of garments conformed more and more to Parisian models.[8]

We have gone into the Venetian fashions in some detail because society life at Venice was most brilliant in the eighteenth century.

At Genoa, President de Brosses noted that "all the nobles are uniformly dressed in black, wear a small wig tied to the ears, with a small cloak', in the same way as the majority of the townspeople (in winter this cloak was of black velvet, in summer of taffeta among the aristocracy). The wives of nobles were forced to wear black, unless it was their first year of marriage.

At Lucca, too, black was the only colour worn by the nobility, except in the country.

In Rome and its environs Father Labat noted towards 1715 that the normal dress for men—few of whom wore wigs—was in the French style or nearly so, but 'as it was worn in the time of the war with Holland', i.e. thirty years behind the latest fashions. The same observation was made in Sicily towards the end of the century by Roland about women's clothes, even those of high rank, but with a time-lag of only a few years.

Moreover the islanders liked to preserve some originality in relation to the mainland. Their elegant women wore dresses of muslin embroidered or bordered with very distinct colours and embellished with gilded or silvered trimmings. They were equally as fond of the lace, jewellery and frippery of London and Paris as their contemporaries in Venice and Rome, but they also wore bracelets of fine pearls, with portraits of the king and queen in cameos, other cameos as earrings, and necklaces of amber or coral from Trapani which marked them down as Sicilians. On their bare heads a silk or coloured gauze ribbon embroidered with silver was tied round their unpowdered tresses. The French sketcher Jean Houël, who was in Sicily at the same epoch as Roland, but spent four whole years there from 1776 to 1780 and brought back a mass of engravings and gouaches, saw ladies wearing a broad braided hat, turned up at the sides and down in front, their dark hair plaited in a pigtail behind in accordance with the masculine fashion of the epoch in France: that had nothing in common with the Venetian tricorn or *tupe*, nor did the frequent absence of body linen which surprised and shocked foreigners. It was only for their devotions that the Sicilian women differed slightly from the Bolognese and other southerners: a large cloak of wool or black silk, often falling to the ground, covered their head and body, only leaving an opening at eye-level, when they went to church. The women of the people wore the same garment, only of coarser material; everyone carried a rosary hung outside the cloak.

At Florence and Bologna 'a craze for English fashions' raged, but the fashions themselves came from France. So they were always Paris fashions. The middle classes wore blouses hugging the waist, with close-fitting sleeves and buttoned from chin to waist. Their headgear was a 'butterfly coif pointed at the sides and excessively long' (Lalande). Young women, who were not allowed to go out walking until they were engaged and then only with their husband-to-be, had a small head covering of transparent black gauze turned down over the face to the bottom of the nose.

At Milan, towards the middle of the century, Maria-Theresa issued edicts, like those of the Council of Ten, aimed at checking luxury. One of them forbade embroidered cloths, gold and silver lace and foreign fabrics under penalty of severe fines. The tailor who made the clothes lost his licence and became liable to three months in prison. It was forbidden to gild carriages, frames, mirrors and panelling, to buy imported precious stones or even to offer them as wedding presents. The tassels, plumes, knots of ribbons and other trappings for horses were only permitted on the teams of Excellencies and Senators.

They also attempted to regulate mourning, which entailed unnecessary expenditure. Detailed edicts on similar lines appeared in Milan and Florence, signed in Tuscany by the Prince de Craon, the representative of François de Lorraine. The maximum duration was fixed at six months for spouses, parents and grandparents; at three months for children, grandchildren, sons-in-law and daughters-in-law, brothers and sisters, uncles and nephews; at one month for a brother-in-law, sister-in-law or cousins; at eight days for other relations.

At Florence, all the heirs who did not belong to the first four degrees of kinship were authorized to wear mourning for one month. On the other hand, mourning was forbidden for children of both sexes of less than eighteen years, unless they were married.

In winter the clothes allowed had to be made of black broadcloth or some other woollen fabric for men, with crêpe on the hat, sashes of undressed leather or reversed fur, sleeves with white bands (reserved for nobles) for six weeks; for the remainder and for mourning of less than six months black clothes of wool, velvet or silk with no ornamentation. Women, whatever their social status, were not allowed to own more than two deep mourning costumes at any time of the year. At Florence the way they were to be worn was laid down in great detail: no lace or jewellery during the first three months, afterwards with black silk or Cambrai linen, white veils, fine muslin and ornaments of burnished steel 'which did not come into the class of jewellery'. It was forbidden to dress domestic staff in mourning clothes, to paint carriages black and to put black ornaments on the walls of churches for funerals.

These provisions and others of the same kind were less ineffective at Milan than at Venice. Nevertheless Milan, which together with Paris supplied the Peninsula with cloth spangled with gold and silver, was not the last city to use it; the *tupe* covered with gold powder and wigs containing silver thread enjoyed a great vogue there. An irresistible movement drove all the rich classes towards luxurious display until the Revolution.

Simple charm, on the contrary, characterized the clothing and hair style of the people, especially the peasant girls. The observations made by foreigners are unanimous on this point, although the great lords such as Caylus and Montesquieu did not pay much attention to it.

Lalande showed himself much more attentive to the popular classes. He thought the Tuscan peasant girls very beautiful—more so than the Roman girls—rather coquettish and very clean. At the end of the century Young confirmed this. They had beautiful complexions, very expressive eyes and were 'most charmingly dressed' with bodices with gathered puffed sleeves, trimmed with coloured ribbons, and wide-brimmed hats 'like those of the Amazons in England'. Lalande had seen them twenty years earlier in the neighbourhood of Pisa and Florence with blue or scarlet skirts, sleeveless bodices showing the sleeves of their chemises, a collar of scarlet wool round the neck and falling half-way down the back behind. They wore a very small straw hat at a tilt, artificial flowers in their hair and two rows of silver pearls above their chignons, plaited and held in place with a large silver hairpin. At the same epoch Mme du Bocage, surprised to see them with such pretty faces and figures, was astonished that they frequently went about bare-footed and bare-legged but with 'necklaces and bracelets of all kinds' and said that they were comparable to the country girls in the choruses of operas on the Paris stage. In Emilia the country girls also had plaited hair and straw hats, and their throats were covered with a batiste collar bordered with fine lace.

In Campania the women of the Gaeta region were tall, well built and had a charming hair style: hair plaited with ribbons which they passed from the side of the head to the nape of the neck where they ended 'in a way which suits them perfectly'. The wives and daughters of sailors wore open corselets with blue and red skirts. The same hair style had also been noticed by Lalande among the very pretty peasant girls of Vicenza, which proves that it was not confined to a particular part of Italy. Under their straw hats they stuck a rose or a carnation in their hair. Around Venice he saw the same flowers with their stems worn behind the ear, together with large pendants. President de Brosses also noted in his exaggerated way that the women of Vicenza covered their heads 'with three or four thousand pins with large tin heads'—following the example of the patrician ladies who used pins of precious metal—and that the women of

Padua wore a large mantle of black satin falling down the back and worn like a scarf in front.

The pictures of the minor Venetian masters tell us far more about the costumes of the people of Venice than any of the travellers' accounts. For women the distinctive feature was the fullness of the ankle-length skirts, generally worn with a charming apron, short sleeves, pointed corselets and very low cut if the wearer was a coquet, sometimes a white veil around the shoulders or a small shawl ending in a point behind, elegant shoes as if the wearer was always ready for the dances which so frequently attracted the *popolane* to the *campicelli* with which Venice was dotted.

At Rome and in the Papal State the dress of the men of the people consisted of a velvet vest which did not reach to the waist and was most often thrown over the shoulders, a waistcoat of the same material barely covering the chest and a white shirt with no tie. The waist was held in by a large coloured belt; the breeches, similar to the vest, were fastened by a buckle below the knee. They wore coloured stockings and leather shoes with large silver-plated buckles curved at the sides and touching the ground. The hat was tall, hard and round like those worn by coachmen of old, but with brims turned up high at the sides and often with freakish trimmings on the crown. Carters had their legs protected by a leather gaiter fastened with a clasp and wore a pointed hat of the 'Calabrian' type decorated with cocks' feathers, with a long net hanging down to the shoulders.

The women's jacket of coloured velvet cotton, with collar and lapels decorated with lace, was called a *carmagnola*; the Spanish-style sleeves, full at the shoulder, were gathered at the wrists. The dress, of the same material and colours, fell to the instep. Women wore the same shoes and stockings as the men, with the same sort of decoration. Usually a broad apron of embroidered voile was worn over the skirt. A big silver comb curved back towards the neck held the bulk of the hair in which was inserted a long pin (*stiletto* or *spadino*), serving both as an ornament and a weapon of defence. Their jewellery consisted of pearls or coral earrings and gold or coral necklaces.

In Sicily, a land of great poverty, the cheerful note which flowers or ribbons added to the everyday dress of the women of

6   Venice: A Reception, by F. Fontebasse

Venice: Masqueraders by Pietro Longhi, 1702-85

7 Venice: The Nun's Parlour by Francisco Guardi

Photo: Mansell

the people disappeared. They wore a dress of black serge (*orbace*) or linen with dark stripes, recalling the colouring of Greek vases, and a bodice of fleecy cloth with small red and black checks. They covered their heads with a linen handkerchief tied under the chin, or went about bareheaded and ill-kempt. Their large mantle for church-going was often white instead of black—sometimes blue in the region of Etna—and when they were too poor might consist only of a white sheet or the cloak with a long pointed hood (*palandrano*) belonging to their husbands, for in Sicily, in the same way that clothes were hired for a farthing an hour, it was common for a household only to own one cloak.

Male costume was equally austere. The short sleeveless waistcoat, barely reaching to the waist, and the breeches were made either of thick serge, which was usually brown, or goat skin. The stockings—when they were worn—and the small forage cap covering the head were of the same material or brown knitted wool. The ample cloak of heavy black or brown wool was of three types: the *capotto* with a collar; the *palandrano* already mentioned and the rarer *salimarco* or *scappulara*, similar to a monastic scapular, which hung down on four sides instead of two and through which the head was passed. It was a suitable garment for winter journeys on horseback. Only on Sundays and holidays did a few coloured ribbons or braids brighten up the drab uniformity of this costume for the wealthier peasants and workers in the towns.

D

CHAPTER IV
TRAVEL AND ACCOMMODATION

PEOPLE travelled a great deal in eighteenth-century Italy, but in extreme discomfort. Foreigners especially were forced to use inns in the small towns which were always third rate, rarely excellent and often detestable, if indeed they found any at all. In Sicily inns did not exist, except at Palermo, Catania and Messina, and the traveller had to lodge with one of the inhabitants in conditions of extreme rusticity.

As in the rest of Europe, transport from one place to another consisted of the post-chaise and the private carriage, with relays of horses, and sometimes boats in regions where there were canals. Travellers usually stated that they were satisfied with the post-chaise, which had universal priority—anyone who did not give it right of way incurred a fine of twenty-five écus in Lombardy and was immediately arrested—at least as regards the speed, but complained of the discomfort and dearness of the journeys.

Goethe compared this carriage to the old time litters in which women and important people were carried by mules. 'They have put two wheels on them, without adding a single improvement,' he wrote. 'You are tossed about as you would have been centuries ago.' In addition there was scarcely anybody who did not fulminate against the dishonesty, clumsiness and rusticity of the postillions employed at the *cambiatura* (posting-houses).

At Piacenza in 1714, the Comte de Caylus bought two carriages for twenty-five louis in order to make himself and his friends more independent. He even had to rent the horses, for the postmaster refused him a team at the stage in that town, but the postillions were so drunk that the carriage turned over three times between Palma and Modena. At Modena he lodged 'in an unspeakable tavern, although it is the best in the town, with a host called Laurens, who is said to be a very good pimp'. On approaching Rome, at Narni, he wrote that the posting-house was 'infamous'. The road from Narni to Otricoli was one of the worst imaginable owing to the loose stones. By the time he had reached Naples, he had become philosophical about things and no longer got excited over such trifles: 'We lodged at the *Three Kings* which was bad, but good for the country'.

Father Labat experienced the same disillusion at about the same date. He had been greatly taken by Siena, both by the fertility of the surrounding countryside and by its streets, which were always very tidy, well paved with bricks set on edge, and cleaned by the waters of numerous fountains; but he changed his tune at the inn where he preferred to sleep on a table wrapped in his cloak with his valise for a pillow rather than in a bed full of bugs and fleas. His less prudent travelling companions spent the night scratching themselves and complained to the valet to no purpose; he replied insolently 'that the only bugs in the beds were the ones they had brought with them'.

President de Brosses found the inns of Florence 'detestable beyond measure', worse than anything which people had told him about Italian taverns, especially at night: 'small midges a hundred times more damnable than the ones in Burgundy', he grumbled, 'made it their business to make me miserable'. Apparently mosquito nets were unknown there at the time. While going from Rome to Naples, apart from the discomfort of bad roads, he endured that 'of not finding even a semblance of a bearable lodging'.

For Jérôme de Lalande, who paid a long visit to Italy in 1765-6, the discomfort of the majority of inns, except in a few large towns, was firmly established. In them one slept badly, was badly served, poorly fed and yet shamelessly fleeced. 'Men of the people . . . look on foreigners as their dupes and frequently cheat them outrageously, not caring twopence what one says to them.'

As soon as he had entered Italy by the Alpes Maritimes, Arthur Young, used to English correctness and very happy about his journey through the French provinces, burst into violent criticism. Tenda seemed to him one of the most horrible places in this desolate district. 'The only inn is frightful, black, filthy and stinking; there are no window panes.' At Coni, the hostelry of 'The White Cross' had been pointed out to them as excellent. In fact he was given a good room but not a single window with panes—there was nothing but torn paper. At Turin and Milan he was reassured on finding inns as good as in France, but his lamentations began again when he had to take a decked boat to go from Venice to Bologna, the roads being so impracticable that the *vetturini* would not venture on them. The filth and discomfort on board this boat were indescribable. 'The skipper takes snuff, wipes his nose with his fingers, cleans his knife with his handkerchief at the same time as he is preparing the food he offers you.' (The other travellers seemed to find this quite natural.) At Bologna, he found the hostelries of *Pellegrino* and *San Marco*[1] full and had to fall back on the *Tre Mauretti*, 'an appalling hovel'.

After the surprises of Torbole, Goethe had some extraordinary experiences when seeking lodging in Sicily. At Girgenti, on April 24, 1787, as there was no inn at all an obliging family made over a part of their house to him and let him have a tall alcove separated by a curtain from a large room in which the women of the family skilfully manufactured by hand a fine variety of snail-shaped vermicelli. At Enna, things were even worse: he had a tiled room with outside shutters, but only a gaping opening to serve as a window, so that he either had to remain in darkness or allow fine rain to fall into the room. There was a new change of scenery at Caltanissetta. A room was found, which first had to be cleaned, with no other furniture except hard wooden trestles. To turn these trestles into the base of a bed, one went to the carpenter and hired the necessary number of planks. Chopped straw in the large leather sack, which our German friends carried with them, formed the mattress. They had taken the precaution of buying a chicken *en route*, but 'the inn' had none of the utensils for cooking and preparing it! An old citizen was willing to supply wood and a portable stove at a reasonable price and the coachman went off to buy rice and salt, after which Goethe could dine and sleep.

To tell the truth, Sicily being without roads (in 1787, from Palermo southwards there was still only one, which ended twenty miles from the capital), the island had little else but tracks for muleteers and their beasts. Roland discovered large stables 'without fireplace or stoves, where one eats and sleeps either on stone benches, arranged lengthwise in the middle, behind the horses, or in the manger when there is room'. There were no plates and dishes or provisions. Everybody drank out of the same jug, they sometimes served themselves with their fingers and the muleteers carrying wheat or other provisions provided their own food; so one had to buy 'bread here, eggs there and grapes somewhere else . . . there were never any fireplaces; a few large stones served as a hearth, the smoke filled the room and later disappeared through the roof which was of rushes, although they were fairly closely set, with tiles above'. Nevertheless good humour and affability reigned among these extremely primitive but worthy folk. Since they were never visited by foreigners, they could not organize hostelries to receive them and would not even have known how to set about such a task.

In fact at that epoch they would not have had any clients. When noblemen travelled in Sicily, they took with them all the necessary bedding and kitchen utensils: in the enormous half-empty palaces occupied by members of their caste they were always sure of finding lodging. Men of the people were put up in monasteries and most of the foreigners resigned themselves to a similar fate, unless they installed themselves luxuriously in a large town for several months at their own expense, as President de Brosses and his Burgundian companions did at Rome. But traditional Sicilian hospitality, which was extraordinarily generous and thoughtful, did much to facilitate travellers from Catania to Palermo.

A Catanian nobleman sent mules and muleteers to Palermo to escort as far as Catania a German traveller whom he did not know but who had been commended to him by one of his friends. 'On the prince's territory they organize stages, they do their utmost to modify the discomforts of travelling. At Catania the prince puts at the disposal of the foreigner a series of well-furnished rooms, a brilliant equipage, servants in handsome livery and offers him magnificent banquets to which friends and relations are invited: all this with such sincere and cordial affection that the German thought he was dreaming. The friendly prince never left him, showed him Catania and found a thousand and one excuses for detaining him.²'

In their absence, noblemen frequently left halls in their villas and palaces open, for the sole purpose of receiving either their friends who were travelling or foreigners of distinction of whose passage they had been warned: Count Stolberg, a Dane of German upbringing, had experience of this at Palermo in 1792. On occasion modest citizens or municipalities imitated this generous behaviour. In his youth Frederic Münter, who later became famous as an archaeologist and Protestant theologian, received a room in the Town Hall; the population fetched beds, linen and a large brasero to heat it.

The hospitality of the monasteries depended naturally on their resources. Cordial but very modest with the Franciscans, it was refined with the aristocratic Benedictines of San Martino, near Palermo. Goethe and his friend Kniep found some compensation there for the bucolic atmosphere of Caltanissetta.

Since it was much easier to lead a society life in the large towns than in the country districts where means of communication were difficult, the Sicilian nobility preferred to leave their castles for their palaces at Palermo, where they always assembled at the latest by September 4th, the feast of Saint Rosalia, the patron saint of the town, celebrated with an exraordinary display of popular rejoicing and religious ceremonies.

At Rome, Florence and Bologna the patrician villas were situated close to the city. They were occupied as soon as the first hot weather came and their owners stayed there until late in the season. At Genoa they were spread out along the sea front, also in the immediate environs of the town, whereas at Milan, although some of them were situated in the luxuriant countryside of the plain of Lombardy, the most luxurious and the most sought after lined the shores of Lake Maggiore and Lake Como.

At Venice country holidays did not normally begin until the beginning of autumn. Her situation close to the sea made the temperature bearable at all times of the year. In order to reach the residences which lined the Brenta Canal, but also for longer journeys by river, the nobles had their own *burchielli*, small elegant boats whose wooden cabins hung with precious cloths or leather were decorated with mirrors, engravings and pictures.

The Venetian parks, like those of the Roman villas, swarmed with fountains, fishponds, statues, and French-style gardens with rich flower beds and skilfully clipped yew and box trees. Sometimes animals, pheasants or turtle doves were kept in them, or even eagles captured in the Alpine summits. The life in these princely villas and the receptions given there were just as splendid as at Venice, but it was also the custom to dance in the fields and dine in the open air while listening to simple country songs, less from love of nature—there was no Italian Jean-Jacques who enjoyed any following — than out of caprice and a taste for variety in their pleasures.

A Venetian parasite called Longo, a poor writer but an acute observer, has left us the story of the kind of life which Marquis Albergati, an Emilian patrician won over to Venetian customs after long residence in the city, provided for his guests in his villa near Bologna during the summer of 1788. With variations, it enables us to imagine the last charms and unconscious anachronisms of a society which, on the eve of the Revolution, had cultivated the so-called 'dolce-vita' as an art and carried it to the highest point of perfection before disappearing.

At 9 a.m. a bell rang and summoned the marquis's male guests to come and be shaved and have their hair dressed by two servants. Afterwards they passed on to what would now be called a bar, a room which was always open, where they had a drink. At exactly ten o'clock another bell announced that the master of the house was in a conversation room known as 'the coffee room' in imitation of those of the procurators of San Marco, where they all drank the ritual cup of chocolate together. At eleven o'clock the guests accompanied the marquis to hear mass in his private chapel, after which pretty village girls came to offer their lord bouquets of flowers and received thanks and presents in exchange. Then some guests returned to the coffee room and began to play cards, but without heavy gambling; others preferred billiards, the seesaws or the library. Everyone's time was free until at two o'clock another bell announced that soup was being made in the kitchen and a few minutes later a second bell that the meal was about to be served.

It was a copious and choice meal during which serious conversation was forbidden. Once it was over, depending on the weather and season, a short siesta in summer or gallant conversation under the arbours surrounding the gardens formed the prelude to a long excursion together. During the autumn, the excursion began immediately after dinner. The guests chose between horses, sedan chairs and barouches unless they formed a caravan of the same type of vehicle. Each one was loaded with one of the utensils or hampers of provisions for preparing a picnic supper whose main feature was *polenta* made of cornflour, served with small birds. On returning from the excursion they started playing cards again, and at 2 a.m. the guests of the marquis retired to their rooms.[3]

Part II

SOCIETY, MORALS
and MANNERS

CHAPTER V
THE CUSTOMS OF THE NOBILITY, AND THEIR ROLE IN LIFE

THE PRECEDING chapters have already shown the predominant social role played by the Italian nobility in the eighteenth century. In fact the nobility held the majority of positions of any importance and sometimes even very humble ones, and it alone made up civilized 'society'. Foreign travellers, mostly titled and wealthy themselves, mainly visited the nobility, among whom they might conceivably meet certain men of letters and scholars of distinction whose merits opened the doors of the salons of the aristocracy to them, even if they did not belong to it by birth. Transient guests were nevertheless cut off from many contacts which might have been useful in their search for information. Moreover, the hardship poor people suffered in taking long courses of study meant that a large number of university professors themselves came from the nobility, such as Marquis Poleni, a Bolognese, editor of Vitruvius, who taught astronomy, physics and mathematics at Padua, and whose library of five thousand volumes devoted to the exact sciences excited the admiration of President de Brosses. The majority of the others were members of the clergy, itself a privileged class. The example of Vico, unappreciated in his lifetime anyway, remained a very rare exception.

If all the power was in the hands of the nobles, it should have been true that all the nobles held some amount of authority. This was not even strictly true in an oligarchical state such as Venice where a severe hierarchy reigned within the noble castes depending on ancient lineage and fortune and where the ruined nobles, the *Barnabotti*—so-called because the majority originally lived in rented apartments in the Via San Barnabe—sold their voting rights to the Grand Council and lived by gambling, intrigues and miserable expedients. These outcasts immediately adhered to revolutionary ideas, but Bonaparte found very few reliable allies among them at the end of the century. Genoa, on the other hand, included a few among the younger sons of great families excluded from public office. In the other States, especially the Kingdom of Naples, where the nobility was over-abundant, many of its members were perpetually idle and uncultured and were only distinguished by their arrogance. They constituted a dead weight for the country.

The proportion of nobles in the aristocratic republics was relatively high, but tended to diminish in the seventeenth and eighteenth centuries. At Venice it was 4·3% in 1586; it fell to 3·7% in 1642, to 2·5% in 1766—when it numbered 3,577 persons—and to 2·3% in 1790. There were also a number in the 'towns on *terra firma*' forming the crown of the Venetian State, but the nobility of the 'Dominante' looked on these provincials attached to their counties and marquisates with the greatest disdain.

In Venice itself no noble titles were carried. The antiquity of a name was enough to establish its splendour. Twelve houses could prove their descent from the twelve citizens —'the twelve apostles'—who elected the first doge in 697. They were the Badoer, Contarini, Morosini, Tiepolo, Michiel, Sanudo, Gradenigo, Memmo, Faliero, Dandolo, Barozzi and Polani, the last named extinguished in the eighteenth century. Twelve others were famous long before the establishment of the Grand Council with its 480 members (twelfth century), notably the Cornaro, Giustiniani, Bragadin and Querini, etc. During the naval wars between Venice and Genoa at the end of the thirteenth century in the eastern Mediterranean, the custom of granting nobility to many families in exchange for a cash payment began, but the ducal families (who had included at least one *doge*, just as those at Rome had given the church a pope) always preserved a higher rank than the others, although nothing distinguished them officially.

Election to the highest positions, such as senator or procurator of San Marco — an office responsible for administering the property of the church of San Marco and of orphans, and keeping the town archives—provoked intrigues similar to those of ancient Rome, save that the electoral body was not formed of the people but of the patricians alone. Instead of the Forum, the candidates used to stand in the Broglio (today the Piazzetta situated between the Palace of the Doges and the Libreria Vecchia). The nobles made a sweeping bow, their wigs touching the ground, and even kissed the hands of the people whose votes they were soliciting, although their rank was often much lower than their own.

The noblemen had mainly acquired their fortunes in the past from trade with the Levant and from the chances which remote proconsulships, or even more humble employment on *terra firma,* gave them of making profits to which the Senate was accustomed to turn a blind eye.[1] However these offices were of short duration. An ambassador, for example, was only appointed for a maximum of four years, the senators members of the Council of Ten for one year and the doge's councillors for eight months.

As for the College of Sixteen 'Wise Men' which the Senate commissioned to study and submit to it matters concerning the State, membership only lasted for six months and its spokesman in the Senate changed every week! The precautions taken by the Venetian Government, which was served by a swarm of spies, against any citizen suspected of aspiring to personal power were so many and so far reaching that they would have discouraged Caesar himself. Although he was surrounded with the highest honours, they made the Doge a veritable prisoner of state, forbidden to travel or undertake any spontaneous action. His opinion on the conduct of public affairs was held suspect *a priori* and the opposite course was generally taken. Noblemen were forbidden, under the severest penalties, to frequent foreign embassies for fear that a careless remark might give away a state secret. The penalty laid down was 1,000 ducats and two years' exile from Venetian territory. In 1542 it was increased to five years' deprivation of any public office and could even mean death if the State Inquisitors had serious grounds for suspecting the honesty of purpose of the offender. However, only one capital sentence was carried out against an ex-ambassador to London, Antonio Foscarini, who was denounced by personal enemies, but rehabilitated in the actual year of his execution, 1622, when his accusers were punished with death in their turn.[2]

Since the commercial and industrial role of Venice had greatly diminished in the eighteenth century, the great fortunes were mainly maintained by landed property. Whole villages with their dwelling houses, inn, mill and hundreds or thousands of fields belonged to the same family; the lord collected a tax on the few pieces of land which he did not own in his own right.

The incomes, sometimes enormous, served primarily to help their owners cut a figure at the great receptions and maintain a swarm of domestic servants in brilliant livery. The Contarini, Mocenigo, etc., had 40 to 50 servants and 6 to 10 gondolas. The Martinengo at Brescia had 84 towards the end of the century. At Florence, Arthur Young saw 40 servants in the palace of the Marquis Riccardi, each of them with his own family and often other domestics in his service. The Roman princes had as many as 200 servants and 100 horses in their stables. But as the nobles did not want to ruin themselves, Abbé Coyer noted 'they cut down on food to keep up the splendour' and when a public holiday approached, he added amusingly, even the middle classes 'condemn themselves to two or three days' fast so that they can hire lackeys and show themselves in a carriage'.

In order to keep up their rank and because a keen sense of family was current in Venice, brothers and sisters lived together as co-heirs, even after the death of their parents. They had a steward who was often a priest and gave each of them a monthly sum for his maintenance and that of his personal servants. When one of them contracted debts his share alone was mortgaged. Normally only one member of a family married—the clergy and the monasteries usually receiving the others—and the brothers allotted him a larger share than their own. If one of them held an employment incurring large expenditure, the excess was borne in common.[3]

Genoa had similar institutions, but her nobility displayed much less luxury. Its economy, carried to extremes, excited Montesquieu's mocking vein. 'All the noblemen of Genoa,' he wrote, 'are real *mercadans*,[4] often the Doge himself takes part in trade . . . There are private individuals here with several millions. This is because they do not spend anything; and in their beautiful palaces there is often only one serving maid, who spins. The lower part is full of merchandise and the upper storey is occupied by the master . . . In the great houses, if you see a page it is because there are no lackeys . . . They possess palaces because they can find marble on the spot.' President de Brosses was equally surprised on his arrival in Genoa to see 'a large gathering of noblemen seated at the corner of a street in shabby armchairs, holding a serious assembly'. He felt that it was ridiculous to build vast palaces on tiny sites with no courtyards or gardens for lack of space. However, he did not spare his admiration for the villas built by the aristocracy on the Genoan Riviera which he described as 'magnificent country houses all painted with frescoes', infinitely more beautiful than those in the environs of Paris, Lyons or Marseilles, whereas Montesquieu mentions them in passing as 'little country cottages . . . , pretty enough', but whose beauty consisted in their position by the sea, 'which costs the proprietors nothing'. This example clearly proves that it is necessary to mistrust the impressions of travellers, even the most famous, and to check them with each other.

The institutions of Genoa, like those of the small republic of Lucca, combined the principal of election with the concentration of all the offices in the hands of the nobles. Genoa possessed two councils, a smaller one with 200 members (*Minor Consiglio*), who chose the majority of the magistrates, decided on peace and war and could either enact laws if they received two-thirds of the votes, or propose them to the Grand Council. The latter, which numbered rather more than 300 members in the middle of the eighteenth century, was composed of noblemen with a good reputation aged at least twenty-two. It represented the supreme power; it alone could fix taxes, change the fundamental laws and fill the highest offices; but in fact, being two-thirds composed of young patricians who were the sons and nephews of the members of the *Minor Consiglio* and obedient to their opinions, it generally carried out its desires.

The election of the Doge, who had to be fifty years of age and own a handsome fortune, was carried out by selection with several stages from among the members of the two councils. The Grand Council drew fifty names by lot which they themselves reduced to twenty, later limited to fifteen by a second debate of the Grand Council. The Small Council then reduced them to six, one of which was chosen by the Grand Council.

The Doge was elected for two years, not only to the very day but to the very hour, and could not hold the office again for ten years, but in practice he never held it twice. After handing over his powers, he was liable to charges by any individual for eight days; these charges were submitted to a sort of supreme tribunal, the *Sindacato dei supremi*. If it held him free of all serious accusations, the ex-Doge became a perpetual procurator, i.e. a member of a higher Finance Service of eight people and all the ex-Doges known as the *Camera*. As for the government itself, or Senate, it included, together with the Doge, twelve governors (or Senators), drawn by lot five by five every six months from 120 names extracted from an urn which contained 400, a figure probably reached with the names of dead persons left in the urn and eliminated only when they were taken out during a draw.

No governor could return to office for five years. In addition there were three posts of Secretary of State, the most lucrative of all, for they brought in an income of 30,000 livres* (about £1,250) a year and conferred nobility. Thus they could not be held for more than ten years.

A curious custom dating from 1620 required that the names of noblemen in Genoa be drawn by lot every month, five on each occasion, and as there were only two draws laid down by the Constitution on the ten other occasions it was only a sort of dummy operation, simply legalizing the universal Italian fashion for gambling. This was the *lottery of the seminary*, leased out for 306,000 livres a year. It must have been the origin of the *Regio Lotto* of united Italy. The gamblers who had bet on a name which was drawn received thirteen times their stake, 230 times if two names were drawn and 2,857 times if three were drawn. A very simple calculation shows that the operation was highly profitable for the banker.[5]

Lucca, a town of about 22,000 souls, possessed 240 noblemen over twenty-five years of age and as such capable of joining the Council. The Council comprised two groups of ninety people with thirty deputies and each group alternated in office from one year to another. A sort of higher government commission, composed of nine *anziani* and one gonfalonier, was changed every two months, always by drawing lots, from a delegation of thirty-six members with eighteen deputies elected for three years. The scrutineers added ten new names to replace ten outgoing members every two months among a selection of 180 noblemen nominated every three years, in such a way that none of them could

*An old French coin superseded by the franc in 1795. Translator's note.

hold office twice during these three years. This system was closely akin to that of the *Priori* who governed Florence in the Middle Ages, but then the public offices, of very short duration, were accessible to all, whereas with time they had become the privilege of the nobility in the merchant republics. Nevertheless there were neither counts nor marquesses in Lucca in the eighteenth century and nobody wore a sword there. As in mediaeval Florence, the podestà (and four commissioners of justice) were always citizens of some other part of Italy so that they would have no relations or acquaintances there.

Even in very small towns such as Tivoli, which was not an ancient republic, the population, divided into five orders with different numbers and different rights, left the whole responsibility for a municipal administration by statute to the local nobility, which was divided into patricians of the first and second order. Manufacturers formed a third category, shopkeepers and craftsmen a fourth and the small farmers of the outer suburbs a fifth.

With minor variations, this system of communal administration taken from the Middle Ages was the rule in practically all the towns. There were generally two councils, the general and larger Council and another smaller one, the *anziani*. In order to belong to the first, it was necessary to possess a high income and not to practice a profession, which reserved access to it in practice to the aristocracy; it was recruited by co-option. The second was composed of members nominated by the General Council and exercised the executive power under the title of 'guardians' but always with a mandate of very limited duration, two or three months. The podestà, elected by the two councils, was responsible for controlling markets, fairs and taverns, in other words everything connected with police matters, keeping public order and calling up the militia if war threatened.

The nobility of Florence, which was much less ancient than the Venetian, owed the major part of its brilliance to families of bankers or traders in wool and silk cloths, contemporaries of the Medici, such as the Peruzzi, Strozzi, Corsi, Rucellai, Antinori, etc. Those against whom the *popolo minuto* had struggled in the Middle Ages (and later Lorenzo de' Medici), or of feudal origin or illustrious owing to high magistratures — Pazzi, Salviati,

E

Cavalcanti, Donati, etc. — were mostly extinct or reduced to relatively modest circumstances.

Montesquieu, always very attentive to the 'standard of living' in the circles to which he was introduced during his travels in Italy in 1728, took careful note of the incomes of the great Florentine families as quoted by public report. The Marquis Riccardi—who occupied the former Medici palace and founded the rich library which has retained his name—was supposed to have an income of 200,000 livres (over £8,000), the Rinuccini, Corsini, Corsi, Salviati and Strozzi families 20,000 écus or 100,000 livres (over £4,000), the marquesses Incontri, Niccolini, Gerini and Ximenes from 12,000 (£2,500) to 15,000 écus (over £3,000), or even a little less. But he added: 'All this is popular exaggeration. Cut it in half or even more.' In which he was certainly mistaken, for all these families possessed vast domains in the Tuscan countryside. He was struck by the modest way of life of these patricians whose houses, when there was no gambling in progress, were lit only by a lamp or lantern and 'when people come in, they light the three lanterns, for the lamp has three branches, and place it on a sort of chandelier'. But Florentine society appeared quite differently to President de Brosses, because he saw it in different circumstances on the occasion of two great marriages 'which had gathered the whole town together'. He was dazzled by what he saw. 'The extravagant magnificence of the Florentines in equipages, furniture, liveries and clothing is something incredible,' he wrote. 'We have seen assemblies or conversazioni here every night in various houses whose apartments are so many mazes. These assemblies are composed of about three hundred ladies smothered in diamonds and five hundred men wearing clothes the Duc de Richelieu would be ashamed to wear[6] . . . Incidentally I was informed that these rich clothes only appeared on important occasions and lasted all the owner's life.'

The nobles received an addition to their income from the minor offices granted them by the Grand Duke which brought in from fifteen to fifty écus a month. Montesquieu was very shocked by this. He observed disdainfully: 'The most wretched occupations in France, such as a post in the Customs, are performed by noblemen and normally only by them'.

The Grand Duke virtually stopped granting letters patent of nobility. But it was possible to get round the difficulty by founding a commandery of the order of Saint Stephen for 10,000 écus (over £2,000). It passed to the founder's heirs on death and was equivalent to a title of nobility; but when a *nouveau riche* founded such an order, he was not allowed to continue trading. Montesquieu attributed the decline of Florentine trade to this vainglory. At Lucca nobility could also be bought for 12,000 écus (£2,500).

Towards the end of the century, Dupaty noticed the same venality over titles at Genoa. It cost 10,000 livres (£400) to have one's name inscribed in the Book of Gold (which was not gold, even in those days). He considered this as a precaution taken by the nobles of ancient lineage to conciliate the up-and-coming middle classes and keep them from any stray revolutionary tendencies. 'They prefer to attract the bourgeois who have made a fortune into the nobility where they can continue to despise and cease to fear them.' Even at Venice, it was decided in 1775 to admit forty families with an income of 10,000 ducats to the patriciate, but only a dozen put themselves forward, for their flight from the responsibilities of public office fought with the vanity of knowing they could be invested with it.

The Kingdom of Naples and Sicily possessed a large feudal nobility of whom only a minute number were required by important appointments to reside in one of the two capitals, Naples or Palermo. However, more and more of them flocked there in the eighteenth century, drawn by pleasure, and at Naples by the proximity of the court which shone under Charles III, with an undertone of seriousness maintained by his principal adviser, Marquis Tanucci—who was Tuscan, not Neapolitan, incidentally—but became one of the most frivolous and corrupt in Europe under Ferdinand IV and Maria-Caroline. Thus the seeds of contempt and hatred of monarchical institutions were unconsciously sown in the minds of the élite, who were not lacking at Naples.

At the beginning of the century the nobility in the Kingdom of Naples numbered 119 princes, 156 dukes, 173 marquesses, 42 counts and 445 barons, the majority beholden to the Spanish monarchy for their titles, at least as far as the highest ranks

were concerned, for the Norman and Angevin kings never
created dukes or princes. Five thousand other families comprising
some 20,000 people out of a total of about five million inhabitants, 400,000 of them in the capital, aped the genuine nobility
or *nobiltà generosa* by their way of life and by usurped or bought
titles. These formed the *nobiltà di privilegio* and strove to justify
their name by cornering the maximum number of posts, which
were in fact privileged, in the magistrature, the bar and the civil
service when they gave up trade and often more nefarious
dealings.

The evolution of the Sicilian nobility was similar. At first it
was feudal land, divided between powerful barons and ecclesiastical domains, then Frederic appointed a few counts there in the
thirteenth century; Alfonso of Aragon, in 1440, marquesses;
Charles the Fifth, in 1554, dukes; Philip II, nine years later,
princes. Towards 1785, there were fifty-eight princes and twenty-
seven dukes; in addition there were thirty-seven marquesses,
twenty-six counts and seventy-nine barons, who formed the
'military arm' of the Sicilian Parliament. But this appellation no
longer had any meaning. The nobility of the Kingdom of Naples
in the eighteenth century was completely unaccustomed to the
profession of arms and showed not the slightest desire to return
to it. But it preserved its prerogatives and through its cadets who
appeared in the 'ecclesiastical arm' of Parliament while other
members of the caste were supposed to represent towns, many
of which were themselves fiefs, on a 'domanial arm', which
could have been a sort of third estate, it in fact concentrated all
the powers in Sicily which were not effectively exercised by the
Viceroy in the name of the Neapolitan sovereign. Even the
biggest 'royal towns' (Messina, Catania and Syracuse) had noble
governors who administered them in the name of the king.

Nevertheless a veiled and sometimes open struggle went on
between the barons and the monarch, under marquis Caracciolo,
Viceroy from 1781 to 1785, after he had spent many years as
ambassador in London and Paris, from which towns he returned
a partisan of the ideas of the philosophers. The barons were
overwhelmed with taxes, which could take away as much as a
third or a half of their incomes. Caracciolo reduced their feudal
rights, taking away in particular the right of imprisoning

insolvent peasants and withdrawing the privilege of appointing magistrates in the baronial towns. But when he wanted to go even further, put the financial system in order by forcing ground landlords to make an exact evaluation of their property, imprison a prince who protected bandits or reduce to two days the festivities of Saint Rosalia, patron saint of Palermo, which the entire population made into a brilliant spectacle, he found all classes united against him. Although exploited by his overlords, the peasant saw in them his natural defenders against the foreigner, in accordance with feudal ideas. Enlightened despotism had no chance of imposing itself in Sicily; even at Naples it only succeeded, thanks to marquis Tanucci, in the field of ecclesiastical jurisdiction, without making any impact on the mass of popular superstitions.

Milan also had a few Spanish Grandees,[7] but on the whole its nobility had lost less of its ancient virtues than that of the south, in spite of the swingeing satire on it by Parini in his poem *Il Giorno*. An austere brain like his, a character hardened by the fetters of poverty could not help being shocked by the luxurious and empty life of the gilded youth, their idleness, their vain pastimes divided between gallantry, gambling, dancing and excursions, the last-named still combining vanity with tender simperings since it was not a question of enjoying nature but of being seen by ladies in their carriages and holding amusing conversations with them.

Let us revert to the impressions of foreign travellers on their contacts with the nobility. One custom against which great gourmets such as Charles de Brosses and Montesquieu never stopped protesting, which angered them as if it was a scandal, was that Italian noblemen, whether rich or only fairly rich, never gave an invitation to dinner. Exceptions prove the rule.

'They do not know what it means to offer a meal,' the President from Dijon grumbled on many occasions. Even at Venice, where money was by no means lacking. 'I have sometimes been at a *conversazione* of the Procuratress Foscarini's, a house of enormous wealth, and she an extremely charming lady; as the only titbit, at 3 p.m., i.e. about eleven o'clock at night in France, twenty valets bring in, on an immense silver platter, a large sliced pumpkin known as *anfouri* or water-melon, a detestable dish if ever there was one. A pile of silver plates accompany it; everyone grabs at a slice, washes it down with a small cup of coffee and leaves at midnight with empty head and belly to sup in his own home.' At the end of his stay in Rome he concluded in the same way: 'I'll be damned if I have yet seen anyone offered a glass of water'. But at that point he must have known that he was exaggerating.

Montesquieu was even more chagrined by this stinginess. The poverty of Piedmontese gentlemen, about which he was well-informed, did not seem to him to excuse the fact that 'no one eats anything in Turin: a dinner given for a foreigner is a great novelty in the Town'. And he methodically quotes several examples: 'M de Cambis was never invited anywhere in three years . . . the Marquis de Prie, who had kept five or six Piedmontese with him for years in Flanders and Vienna, was at Turin when I was. Not one of them offered him so much as a glass of water[8] . . . One day when he left for the country the Marquis de Carail said: "I'm so sorry, for I wanted to ask you to dinner".' Now the Marquis de Carail was the richest lord in Piedmont: he was supposed to have an income of 40,000 to 50,000 livres when 'all the rest (of the nobility) lived on 10,000 to 12,000 livres'. At Genoa 'to give one a meal is unheard of . . . You would not believe how far the parsimony of these princes goes,' concluded Montesquieu. 'The Venetians rarely offer anything to eat,' Lalande noted in his turn.

At the end of the century, Arthur Young made the same observations at Florence, but admitted that it was quite a different matter at Milan. 'I would not give a farthing,' he concluded, 'for a society in which no one ever received guests for dinner.' After remarking on the great style in the house of the Marquis Riccardi, he added that 'the Ranuzzi are even richer and more people live at their expense; but there are no dinners, no parties, no equipages and no comfort'. However, in some good houses he had appreciated perfectly served dinners, accompanied by excellent wines. In the splendid villas of the Venetian patricians, the luxury and abundance of the table was part of the background, all the more so as one might be surprised by the quite unexpected arrival at one's house of a large company of country neighbours. Lady Montagu related that 'during the holidays I received a visit from a cavalcade of twenty people, men and women . . . (who) had come with the kindly intention of spending a fortnight with me, although I had never seen a single one of them before'. These neighbours of high lineage often had an admixture of parasites, who abounded in Venice and were tolerated for their wit and jokes.

At Rome the presence of foreign ambassadors, with the French ambassador in the lead, who kept open house and a very good table, e.g. the Duc de Sant-Aignan in the time of President de Brosses, and later Cardinal de Bernis, could not help influencing high society. In fact President de Brosses contradicts himself when he tells the story of his first unannounced visit with his friends to Cardinal Firrao, Secretary of State to Clement XII, who nevertheless made them stay to dinner and served them 'a superb banquet'. 'The ambassador and he are the only lords in Rome who keep up this custom,' our memorialist noted immediately. Later they had a few imitators.

He explained the lavish hospitality of the nobility at Naples by the fact that they lived in the Spanish rather than the Italian style. The Duke of Monte-Leone daily held 'the largest and most magnificent assembly in the town, which costs him, so they claim, more than 50,000 francs in candles, ices and refreshments; he is the richest man in the State'. There follows a longish enumeration of other grand houses where our Burgundian friends were handsomely treated, with 'very good wines, all the more acceptable because everywhere else they are unbearable . . . excellent beef . . . melons in the middle of winter . . . pigeons, which proved to be exquisite as early as Milan, but increase in size and quality the further one penetrates into Italy'.

In short, on condition of being well-born, it was still possible to provide good cheer in eighteenth-century Italy, but as a general rule, 'the houses do not worry too much about the table', as Abbé Coyer also observed. At receptions all they offered was chocolate and iced water which did not weigh too heavily on the aristocratic budgets.

We may also add to the customs of the nobility the fashion for leaving visiting cards which established itself in Italy towards the first third of the eighteenth century, for the practice was almost exclusively confined to the nobility; but they quickly adopted the habit, which was used with a pleasing note of fancy, for the cards, which were quite plain at first, later became little works of art, carefully engraved with the name of the sender accompanied by garlands of flowers, heraldic, military and mythological emblems, or even country scenes and landscapes containing the name of the person who sent them discreetly in one corner.

Historians do not agree about the exact origin of this fashion. In Florence they claim that it coincided with the arrival in Tuscany in 1731 of the Infante Don Carlos and the Spaniards who escorted him to Parma, where he was to take possession of the Duchy before ceding it to his brother Philip when he became King of Naples. But elsewhere they claim that the French were responsible for its introduction into Italy. Goldoni, in his comedy *Il Cavaliere giocondo*, performed at Venice for the carnival of 1735, makes his hero say: 'in the past I spent the whole day paying calls; now I fulfill all my obligations with visiting cards. Oh! the French are really very ingenious.'

However that may be, the new fashion helped people to show imagination and their good or bad taste. For some of these cards, swamped with human figures or decorative motifs in the baroque style, were not always free from affectation. They became simpler towards the end of the century under the influence of neo-classicism. Sometimes the card stated in writing, engraved with the name, the reason for which it had been left, for example: 'Count N . . . , *pour prendre congé* the Marchioness A . . . , *née* V . . . , *pour remplir ses devoirs*'. Subsequently these were expressed more simply and expeditiously, as we know.

Notifications of funerals were fairly similar to French ones, but only mentioned the closest relatives, with their titles in full, for the custom of complying with all the most exaggerated requirements of etiquette, still nearly as prevalent today, was then absolutely general in Italy.

CHAPTER VI

RELIGION AND THE CLERGY

THE FIELD of religion in eighteenth-century Italy undoubtedly brings out most clearly those contrasts which seem to us to characterize the epoch and which are so obvious in the antithesis between the social conditions of the aristocracy and the rural or urban proletariat, to use a term which had not yet been invented.

Religion permeated all the outward expressions of public and private life. The clergy, excessive in number, the largest owners of landed property in every Italian state, benefiting from exorbitant privileges especially in judicial matters and holding absolute sway over people's consciences, exhibited such a large variety of prototypes in every category from the highest to the humblest that it discourages any classification or overall judgment. It included sybaritic prelates and genuine saints, great men of letters and ignorant priests, dissolute or slothful monks[1] and excellent teachers, confessors indulgent about the worse moral lapses and inflexible preachers, steeped in Jansenist maxims.[2] It is impossible to do more than give a general sketch of this complexity of attitudes in everyday life. But it is essential to point out that it would be as wrong to judge all the eighteenth-century clergy by the elegant and bedizened priests in contemporary engravings as by the erudite editors of the ecclesiastical gazettes or the countless crowd of agents of the pontifical government.

As to their numbers, statistics give a percentage of priests and monks or nuns, which as we have seen (cf. Part One, Chap. I, note 1), made up about one-fifteenth of the population of Rome at the beginning of the century. At Bologna the proportion was similar: it contained one ecclesiastic per seventeen inhabitants, and in 1796, when the French arrived, convents and monasteries occupied one-sixth of the area of the town. Naples, with some 12,000 ecclesiastics, including 5,000 priests to serve its 400 churches and chapels and undertake the multiple responsibilities put into their hands, had a proportion of about one-twenty-eighth, the same as at Turin in 1755, where there were 2,482 priests or monks and 412 enclosed nuns for a steady population of between 80,000 and 90,000. At the same epoch, Taine fixed the proportion of ecclesiastics for France at one in two hundred.

Every traveller bore witness to the swarms of men of the church and praised the fact or were indignant about it according as they were themselves believers or not. Even good catholics deplored the abuse of masculine, and especially feminine, *monacazioni* without vocation; the superfluity of priests without a definite ministry, holding several livings and employed in all sorts of profane tasks; the almost general slackness of discipline in the monasteries[3]; the mediocre intellectual standard, for lack of serious study and qualitative selection of the candidates, of the actual parish clergy, particularly in the south.

The diocese of Imola, which was Pius VII's before his elevation to the pontifical throne, a diocese of average size (94,000 souls), can be taken as an example of the usual distribution of ecclesiastical categories in Italy towards the end of the eighteenth century, in the present case in 1785. Out of 979 priests and secular clerks, only 200 to 250 belonged to the parish clergy as priests or curates. Forty canons formed the two chapters of Imola and Lugo, the two main towns. The remainder were divided into 130 beneficed priests and clerics, 101 of them for Imola, and 458 unbeneficed clergy, who were consequently obliged to live—for ecclesiastics of wealthy families were nearly always the most favoured — by jobs which were often far from sacerdotal in character. They became tutors, but also stewards, agents, secretaries to aristocratic families, compilers of heavy treatises, or members of the subordinate staff of public or private libraries, etc. Only a small number acquired fame by their exceptional qualities on the teaching staff of colleges and universities, which incidentally was almost exclusively made up of monks. The diocese of Imola contained 246 regular monks divided between twenty-three monasteries.[4]

Even if many of the houses of the mendicant orders were poor and their monks lived by the alms which they begged in the outside world, the secular clergy as a whole was very rich and remained better off than the nobility itself. In the Kingdom of Naples, where it formed 2.5 per cent of the population, it collected a third of the revenues of the State. In the Duchy of Parma more than half and in Tuscany more than three-quarters of the territory was in the hands of ecclesiastical bodies during the first half of the century, before the reformist policy aimed at reducing the general spread of mortmain was applied in Parma by the minister du Tillot, in Tuscany by Grand Duke Leopold, in Naples by Tanucci, in Milan by the representatives of Emperor Joseph II, and in Venice by the reigning patriciate.

The following figure will give an idea of the rapidity with which mortmain extended: in the town of Venice alone, in ten years, from 1755 to 1765, legacies and endowments in favour of ecclesiastical bodies amounted to 3,300,000 ducats (about £850,000), largely owing to the dowries demanded from enclosed nuns. The movement for limiting property in mortmain began at Venice around 1770 but made little impression on the enormous extent of church land.

The endowments of bishoprics were obviously most unequal, for a great number of factors came into play when they were decided. Monreale, in Sicily, was one of the most richly endowed; it brought in 70,000 écus (about £14,500) to Cardinal Aquaviva of Aragon, *chargé-d'affaires* of Spain and Naples, and enabled him to maintain 'the style of the greatest lord in Rome'. The *conversazione* which was held in his house twice a week was 'well attended and magnificent' and gave Charles de Brosses special pleasure because of 'certain absolutely delicious cinnamon-flavoured water ices'.

Palermo, Catania and Girgenti guaranteed their archbishops an income of 60,000 écus (£5,000). To these lavish revenues were added taxes in kind, for example a tithe on tunny fishing for the Archbishop of Palermo worth about £500. Once unloaded on the shore the fish were laid out in rows of ten. The archiepiscopal steward made the master of the *tonnara*[6] draw a numbered ball from a bag containing ten and marked the fish corresponding to the number drawn in each row with a special sign: these fish belonged to the Archbishop. In Tuscany, the Bishop of Arezzo had an income of about £2,000. The revenues of the vast dioceses in the north, such as Milan, Padua, Brescia and a few others were also considerable.

But it was not unknown that instead of using the privileges of their situation to lead a life of luxury, certain prelates, imbued with the evangelical spirit and persuaded that excessive wealth was not fitting in their status, abandoned it: e.g. the Bishop of

Asti, Count Caissotti di Chiusano, who governed this average-sized diocese for twenty-four years during the second half of the eighteenth century; he covered it on foot after having reassigned a large part of the property owned by the bishopric to his sovereign, the King of Sardinia. Another example was one of the last bishops of Monreale before the Revolution, Monsig. Testa. He lived like a hermit, slept on straw, ate frugally, only keeping a bare thousand écus for himself out of the enormous revenues of his bishopric and devoting the remainder to succouring the poor or making roads in a country which had none so as to provide work for the destitute masses for the benefit of the community. When he died in 1773, venerated by the whole of the population, he had *none* of his patrimonial fortune left.

Nor should one forget that eighteenth-century Italy saw the growth of congregations preaching the austerest of penitences, side by side with scandalous laxity. For example the Redemptorists, founded at Naples by a young lawyer of noble birth, Saint Alfonso di Liguori, and especially the Passionist fathers, whose founder, Saint Paul of the Cross, was literally obsessed by the memory of Christ's Passion and personally practised the most rigorous asceticism. It was also the time when Saint Leonard of Port Maurice, a Capuchin, spread the practise of the Stations of the Cross at Rome, particularly inside the Coliseum.

These examples of heroic detachment even compelled the esteem of non-believers, but it does not seem that the people as a whole suffered or were profoundly shocked by the multifarious powers invested in the clergy, its proliferation, or the frequently blameworthy behaviour of its members. Familiarity and a sort of passivity in the face of established order explained their attitude. Perhaps ultimately because ecclesiastical status and its privileges were available to all; because the religious and profane holidays tended to merge into the same display of picturesque and boisterous gaiety, creating 'entertainment' in the Pascalian sense of the word for everyone; because lastly the Church was not generally very exacting in moral matters and only required the formal adherence of the faithful to its ritual practices. Lalande noted in 1765: 'The people are attached to their religion (at Venice) as in the rest of Italy, but that has little influence on their behaviour. The people give way to their passions quite naturally, then go to confession and begin all over again.' At the end of the century a priest said to Dupaty: 'These people are all sensation; a refined religion would not have enough body for them; they have to be able to touch it, feel it, see it, therefore it must be mixed with superstition'. And again: 'If we are so weak about love, it is in the interests of our religion; if we were more severe about this article, our faith would be abandoned; we have tried strictness more than once and it has been highly unsuccessful.'

Why should anyone blush at such a businesslike religion? Not only was there no deference to public opinion in eighteenth-century Italy—that fear of the mockery of unbelievers wherever they are in the majority—but also devout observances were kept with naïvety, or even an impudence which could be called cynicism elsewhere. President be Brosses saw a theatrical performance at Verona which was interrupted because the angelus was ringing: all the spectators knelt and turned to the east, the actors did the same in the wings, while on the stage an actress who was supposed to have fainted got up to pray and then returned to her fainting pose. Later, Abbé Coyer wrote:

'The outward show of their religion has penetrated national education so deeply that on Saturdays, in actual houses of prostitution, candles are burnt in front of an image of the Virgin and an extra fee is charged with which to have a mass said.'[7]

The majority of religious services were held with music and an abundance of lights. People walked about the church, laughed, chatted and formed crowds around orchestras.

'There is not one day in the year without two or three of these spectacles and all of them are thronged alike . . . After coming out from the evening service, people go to the Corso to eat ices, sup at an inn with women, watch a firework display or attend a ball at the home of a devout member of the parish or a protector of the monastery.'[8]

Moreover there was a similar alternation between laughter and penitence, as between the sacred and the profane. 'On Ash Wednesday, the day after every imaginable kind of folly,' Comt de Caylus noted at Venice, 'one sees nothing but sanctity and quiet in the streets.' The most serious historians confirmed his observation: 'At the end of carnival, at the sound of the bell of

San Francesco della Vigna announcing matins for Ash Wednesday, all noise ceases throughout the town as if by magic' (Ortolani).

In many Roman families, especially in humble circumstances, parents, children and servants recited the rosary every day in front of an image of the Virgin exposed on a small altar which, together with the crucifix, was often the main ornament of the comfortless apartments inhabited by modest households.

Fasting and abstinence in Lent and on the days of example——Fridays, Ember-eve, vigils—were strictly observed. If needs be, the civilian authority helped to ensure this. At Rome, a medical certificate was needed to obtain authorization to eat meat on those days and if some innkeeper, to meet the wishes of a free-thinking client, agreed to serve him a meal with meat on a forbidden day, it could mean prison, the pillory and the *cavalletto* for both of them.

But the observance of the Easter precept was what occasioned a veritable inquisition throughout Italy. On the last Sunday of the Easter fortnight priests announced from the pulpit that on checking the forms they gave to communicants, of which they kept duplicates, they had noted with grief that not all their parishioners had 'made their Easter' and they urged them to do so. This exhortation was repeated on the following four or five Sundays under threat of excommunication; then excommunication was pronounced without listing the culprits, but afterwards they were named and finally a list was attached to the church door giving their full names, occupation, age and domicile. The names of those who showed repentance were struck through but remained legible. Grosley, who gives these details, claimed that excommunications only took place in small towns or villages, for in the large towns, especially Rome, control would have been impossible, since people could communicate in the conventual churches; but Duparty asserts that even in Rome the custom was established and that priests sent the list of refractory worshippers to the government, whose excommunication was fulminated on Saint Bartholomew's Day (August 24th). At that period the sanction only had spiritual effects; thus certain priests to whom the procedure was repugnant tried hard to get round it, but not always very scrupulously. One of them confessed to

Dupaty that he never sent the list to the authorities; he tried to make the rare refractory worshippers amend their ways by private warnings, but if he failed he did not hesitate to have those who refused sent to prison. One of his parishioners was held captive for six weeks: 'he communicated in the end!' However the sacraments were refused to courtesans.

Reaction against usages which were inevitably distinguished by hypocrisy came from two circles: from the Illuminists influenced by the Encyclopaedia, which circulated widely in Italy, and more generally by 'French ideas', and from the supporters of Jansenism.

It is barely half a century since growing attention has been given by historians to the extremely important development which so-called 'Jansenist' tendencies experienced during the second half of the eighteenth century, even inside the Sacred College, the high prelature and the religious orders, mainly the Oratory and the fathers of the Pious Schools (Piarists). It appeared not only in the form of opposition to the laxity with which the Jesuits were reproached, but also of support for dispossessing the clergy of property, the reduction of the number of priests and especially of monks, a stricter observance of monastic vows, numerous liturgical reforms which it would be out of place to list in this book, and lastly an even more drastic reform of the customs of the Roman Court and the privileges of the pontifical authority.

As an example of these tendencies we may mention a bishop of broad views and great culture, Mons. Ventimiglia, Prince of Belmonte, who was Bishop of Catania from 1757 to 1773, then Archbishop of Nicomedia and Grand Inquisitor at Palermo—the last person to bear this title in Sicily. In spite of his dreaded office he had in his library the complete works of Voltaire, Rousseau and Helvetius, was fond of the great Greek and Latin classics, only granted nomination to the prebends in his gift on merit and even considered Calvin to be a great man. He was in epistolary relations with several French Jansenists and was even more in sympathy with them than with the philosophy of enlightenment.

One of the practical ways of applying the 'Jansenist' trend, supported by several governments, particularly those of Tuscany and Lombardy, was a reduction of non-working holidays. There were a hundred of them at the end of the sixteenth century, in addition to Sundays and moveable feasts, and almost all of them were allowed to continue in the seventeenth century. In 1770 there were still a good fifty, including thirty-six of obligation on top of the fifty-two Sundays. In the month of December alone, there were twelve holidays. On August 23, 1783, Pius VI reduced the feasts of obligation to nineteen: Christmas, Circumcision, Epiphany, Easter Monday, Ascension Day, The Assumption of the Blessed Virgin, the Nativity of Mary, the Immaculate Conception, Saint Joseph, Saint John the Baptist, Saint Peter and Saint Paul, Saint Lawrence, All Saints, Saint Stephen and the Patron Saint of each town or country. On other feast days laid down by the Holy See, the Synods or custom, he gave the faithful permission to work, provided that they went to Mass. The law about fasting remained applicable to vigils.

Another capital reform carried out in the eighteenth century was that of the right of asylum which conferred immunity on a mass of criminals; we shall refer to it later. Enlightened despotism issued decrees abolishing the survival, carried to absurd limits, of a measure originally inspired by the spirit of charity. 'The Christian princes,' Father Labat rightly observed, 'had originally excluded from immunity arsonists, assassins poisoners, forgers and some others. The abuse which is deplored at present is that all crimes find sure asylum in the churches, except for matters of faith.' Suspicion of heresy or free thinking in fact seemed the most unpardonable of faults to many licensed or benevolent inquisitors.

Before closing this chapter, mention should be made of the appearance in Italy towards 1730 at Florence, Naples and Rome of Freemasonry, under the influence of English protestants. In spite of the pontifical condemnations of Clement XII and Benedict XIV, who were particularly worried by the secrecy of the meetings in the lodges, it immediately recruited many members among the nobility and a few among priests with illuminist leanings, and even in the lower classes. Grand Duke François de Lorraine, in ill-favour with the Tuscan clergy who sympathized with the Bourbons, was a Freemason. However, under pressure from Cardinal Corsini, a nephew of the Pope, he had to agree to close the lodge at Florence and hand over to the Holy Office a priest called Bonaccorsi, while proceedings were taken against other Florentines suspected of heresy. The atmosphere of intrigue, charlatanry (Cagliostro was one of the main introducers of masonry into Italy) and erotic epicureanism developed by the lodges, to which women were soon admitted, could not fail to worry Rome, at the same time as fraternization between noblemen and craftsmen, soldiers and civilians, Italians and foreigners united by the same reformist and egalitarian views. Masonry also had a considerable development at Genoa, but none of the religious leaders of the Jansenist movement—very opposed in general to illuminism—were members. Things were quite different in the south and later in Piedmont. At Naples, Father Perocades, a champion of Jacobinism in 1799, had first distinguished himself as 'the poet of masonry' (E. Rota).

F

CHAPTER VII

THE MIDDLE AND LOWER CLASSES

ONE CAN scarcely talk of a middle class in eighteenth-century Italy. In richer and more densely populated countries, it was mainly made up of traders, industrialists, legal men, proprietors working their own land and that ascendant bourgeoisie which produced the Revolution in France. In Italy its general outline was very much the same, but it led an unostentatious life and was numerically small, except in a few large towns, between a superabundant nobility and a multitude of poor people, whether they were cultivators, craftsmen or *lazzaroni.*

At Rome, where titles immediately assumed the superlative form, a fraction of women of the people called themselves in dialect *minenti* (eminent), but their husbands were carpenters, cabinet makers, turners and smiths, in short, skilled workers. Others natives of the provinces of the Papal state (masons, tailors and hatters), Genoa (innkeepers), Friuli (bakers) or Switzerland (grocers and pastry cooks), were really only distinguished from the lower classes by their habits, but possessed more regular and generally larger resources.

The middle class proper was composed of the numerous employees of the Curia, whether they were priests wearing the small collar, or fathers of what were usually large families, careful to observe scrupulously the pious duties laid down by the church for its members.

At Venice there were also the well-paid secretaries of the ducal Chancellery, citizens by birth inscribed in the *Book of Silver*, who formed the élite of the middle class. They played a very important role in it owing to the complicated machinery and the high political worth of the Venetian government which remained without an equivalent in Europe until its fall. This body of officials was entrusted with all the technical work which gave shape to the decisions of the senate: drawing up draft laws, drafting instructions to ambassadors, letters to foreign Courts and reports on a multitude of questions. These 'gentlemen of the people'—who treated the nobility of the province as their equals, wore the toga and the wig and were invited with their wives to

82

ducal receptions—could even represent the Most Serene Republic as Residents in places where no embassy was maintained, command gallies and, as chancellors, accompany governors and ambassadors on distant missions and at Venice even become secretaries of the Council of Ten, i.e. be admitted to sharing the most dreaded secrets of government.

The census of 1766 enumerated in addition 5,500 merchants in Venice. Together with the lawyers, magistrates, public officials and directors of undertakings, this middle class represented about one-fifth of the population, the humbler classes of gondoliers, porters, servants and craftsmen of all kinds making up the other four-fifths.[1]

The life of the working classes was rough, the men left home at sunrise, attended mass, gulped down a cup of coffee and went off to their place of work. At Venice the *fondachi* (warehouses) opened before 'tierce' — i.e. about 10 a.m. in December and January, and 8 a.m. in June and July—the retail shops shortly afterwards and a little later still the centres of commercial transactions and the large shops. The legal profession also had their office hours from before tierce until an hour after noon and sometimes until night.

At Milan, the middle classes assumed a more important role in the eighteenth century, because industry was more highly developed there than elsewhere and the nobility was not so predominant. In spite of successive losses of Lombardic territory to the House of Savoy which in the middle of the century had only left about 1,300,000 inhabitants in this then Austrian province, Milanese banks had flourished abroad, founding branches in Vienna, Paris, Amsterdam and Cadiz. As the result of a campaign undertaken by Pietro Verri in 1764 against the privilege of private farmers, which enriched individuals to the detriment of the State, the administration of the excise was directly assumed by the government in 1780. In 1777 new coins were minted in Milan. They were the most beautiful and the most accurate in Italy. All these things had increased the town's reputation and developed trade, and consequently the middle classes.

Extremely accurate statistics of the various trades practised at Florence in 1765, when Grand Duke Leopold acceded to the throne, listed no more than a thousand men practising a liberal profession out of an active population of 47,662: lawyers, attorneys, notaries, doctors, surgeons, engineers, architects, bankers, professors (of both sexes) and chemists. Together with their wives and children, included in the non-working section of the population—which then totalled slightly more than 78,000 souls—would they make a total of 4,000 people? It is doubtful, and how many of them were really families in comfortable circumstances? By adding tradesmen or employees such as booksellers, bookkeepers, transcribers, watchmakers, goldsmiths, jewellers, printers, musicians and music teachers, sculptors, painters and draftsmen, i.e. trades raising their practitioners above the vulgar mob and putting them into the middle class at a pinch, we should have another 2,000 active citizens. The total remains low and certainly it does not permit us to postulate capital savings of any size between the exaggerated wealth of the aristocracy and the admitted poverty of the working-class population.

At Naples industrial activity was too handicapped by obsolete and tyrannical regulations, obstacles to export, lack of fluid capital and raw materials to be able to create wealth derived from production and trading. Business circles there remained the field of middle-men with no position: money changers, awarders of public works, tax collectors (a large number), etc. The complicated system of customary rights and legislation applied by a dozen successive governments — Roman, Byzantine, Swabian, Angevin, Aragonese and Spanish—had made Neapolitan law into such a jungle that it 'offered the most propitious atmosphere for roguery'. So legal men were more prosperous there than anywhere else. 'The town included a lawyer or a notary per 150 inhabitants, a higher proportion than all the other towns in Italy' (René Bouvier). At the end of the eighteenth century, they were estimated at 30,000 for the whole of the kingdom, except Sicily, a figure of approximately the same order. Certain cases lasted for centuries. However, many diplomas or doctorates in law were no proof of serious studies or genuine competence. They were bought like an office at the *Collegio di dottori* without any examination by the Faculty. Nevertheless, by no means negligible fiscal and honorary privileges were attached to the title, as they were to that of doctor—which also abounded. Thus their holders were close to the nobility, but far from giving the country a genuine brilliance they brought discredit on their social class and served as a pretext for the satirical zest of the *commedia dell'arte* until Manzoni immortalized in doctor Azzeccagarbugli of his novel I *promessi sposi*[2] a type of barrator who became as classical in Italy as Molière's Diafoirus in the medical field in France.

These advocates, both at Venice and Naples, gave their pleading a theatrical aspect by their exaggerated mimicry. They began by setting out their argument and drawing their conclusions in a moderate tone of voice, but soon, in order to refute the opposing counsel, they got excited, raised their voices, gesticulated and struck the edge of their boxes, darting in and out of them impulsively. They made themselves look ridiculous to foreigners but the Italian judges did not appear to be affected by their behaviour. A few members of the legal profession nevertheless maintained the high juridical reputation of the University of Naples (comparable with that of Bologna). Several figured among the victims of the repression of the liberal movement in 1799. Four hundred lawyers of the first order were markedly superior.

In the villages and market towns, innkeepers could also be assigned to the middle class, in spite of the mediocrity of their establishments. They often held fairly large sums of ready cash and acted as pawnbrokers. Next to the lord they were often the richest figure in the place. The many different varieties of agents and stewards joined them in an intermediate rank between the nobility and the agricultural proletariat. The most fortunate were the yeomen — especially numerous in the south — who worked the great domains as stewards for a fixed rent. Others administered the more modest landed property of the urban bourgeoisie.

The largest section of the people was that of poor peasants and agricultural workers. In the south there was virtually no other, apart from the craftsmen. In the first place properties were neglected and devaluated — livestock on the decrease, plantations abandoned, excessive tree felling—in which case the farmer had to give up working the land and leave to swell the ranks of the proletariat. In Venetia the cause lay mainly in the shortness of the leases which only lasted for five years and were often limited to three; moreover, the farmer received no indemnity for improvements made on the domain when he left; consequently he was discouraged. We have seen that Young also blamed the excessively small size of rural properties, even in several zones of Lombardy. Dismissed, the cultivator passed from one village to another looking for a plot of ground, however modest it might be, to work on his own account. Only the ecclesiastical bodies kept the families who farmed their lands for very long periods, often even for several generations.

Next to the peasants, the most numerous working class category was that of domestics. In Venice in 1760, they numbered nearly 13,000 of both sexes, or ten per cent of the *popolani*. In the country, where craftsmen were frequently lacking in the castles and villas, they were replaced by a mass of servants, in addition to the cooks, gardeners, market gardeners, stable lads, gamekeepers, bookkeepers, washerwomen, etc.

In Rome, Naples and especially in Sicily, the domestic staff was augmented by the runners who accompanied the carriages at night carrying large torches. These fellows were very badly paid and undernourished, sometimes in rags at home but looking well in their livery when with their masters. Roland wrote that the occupation of runner could seldom be continued for more than ten years. 'It is a terrible occupation in these climes; several of them have been seen to fall dead in front of the carriages . . . They are very lucky if, after having run ahead of the carriage for this time, they are still fit and their masters allow them to climb up behind. Often they are kept on until death out of pity.' According to Dupaty, 'the profession of 15,000 people at Naples is to run ahead of a carriage and of 15,000 others to run behind'.

These domestics felt that they shared in the splendour of the houses they served and made it a sort of point of honour to observe a strict order of precedence. Hence among the coachmen, who held a high rank in the hierarchy of servants, and even among the runners accompanying the heavy carriages, a jealously-guarded insistence on not giving way to less worthy colleagues. On the occasion of a grand reception given one night in March 1782 by Cardinal de Bernis, French ambassador, in his palace on the Corso, the coach of the Cardinal of York, suburbicarian Bishop of Frascati, whose luxury was proverbial and who kept runners faster than his actual horses, appeared at the entrance to the palace at the same time as that of Princess Rezzonico, *née* Boncompagni-Ludovisi, wife of the senator of Rome. To ensure the English cardinal's precedence, the most agile of his runners, Gigi, nicknamed the *Moretto*, threw his lighted torch in the nostrils of the horses of the 'senatress' who flew into the rage one can imagine. After domestic staff and before the skilled workers it would undoubtedly be legitimate to place the beggars. Sometimes the two functions of valet and begging for favours were combined. Foreign travellers frequently complained about this in the eighteenth century. Montesquieu was enraged at such behaviour. From Rome he wrote: 'You go to see a man: on the spot his servants come to ask you for money, often even before you have seen him. Better dressed men than I have often asked me for alms. In short, all this rabble is constantly after you.'

In truth, domestics were not the only people to solicit the generosity of foreigners who were supposed to be wealthy. As Montesquieu noticed at Verona: 'You cannot see a man who does not ask you for money; a shoemaker asked me for alms after selling me a pair of shoes; a man who has sold you a book asks you for the *bona man*; the man who tells you the way or a piece of news asks for a reward. This is quite different from Holland where they ask for money for drink; here it is to live. Cheating, the companion of poverty, is rampant: if you have agreed on a price with someone, he will make you pay more.'

Grosley noted that on entering the towns of the Milanese territory you were not asked to open your baggage, but for *la buona mancia per il signor officiale della dogana*[3]; likewise on leaving. At first requests were polite and then threatening if one pretended not to understand. In the Papal States, at the gates of each town, travellers were presented with a printed certificate marked *gratis* but which they had to pay for. President de Brosses also showed his exasperation at always having to put his hand in his pocket: 'For the smallest things, you are surrounded by people asking for tips; even a man with whom you have made a bargain for a *louis* would find it very odd if he was not given an *écu* as a tip when he had carried it out'. He told himself that he was exploited because he was a foreigner and that he would put a stop to it when he knew the language better.

In fact, although the foreigner known as such was frequently fleeced, the native was equally so. Especially at Rome, the prelate of the *annone*, who presided over the holding of markets, found it necessary in 1770 to issue detailed provisions about how meat should be cut up and fix the quantity of bone to add per pound, etc. In spite of these fine regulations, 'the traders thieved, robbed and falsified the weights and measures in the midst of a fiendish din' (D. Silvagni). Normally this did not give rise to serious troubles. As the people's needs were extremely few, they put up with their lot. The mildness of the climate did the rest, so much so that it enabled the Neapolitan *lazzaroni* to live in complete idleness watching the enchanting views of their gulf and feeding on a few pence worth of macaroni. They could always come by these few pence by begging. Even at Genoa, 'there is not a single beggar who is not sure of eating and drinking every day; the craftsman is by no means sure' (Dupaty).

'The people of Calabria have a cloak, with which they stay on one spot throughout the day, having enough to live on with two sous a day,' said Montesquieu once more. The costume is not only Calabrian, but also extended to Apulia and the whole of the extreme south of Italy. However, what Montesquieu did not notice was that it was the result of the agricultural labourer's endemic unemployment, not of laziness. The *braccianti*—who had no capital but their arms—used to wait from dawn onwards, collected in the centre of the village, for a steward to come and hire them for seasonal work or even only for the day. It is still so in our own day, in spite of the efforts already made to rationalize southern agriculture and cure the scourge of unemployment in the overpopulated provinces.

As for the body of craftsmen in Italy, it experienced a development prolonged by the belated rise of large-scale capitalism. Even today, in Florence for example, we find workshops producing embossed leather, hard stones, fancy jewellery and embroidered fabrics which, with a very small work force, keep up the old traditions which delight foreigners. The movements of emancipation in the nineteenth century recruited their cadres and militant workers far more from among the craftsmen than the peasants and even the bourgeoisie. But throughout Italy in the seventeenth and eighteenth centuries, the ancient structures of society underwent the assault of new techniques: in the same way that the smallholder or farmer often arrived to swell the ranks of the *braccianti*, many craftsmen became wage-earners in the growing industry which we shall study in another chapter.

What are we to say of the character of these lower orders? Once again a clear distinction between regions must be made.

The Venetians were famous for their gentleness. There is not a brutal action in the comedies of Goldoni. 'The people of Venice,' wrote Montesquieu, 'are the best in the world: there are no guards at all at the spectacles and no rowdiness is heard; nor does one see any brawling. They endure patiently the fact that a lord does not pay them at all . . . ' This was all the more remarkable because there were practically no myrmidons of the law at Venice. Police informers, both paid and unpaid—Casanova was one of the former—pullulated and the government knew everything which was said or done in the town, but a large force responsible for keeping order was unnecessary. They could rely on the people's deep attachment to the government, maintained incidentally by the cordiality of the great with regard to it, the honours which the various quarters enjoyed, the parishes, the guilds and especially the stream of feasts at which the people gave full reign to their enjoyment.[4]

Dealing with Italian servants in general, Abbé Coyer was struck by their respectful submission to anyone employing them, even if they were passing foreigners. He attributed mainly to their sobriety the evenness of humour, the 'sweetness of manner' which until recently was still the distinctive feature of Italian domestic personnel. However, President de Brosses was perhaps over-indulgent when he asserted of Venice: 'The blood is so gentle here that in spite of the opportunity given by masks, the night, the narrow streets and especially the bridges without parapets, from which one could push a man into the sea without him noticing, there are not four accidents in the sea; and then only among foreigners'. Charles de Brosses had visited Italy in 1739 and 1740. Now, from March 1st, 1739, to the end of January 1740, not taking into account blows exchanged during brawls, there were seventeen judgments pronounced at Venice for serious wounds and homicides. That is admittedly few if we compare them with the 4,000 murders committed at Rome under the pontificate of Clement XIII, which lasted eleven years (1758-1769), and the 7,000 for the same period in the rest of the Roman States. Stendhal reported that there were supposed to have been 18,000 under Pius VI, from 1775 to 1800. Venice was a little better lit than Rome or Florence. According to Lalande, there were 3,000 lanterns there, a probably exaggerated figure, but reliable men were posted at various points by the Seigniory to guide strangers or citizens through the dark alleys with a lantern.

Romans had livelier blood and a rough humour. We know the disorders and tragedies of which the town of the Popes was the scene in the Middle Ages and the Rennaissance. Whenever the pontiff was changed, and especially when the Conclave was prolonged, pillage became licit and private vengeances were given free rein. It was still seen even in 1774, before the election of Pius VI, when Prince Chigi tried to poison Cardinal Carandini, a certain Father Ceracchi killed his brother, and a doctor —Lunadei—publicly and forcibly removed a woman from the arms of her husband.

The lower classes accepted the pontifical government out of meekness and for the many benefits they gained from it. Their liking for colour and superstition found food in the frequency of holidays and religious processions, and the multiplicity of popular devotions. But they readily put their hands to their knives, even after they had danced the tarantella to the sound of a guitar or a mandoline outside an inn of the *Castelli* or listened to *stornelli* (*ritornellos*) improvised by a rustic poet or poetess. An objectionable word, or too fixed a stare at some other man's wife were enough to start either a duel, incidentally always fairly fought, or a general scuffle, most often followed by reconciliation. But if a man died, the murderer fled to a place of asylum, or joined one of the bands of brigands which were typical of Rome until the middle of the nineteenth century. Even policemen sometimes had great difficulty in arresting a malefactor in the working class districts where, if he escaped from their hands, he found a thousand accomplices who kept him out of their grasp; and faced with certain furious rebellions

of the Roman working classes, the *sbirri* themselves had to turn
on their heels and seek shelter.

We find a very characteristic illustration of this state of mind,
reviving the communal rivalries of the Middle Ages, in the
pitched battles which the inhabitants of the Transteverine quarters, *Transteverini* and *Monticiani*, engaged in periodically with
bricks and stones on the deserted enclosed space of the Forum,
where they only had to bend down to find projectiles among the
ruins. The combat did not end until one of the two camps was
routed or when a squadron of light cavalry arrived to disperse
them. But once the soldiers had gone away, the battle frequently
began again with equal fury. When they tired and night fell, the
wounded were finally transported to the neighbouring Hospital
of the Consolation until the next occasion.

CHAPTER VIII

WOMEN, LOVE AND MARRIAGE

ONCE A society woman of the eighteenth century was married she exercised a sort of sovereignty. Until then she was the slave of tyrannical customs which first of all shut her up in a convent from the age of four or five years and practically forced her to stay there as a nun if she was not rich enough to be sought after by a husband of her own rank. Sometimes a gentleman who had seen her at the receptions, concerts, or even comedies which were given in the parlours of the convents asked for her hand in marriage without a dowry. This was the only condition on which she could leave. At Venice, even when she was rich, she was rarely taken into town, even more rarely to the theatre and then always masked, and never to a ball. Conversations between young lovers were forbidden unless the mother was present.

It seems that the only exception to these customs was in Sicily. There young girls made an early entry into the world after being educated by their mother in families which were much more united than in the rest of Italy. Brydone, an English physician of noble birth, a friend of Priestley and on close terms with Ambassador Hamilton at Naples, wrote in a description of travels in Sicily and Malta, published in 1770, that in the house of the Prince of Partana he saw a group of young people of both sexes playing parlour games on their own without the mothers worrying about it. He compared this freedom of behaviour with that of the English.

A young girl of the middle classes also lived more of a family life, but she was closely watched nevertheless. Once she was married and had children she hardly ever left her house again. Abbé Richard relates that he knew a lady who had never left her own home for more than twenty years except to go to the church situated opposite her house. This was the way the wives of the 'citizens' lived at Venice, the secretaries of the chancellery, for example: they never had *cicisbei*, never frequented the conversation salons (*casini*) on St Mark's Square, where the nobility on the other hand gossiped and gambled until late in the night.

When pronouncing a judgment on the Italian woman of the

eighteenth century it is always necessary to distinguish the class
to which she belongs. Even if a large part of the aristocracy was
corrupted, the lower middle classes—the favourite subject of
Goldoni's comedies—still had simple strict morals and the lower
classes, who formed an entirely separate world, remained healthy
on the whole, even at Venice.[1]

The custom of cicisbeism, peculiar to Italy of the eighteenth
century, which had received it from Spain, was nevertheless
more developed in the Northern States than in the Kingdom of
Naples where a Spanish dynasty reigned.[2] It was always kept
within the bounds of decency. The cicisbeo, or *cavaliere servente*,
was never a lover, although he was allowed to attend his lady's
toilet in the morning, while her hair was done or her maids
dressed her. He accompanied her at meal times, on excursions,
in society and to the theatre, but never spent the night with her.
Parini, whose masterpiece, the poem *Il Giorno*, is entirely devoted
to a witty and swingeing satire on the nobility of his epoch,
when describing the way a young lord spent his time with his
fair one, far from insinuating that he might go too far in his
familiarity, illustrated the origin of cicisbeism by a mythological
allegory: when Eros complained to his mother Venus that he
could not pierce hearts bound by the marriage bond as and when
he wished, she, in order to meet his wishes, granted that his
brother, Hymen, would only retain his sway over mortals during
the night, while he would abandon the day to the arrows of
Cupid. Thus the tiresome servitude of marital duty would satisfy
the husbands and the day would be made over to the tender care
of the cicisbei.

To tell the truth, cicisbeism was originally primarily a way
of protecting married women from ill-intentioned attentions. At
Venice they were often named in the marriage contract and
chosen from among relations or friends of the family, even if old.
Lalande even went so far as to say that he was a man for whom
the lady had little liking and who accompanied her out of
decency. He saw far more of his lady at the theatre and in company than *tête-à-tête*. The Venetian satirist Bondi described him
ironically: 'Supplementary husband during the day, his duty is
to stay constantly by the side of the wife of a third party and by
express contract and obligation to be bored by her for days at a

time'. Goldoni introduced examples of cicisbei into several of his comedies (*The Knight and The Lady, The Antiquary's Family* and *The Prudent Lady*). He particularly emphasized their ridiculous aspect.

It was in the highest nobility that the institution assumed the increasingly frivolous aspect immortalized by Parini. At mealtimes, the cicisbeo, seated next to the mistress of the house, had the task of carefully carving the poultry, choosing her favourite morsel for her or offering her the carving knife with an elegant gesture if she wanted to serve her guests herself. In the afternoons, they both went to visit the lady's friends, drove along the Corso in her carriage, occasionally stopping to chat from one carriage to another; in the evening at the elegant receptions where they met their counterparts, it might happen that they were not seated at the same card table but in any case the husband, who was courting another woman, never played with his wife and it was the cicisbeo who watched her from a neighbouring table and winked and smiled at her.

In the Kingdom of Naples, where a woman of a certain rank would never step out into the street unless accompanied by a lackey and a chamber maid, the former walking in front and the other behind, an equerry, if there were no servants, took her arm to go to church. It was a kind of profession which required, as Father Labat wrote, 'a blameless life and a fidelity able to withstand every sort of solicitation'. The equerry might even serve several ladies: while the first made her devotions, he went to fetch another, then took the first one back home. But that was no longer genuine cicisbeism.

Obviously the only conclusion one could draw from all this was that the Italian women of the *Settecento* did not thrive on amorous intrigues. However, Casanova has given them a highly exaggerated reputation for habitual libertinage. Even Montesquieu recorded the spiteful gossip commonly current in the salons rather than observations worthy of his brilliant mind when he wrote at Rome: 'There is nothing more common than for a husband to sell his wife for money or protection. As soon as a young woman marries, they start looking for the prelate or cardinal who will have her . . . They say that Ottoboni has between sixty and seventy bastards.'[3] This was true in the

sixteenth, but infinitely less so in the eighteenth century. We
have described how widespread Jansenism was, even within the
Holy College of Cardinals. In general the Popes led a very worthy
life and some of them were particularly austere. Charles de
Brosses rather contradicted himself, as he often did, when
writing that all the women of noble birth at Venice had a lover
and added a little further on that, according to the French
ambassador, 'he only knew about fifty women who slept with
their lovers; the remainder were restrained by devotion'. Yet this
ambassador, Count de Froullay, a dissolute and despised figure,
was unlikely to have made an underestimate.

The president's explanation was that the confessors were very
generous about gallantry so long as it was not carried to the
furthest extremes. At Venice there were many gondolas 'which
women always take alone without chaperones; they are a sure
asylum. It is unheard of for a gondolier of Madame to let himself
be caught up by Monsieur; he would be drowned by his com-
rades on the morrow.' Montesquieu also thought that everything
imaginable went on in a gondola : 'Women can only go shopping
or walking in St Mark's Square during carnival time, but . . .
they go where and with whom they wish in their gondolas'. In
actual fact it was generally with their cicisbei and the most
malicious memorialists admit that they were never lovers.

Until the middle of the century, Italian women never wore
rouge. Their natural complexions were charming without any
artificial aids. Montesquieu was astonished by their youthful
appearance at Florence. 'The majority of them look as fresh and
as youthful at forty as at twenty. You see women who have had
ten or twelve children and are as pretty, fresh and attractive as
ever. I think that their regular life, simple diet and something
special in the air keeps them like this.' A regular life and a
simple diet, i.e. moderation in love and at the table.

Nevertheless there were courtesans. They no longer enjoyed
anything like their ancient splendour. In 1714 de Caylus
estimated that there were 8,000 in Naples 'without counting
those who are never mentioned'. President de Brosses, who was
very observant in these matters, noted as soon as he arrived in
Milan : 'you cannot take a step into the squares without meeting
the most obliging pimps in the world, who always offer you

women of whatever colour and country you want; but there is no doubt that the girl who appears is not always as magnificent as was promised . . . ' We know how surprised he was in Venice at visiting a courtesan whose dress and home were so unlike what one would have expected in a member of her profession. In fact, Grosley reported that at the beginning of the century a feast given to the Prince of Denmark by the courtesans of Venice surpassed the one which the *gentildonne* had offered to the same prince in the magnificence of the costumes and the brilliance of the jewels; but when he published his *Observations* he admitted that from about 1730 onwards their prestige had greatly declined. This is confirmed by Abbé Richard and by Cardinal de Bernis in his *Mémoires*. Historians of our own epoch support their views: 'the courtesan, who had gradually fallen to the lowest ranks, no longer held sway in eighteenth-century society' (Ortolani).

They were excluded from the churches and all assemblies at Rome. They were forbidden to receive clients during Advent, Lent, Easter Week, Sundays and holidays, fast days and vigils. The *barigel* (provost of police) and the *sbirri* could enter their houses at any hour of the day to make a check-up and any infraction was penalized by the pillaging of their furniture by the police, in addition to a prison sentence. If they died in sin, Christian burial was refused them. Father Labat reported that at Civitavecchia he had with his own eyes seen one of them dragged to the refuse dump with her feet tied to a horse's tail.

These customs were far from making it an attractive trade. On arriving at Genoa at the end of the century, Dupaty noted 'so much libertinage that there are no prostitutes, so many priests that there is no religion, so many people who govern that there is no government'. It is characteristic of travellers, even the intelligent ones, to make such a dogmatic list of their first impressions. The truth is that the gradual emancipation of married women introduced more delicacy and distinction into social relations and discredited the courtesan, with a consequent increase of amorous liaisons, both licit and illicit, between people in the same world. Jealousy had not completely disappeared, especially in the south, but cicisbeism at least made husbands simulate indifference by trusting in their wives' fidelity. At

Naples, where the custom was uncommon, Lalande observed that husbands took their wives to mass themselves and stood in front of them if anyone looked at them too long; but normally jealousy went no further.

Actresses and especially opera singers attracted most of the attention, far more than the courtesans or even the dancers, whose behaviour was generally extremely free. Many of them were married and lived a settled life, helped by the considerable wealth earned by their talents. But others excited passionate rivalry between the great lords: e.g. the *diva* Caterina Gabrielli, who had a great success in *Didone abbandonata*, of whom Abbé Coyer wrote: 'Pious Aeneas would have had to be very devoted to resist the charms of her voice and figure'. She and her sister Francesca were finally expelled from Naples because of the amorous intrigues they excited, but the whole of Europe was on tenterhooks to hear her. Her impertinent reply to Catherine of Russia, who remarked that none of her marshalls had dared ask her for ten thousand roubles for a few weeks' work, is well known: 'All right! Make your marshalls sing, your majesty.' Another celebrated singer at San Carlo, Elizabeth Billington, a German brought up in Great Britain, was the subject of tremendous rivalry between the Marquis of Caltanissetta, son of the Prince of Paterno, and Prince Augustus of England, who became her acknowledged lover.[4]

CHAPTER IX

MARRIAGES AND FUNERALS

MARRIAGE RITES involved both social conventions and folklore, with one or the other predominating, depending on whether the aristocracy or the lower classes were concerned.

We know that the daughters of the nobility were normally married on leaving the convent to a man chosen by their parents, often long beforehand, without their own wishes being taken into account at all. However, in certain cases at least a show of love was made in Venice; 'once the marriage was fixed, the young man was supposed to walk up and down at a certain hour beneath the windows of his fiancée, who was supposed to return his greeting. He had to give her a present of a diamond which was called a *ricordino* (a little souvenir). Before the nuptial blessing, the husband's mother gave the young woman a pearl necklace which she was obliged to wear continually until the first year of her marriage was over.'

Unions between two great families were normally celebrated at home. On the wedding day, all the relations assembled in the largest hall in the palace, amid a great display of silk, swords and finery. 'The fiancée, dressed in silver brocade, her breasts covered with lace and jewellery, made her entrance, as in the past, by giving her hand to the master of ceremonies or dancer, dressed in black and wearing a small damask cloak with a broad collar on his shoulders. The bride knelt on a square piece of velvet and received the blessing of her father, her mother and her closest relations; then, led by the master of ceremonies to the middle of the hall, she put her hand in her husband's and the priest blessed them.[1] After which the married couple kissed each other, the orchestra began to play and the wife danced a sort of minuet on her own, thus opening the ball which went on until late at night.

In 1752, Catherine Loredan, niece of the Doge Francis, was married to Giovanni Mocenigo in the ducal palace itself. An engraving of the nuptial ceremony exists showing the Doge on his throne; on his left the married pair kneeling on cushions, surrounded by senators and to the right an orchestra.

During the eighteenth century these practices, which already existed in the preceding century, underwent some changes. Ladies invited to weddings uniformly adopted dresses of black silk trimmed with lace for the religious ceremony, while for the banquet which followed they put on coloured dresses. The bride herself changed clothes and replaced the strings of large pearls which she wore round her neck and arms with her white dress by precious stones. A hundred or so gondolas were put at the disposition of the guests with boatmen in the traditional gala dress: silk jackets and stockings, short breeches, white shoes and red belts and bonnets. The same display of pomp was made when young noblewomen took the veil. Madame du Bocage described a ceremony at which half the Senate attended. The sister of the Doge Loredan was the only one to wear a coloured dress; all the other ladies were in black. 'The victim made her vows, supported by two mothers', before going up to the parlour where the women who had come to greet her were served with all kinds of refreshments. The conventional rules did not prevent 'assemblies at the grille every evening' and the dress worn by nuns 'far from effacing their beauty, increased it'. It cost as much as 30,000 ducats for this sort of ceremony.

The proveditors *alle pompe* admittedly try to counteract this excess of luxury, going so far as to compel the dancer, dressmaker and hairdresser to denounce contraventions under oath, for they never found a witness among the nobility who would agree to do so. Even when they had information, they hesitated to deal severely with usages which had become habitual. They limited themselves to forbidding silver underclothes and dresses embroidered with gold. At the same time dowries increased and a marriage entailed such enormous expenditure, even if there was only one son and one daughter per family, that the custom was established of only seeking unions with people of similar wealth—which balanced the endowments—or even between the near relations. In 1766 on the marriage of her son Alvise, the Dogaressa Corner Mocenigo spent 456,487 livres (nearly £20,000), including 5,621 for the dinner alone.

Almost at the same epoch, on May 27, 1762, Abbé Richard witnessed the funeral procession which accompanied the remains of the Doge Loredan from the ducal palace to the Church of

Saints John and Paul (in the Venetian dialect, San Zanipolo). It lasted for three hours. After all the religious schools, the clerics of different orders, the secular clergy, the masters of ships and the guilds of the Arsenal carrying lighted candles, came the shield of the Doge with the Lion of Saint Mark covered with a black veil, the bier covered with gold cloth, the statue of the late Serene Highness under a gold baldaquin surrounded by 200 banners with silver shafts of the school of Saint Mark and an equal number of torch bearers. Also carrying torches came the boys and girls brought up in the town's four 'hospitals'—in reality pupils of genuine musical conservatories which we shall mention later—the notaries of the ducal chancellery, the secretaries of the senate, the three *Avogadori di Comune*[2] (replacing the members of the Most Serene *Signoria*, in other words the government, who could not leave the palace), the brother of the Doge with the senators in black togas and the nobles in long scarlet robes. This magnificent procession first walked round the square to the sound of the bells, and in front of the main door of the church the bier was raised and lowered to the ground nine times, according to the rite. The Doge's relations wore enormous trains and hoods like pyramids which excited the intense curiosity of the great crowds lining the streets and looking out of windows.[3]

In 1779 the procession of the Doge Alvise Mocenigo was even more splendid. Beginning at half past six in the evening, it did not finish until midnight. All the dead man's valets and subordinates, who numbered eighty, wore mourning dress from head to foot and 16,000 livres (£650) worth of wax was used.[4]

The obsequies of official personages, even of a lower rank, were celebrated with the maximum of luxurious display from the beginning of the century. After the burial of the great Chancellor Pietro Businello in August 1713 in the family vault in the church of Saints John and Paul, his family had a statue made which, dressed in a red toga and girded with a gold sword, was taken to Saint Mark amid a multitude of flambeaux, torches and banners. It was laid in the baptistry on trestles hung with violet drapes and the next day the statue, laid on a litter, as if it was the actual body, followed by a procession of noblemen, secretaries of the chancellery in black togas with long trains, nine congregations of priests each dressed in a special colour, indigents from the hospitals and the lower classes, was carried to the church of Saints John and Paul where the funeral panegyric was pronounced and where a catafalque, resting on sixteen columns and finishing in a tall pyramid, awaited the statue. Along the route taken by the procession the windows were covered with damask, tapestries and carpets as if a sovereign were passing by.[5]

The main Venetian churches were full of funeral monuments, usually more sumptuous than beautiful, owing to overloading with decorative motifs, in the style of the catafalque. For example that of Doge Giovanni Pesaro at the Frari Church, and that of the Doges Bertuccio and Sylvester Valier at San Zanipolo.

In Sicily it was the custom to instal the dead man himself in the church, seated on a dais and as richly dressed as he was in life. Roland witnessed the funeral vigil of an important trader at which the dais with several storeys, with galleries, columns, garlands, fleurons, plumes and hundreds of lighted candles, rose right up to the interior of the dome. 'On one of these galleries the body was placed in an armchair; it was dressed in a drugget of reddish brown silk, with white silk stockings and a powdered curled wig; next to it was a hat trimmed with gold. On each side a herald kept the flies away with banners of silk gauze emblazoned with the arms of the defunct . . . nearby thirty musicians played instruments.' The church was draped throughout with gold and tinsel, as if for the gayest of feasts, and full of dazzling lights.

Confronted with this way of envisaging death, the macabre spectacle formed by the catacombs of the Capuchins at Palermo will come as no surprise. They were not dark but brightly lit with the skeletons erect and mostly wrapped in monks' robes, holding in their hands a card giving their name and title. Johann-Heinrich Bartels relates that the Palermans went daily to pay a visit to their dead friends. 'It is quite common to see them choosing their niche and seeing whether their bodies will fit it . . . and often, by way of voluntary penance, standing upright in it for several hours.'[6]

At Novara in the eighteenth century there were ossuaries consisting of a series of chapels in which the bones of the dead were laid out symmetrically in boxes decorated with gilt or marbled paper. Poniards, daggers and stilettos were hung on these boxes at regular intervals; they were left there as evidence of reconciliation by enemies who had renounced their vengeance.[7]

But by the middle of the century a reaction set in against 'pointless expenditure' on funerals in the States where politics were most directly inspired by the philosophical spirit, namely Lombardy and Tuscany. They went from one extreme to the other, not only with the strict regulations concerning mourning dress already mentioned, but also with severe provisions which even defied the most traditional customs concerning the honours paid to the dead. François de Lorraine issued an edict in 1748 that only the nobles and the bourgeois (*cittadini*) could have a funeral service held in the form of displaying the body in the church from morning till noon on a cloth spread out on the ground. The nobles were entitled to twelve lighted candles (six on the high altar, two on the others and four in the *gentilizie* chapels, the bourgeois to six (four on the high altar and two in the family chapel, if they possessed one). In addition noble families could decorate the door of the church, sometimes their own chapel and place their coat of arms on the altar and the coffin, but any exposure of the corpse in private houses, erection of catafalques 'or other funerary contraptions' and display of silk fabrics in the churches was strictly forbidden. As for those who were neither nobles nor bourgeois, in the towns they had simply to have the dead carried from their houses to the church and cemetery 'at one o'clock at night' (about 6 p.m.) with four torches held in the hand. In the country, the obsequies took place in the afternoon.

The Grand Duke Leopold emphasized this strictness by another order forbidding the use of coffins at burials, except for bishops and nuns. At Milan, they were only used during the funeral ceremony and many parishes owned a communal coffin available to paupers. Sometimes the faces of the dead were simply covered during the funeral service before the bodies were carried off to the paupers' graves. Coffins did not become compulsory until 1787.

Nowadays these usages seem tyrannical and unthinkable. But in those days people were less horrified by death and the sight of corpses, and believed more in their glorious resurrection. The bodies were 'mortal remains' in the strict sense of the term. This explains the apparently disrespectful procedure practised at Palermo when preparing the skeletons subsequently assembled in the catacombs of the Capuchins. After death the naked corpse was walled up in a hole carved out of the rock with a base of pierced planks placed cross-wise over swiftly flowing water. Six to eight months was enough to remove the flesh after which the skeleton was dressed and fixed upright in a niche with the aid of hooks.

Sicily, an ancient country still steeped in pagan traditions which had been Christianized, was also the land where the ritual of peasant troth-plighting and weddings was most original and more reminiscent—in some aspects at least—of antiquity.

In the past the choice of a bride for a young man was made by his mother among the young women of the village—often with very large populations, we must remember—and the first notice of it was to drop a brush in front of the chosen girl's door at dawn. She picked it up and around midday awaited the visit so announced. Her mother-in-law to be then knotted her hair with a ribbon ('ntrizzaturi), the symbol of betrothal. The rite was accompanied by the distribution of grilled chick peas, almonds, walnuts and broad beans.

On the wedding day a procession went to fetch the bride-to-be, singing an epithalamium. Bartels, witness of one of these nuptial ceremonies towards the end of the eighteenth century, described one as follows:

'The father of the bridegroom goes in alone, pays the young woman a compliment and takes her in all her finery by the hand to her betrothed, who receives her at the door, while from above they are showered with wheat, bread and salt, signs of fecundity and wealth. The groom's mother-in-law attaches a biscuit of fine pastry to his buttonhole with ribbons, as a symbol of the food with which he must supply his wife. At the church they are censed and the sign of the cross made over them. The priest puts the rings on their index fingers, gold for the groom, silver for the bride; and the father changes the rings from one index finger to the other three times. Then two crowns of bay-leaves, olive leaves, rosemary and flowers are placed on their heads; and their crowns are exchanged three times as for the rings. Then the priest places a veil of white gauze on their heads above the crowns; the spouses link the little fingers of the same hand in which is a lighted candle. A table is laid in the actual church; the priest breaks a piece of bread, dips it in the wine, gives the couple three small morsels to eat, then makes them drink three times from the same glass and finally breaks the glass to show that happiness is fragile. Then the couple, together with the priest and the witnesses, form a sort of circle round the table and dance round it three times. Then all that remains is to form a procession and return to the couple's house singing.'[8]

At the wedding feast which followed a dish was put on the table for the presents given by the bride's friends. On baptismal days, neighbours sprinkled the road to the church and the child itself with wheat and fragments of bread.

In addition a few words should be said about a very ancient institution, by no means peculiar to the eighteenth century, but which continued to flourish then, and which was aimed at providing the poor with burial: the Confraternity of Mercy, founded at Florence in 1240, which subsequently thrived in other Tuscan towns and showed itself to be of vital importance during the great plagues of the Middle Ages, when the dead were numbered in tens of thousands. Similar confraternities also came into being at Milan and elsewhere and lasted under every type of government, advantageously replacing the administrative lack of warmth of present day hospital services and undertakers by the spirit of charity and union between the social classes which inspired them.

The essential characteristic of the confraternity—still active and equipped in our day with the most modern equipment for providing assistance or transport — was to consist of a fixed number of seventy-two members in memory of the seventy-two disciples of Christ mentioned in the Gospels, including thirty priests and forty-two laymen. Of the priests ten had the rank of prelates—and they included a number of bishops and archbishops, and even of popes native of Florence—and the laymen were divided into fourteen noblemen and twenty-eight 'artists' or craftsmen. We know that in the Middle Ages the term embraced all the professions covered by 'the arts'. These seventy-two members constituted the *numero minore* which embodied the confraternity, under the authority of four captains, four councillors and two proveditors, drawn by lot, half from the clergy and half from the laymen. They only remained in office for four months. (We have already emphasized the extent to which public offices were habitually of short duration in Italy in both the Middle Ages and subsequent centuries, and still are today.) To this Directory were added an indeterminate number of plain 'members', people of good will of both sexes, who formed the *numero maggiore*.

The new statutes, drafted in 1501, established a new office, whose name quickly became the most current, that of *Capo di Guardia*, chosen by lot among the seventy-two members, responsible for one month for the burial services or transport services for the sick; in addition they authorized paid 'ministers' to assist the members of the confraternity. In 1574, the office of proveditor, or financial administrator, was extended to one year's duration, renewable by decision of the captains and councillors, and entrusted to a single person instead of two.

All the Grand Dukes of Tuscany were successively numbered among the *Capi di Guardia*, at least in an honorary capacity, and in a practical capacity the most eminent members of the Florentine patriciate during the seventeenth and eighteenth centuries.[9] However, there was some anxiety on the accession of Grand Duke Peter Leopold, whose reformist views in religious matters were not slow in showing themselves. Nevertheless a dozen exceptions were made from the general suppression of confraternities and pious associations in Tuscany decreed in 1785 for reasons of what we would call public purposes today, among them the 'Confraternity of Mercy' which was also allowed by an infraction of a general prohibition to continue wearing the black cape and hood which could be pulled down over the face characteristic of certain mediaeval confraternities, in particular of the Company of Mercy at Florence. The Grand Duke (who, after refusing at first, finally accepted his nomination as *Capo di Guardia* like his predecessors) nevertheless made no exception in its favour to the reform suppressing the right to burial in churches and chapels.[10] The remains of members buried in the Chapel of Mercy were, like the others, transferred outside the town, where various cemeteries were subsequently built.

CHAPTER X
EDUCATION AND INSTRUCTION

I N THE eighteenth century, in Italy as in France, the education
and instruction of young noblemen, who hardly ever saw
their parents, was normally entrusted to tutors who were
generally clergymen, often rather despised and treated almost
like servants.

Alfieri, well placed to know the humours and usages of members of his caste, made them the subject of a satire so racy that
we cannot resist the desire to translate it almost in full:

'Sir priest, can you say mass?'
'Yes, Excellency, I have just been ordained.'
'Then you will say it for the Countess.
But where are you with your studies?
What is your behaviour like? I want to be informed
As fully and clearly as possible in advance.'
'Have me examined by anyone you like.
I know Latin very well; and as to my behaviour,
'I don't think anyone can criticize me.'
'Your Latin is a lot of old rubbish.
I have six sons: the young count is full of wit
and his easy eloquence is astonishing.
You will have a little trouble keeping
the two young priests and the three little knights in order;
So take care of them.
Don't make them into budding doctors for me:
make them talk about a little of everything
so that they won't look like ninnies in society.
You understand me. Now to the main thing,
the question of salary. I'll pay three écus
for I like everyone in my house to be comfortable.'
'But what an idea, Sire! Pay me three écus!
You pay your coachman six! — What impertinence!'
'Is there a dearth of masters, even at two écus?
What is your knowledge after all?
In short who are you to come and dispute the precedence with
my coachman?
He was born in my house, the son of one of my valets;

while thou art the son of a peasant
and your family work other people's land.
Spelling out Latin without understanding it;
a chimer, a long cassock,
a blue collar of dubious cleanliness
suffice perhaps to change your nature?
Enough of words: I pay as well as anyone:
if you don't like it, the door is open.'
    'La, don't get annoyed, Most Illustrious lord:
I will accept three écus a month:
the Most High will provide the rest.
There will be some perquisites at Easter and Christmas,
I trust; and by then I will show you
that you have a not untalented tutor.'
    'You will eat with us; but when dessert comes
you will leave the table; and it goes without saying
that in my house you forget all about "I want" or "I don't
                                                    want" . . .
I forgot one thing: my daughter,
you must make her glance at a book from time to time
Metastasio . . . ariettas; she's mad about them.
She practises them on her own occasionally;
for I haven't got the time and the Countess even less:
but you will interpret them to her
for another couple of years;
for then I am thinking of putting her in a convent
so that her mind is fully embellished.
That's all. I expect excellent tutoring from you.
By the way, what is your name[1] . . . ?'
    It goes without saying that not all education was as useless.
The instruction given by the Jesuits in their numerous colleges
and by the Fathers of the Pious Schools to the children of the
middle classes, had a more solid foundation. But the gilded
youth, whose prototype is the hero of Il Giorno, and whom
Father Parini, in the capacity of tutor, had every opportunity of
studying at first hand in the house of Duke Serbelloni and elsewhere, only aspired to drawing-room wit in conversation with
the ladies or between young lords, all equally devoid of genuine
culture. Add to this the snobbishness of only talking French, of

only praising foreign productions, on which Parini harps, and which offended his rough peasant patriotism, so that he made it another cause for complaint against the nobility of the day.[2]

Here again Venice was distinguished among the Italian states for her preoccupation with giving the young patricians destined to rule the Republic wide experience of foreign parts in addition to sound studies. They did not come out into the world until comparatively late, between twenty-two and twenty-five, and before entering the Grand Council, practised public speaking, drafting memoranda, and familiarized themselves with the laws, etc., under an ex-Senator. Many of them accompanied ambassadors abroad and acquired experience of courts and life in other countries than their own.

The less wealthy nobility and growing middle class entrusted their sons to the care of the Jesuits, whose colleges were particularly numerous in the Papal State, the Kingdom of Naples and Sicily, where even very small towns had them (Sicily alone possessed twenty-nine). In the north they were less in favour; the presence of other teaching congregations and especially the spread of 'philosophism' and later 'Josephism', meant competition for pupils. Nevertheless, until the suppression of the order they owned eight colleges in Venetia, seven in the Milanese territory, six in the Republic of Genoa and ten in Piedmont. When they ran two or three colleges in a fairly large town, one was exclusively reserved for young noblemen; e.g. at Bologna, Brescia, Ravenna, Parma, Milan and Turin.

The education they gave was based on piety and very strict discipline, daily mass, frequent communions, freely given corporal punishment. Pupils generally acquired in them a solid knowledge of Latin and the classical authors. After the suppression of the order in 1773, their colleges passed to the secular clergy or other religious bodies, but their influence often continued to be felt through their successors. Grosley noted on the eve of the event: 'The only body to be feared by the Jesuits, who nevertheless do not seem to fear it very much, is the Congregation of Pious Schools'.

The latter did in fact include several eminent masters won over to Jansenist ideas (the same was true of the Oratory). In the Republic of Genoa, where its activities were particularly far-reaching, it possessed six houses—as many as the Jesuits—and retained the three at Genoa, Savone and Chiavari even after the fall of the aristocratic regime and the suppression of sequestration imposed on religious orders by the new government in 1798. The spirit of its teaching was distinguished by the appeal it made to personal responsibility ('Anyone who teaches should never swear on the word of the masters,' professed Father Assarotti, one of the leaders of the order), to freely accepted and deeply experienced intimate convictions, to a total loyalty in the expression of these convictions.

At the same time as the methods, the actual matter taught was changed by the fathers of the Pious Schools at the end of the eighteenth century. The circle of subjects was extended to concrete examples of economic and agricultural life and a larger place given to the national tongue, of which another great precursor, also of Jansenist tendencies, Father Genovesi, was the first to introduce the usage at the University of Naples instead of Latin, and expressly for teaching political economy.

At the end of the century, a large number of patriots and democrats, who devoted themselves to the emancipation of Italy and opposed the narrow conservatism of the ancient society, came from the Pious Schools.

These hints of a widening of elementary instruction at least and a rejuvenation of traditional culture did not extend to women, however. The convents where they were prematurely shut up taught them little more than social accomplishments and dressmaking, together with reading, writing and a little grammar, sometimes not even that. In a baron's house at Girgenti in Sicily, Houël was present at a dispute between titled people about the orthography of an Italian word. Two ravishing young women were appointed judges by the assembly. Without the slightest embarrassment they replied that they could not read at all. Their mother, who was also unable to read, felt that it would have been dangerous for them to learn and a canon, a sort of director of conscience in the house, who arrived at this juncture, stated that women go astray from reading bad books and that it was quite enough for them to know how to recite the rosary. 'Everybody seemed to be of the same opinion as the canon,' Houël ended. At Rome, household duties and pious exercises bounded the horizon of the women of the lower middle classes in the circles around the Curia.

However there were a few highly cultivated women in the eighteenth century—generally of high lineage—who were even more out of context in their epoch than were the blue stockings in the times of Molière's Chrysale. For example, at Venice, Isabella Teotochi-Albrizzi, somewhat comparable to Mme Récamier for her charm and the number of writers and artists who frequented her salon and praised her beauty, which emerges very clearly in the portrait of her by Mme Vigée-Lebrun[3]; at Milan, Countess Clelia Borromeo, 'who knows not only all the sciences and languages of Europe but also speaks an Arabic like the Alcoran' (Ch. de Brosses); or again *signorina* Agnesi, an infant prodigy who recited the office of the Blessed Virgin in Greek at the age of eleven and in addition to the ancient languages, including Hebrew, and the main modern languages, studied philosophy and history, and won special fame in mathematics for her *Treatise on Conic Sections* and her *Analytical Institutions*, in which she applied the method of Leibniz to the exact sciences for the first time. When President de Brosses passed through Milan, she was in her twenties and he heard her holding forth in Latin with Count Belloni about the causes of the ebb and flow which certain fountains have in common with the sea.

At Palermo another young woman, Anna-Amelia Gentile, the daughter of a lawyer, had translated Voltaire's *Mariamne* at the age of eighteen, wrote pleasant verses and was an excellent musician. She was the pupil of the Prince of Campofranco, i.e. she had escaped from the common mould, which only formed more than mediocre minds. Later she defended the ethics of Helvetius by writing her *Philosophical Letters* under a pseudonym.

A young girl with a genuine gift for letters or the sciences could therefore easily find the means for developing her natural gifts if her family did not prevent her, but such cases were rare. When married, even in the narrow circles of a small town, she could show herself to be educated, or even erudite, without over-estimating her own importance, like the Baroness Rosabia, whom the geologist Dolomieu, later professor at the Museum, met at

Caltagirone in 1781. And in all the capitals, in the same way as at Venice and Milan, there existed at least one salon where a woman of open and keen intelligence received the eminent Italian and foreign men of her epoch. For example, Princess Leonforte at Palermo and at Rome an ordinary middle class woman, Mrs Pizzelli, equally versed in the ancient languages, mathematics and astronomy, whose house was frequented by scholars and literary men. Vincenzo Monti lorded it there, Goethe put in an appearance and Alfieri, already linked with the destiny of the Countess of Albany, read his vigorous tragedy, *Virginia,* which was so different from the gentle idylls dear to academic circles in the century of the Metastasio.

The reader may ask who looked after the instruction of the people. The answer is practically no one, and that is why in the middle of the nineteenth century about eighty per cent of the population of all southern Italy were still illiterate. In the eighteenth century the proportion was even higher and more widespread. But when a zealous priest spotted a naturally keen intelligence in one of the boys in his parish, he sometimes gave him a few lessons or sent him to a small seminary which he did not always leave with an ecclesiastical vocation. In this way a few men of the working classes did manage to acquire at least elementary education. The monks of the Pious Schools (known in Central Europe, where they had many branches, as Piarists) also added primary schools to their secondary colleges in some districts of Italy. But the numbers so affected could not but remain minute in the absence of any planned school system on the part of the States.

CHAPTER XI

INTELLECTUAL LIFE AND THE ACADEMIES

ALTHOUGH NOT an outstanding literary century in relation to the works produced, the eighteenth century in Italy was nevertheless one of intense intellectual activity, both in the scientific and poetical fields, which found its main expression in the academies and gazettes. The fashion for academies went back to the fifteenth century, as did the bizarre appellations which characterized them and the borrowed names under which their members concealed their identity from the profane, as French blue stockings did. The Platonic Academy, a group of humanists revolving around Marsile Ficin in the Villa Careggi in 1459, had escaped these rather ridiculous conventions, but it disappeared at the beginning of the next century. Almost contemporaneously, Siena saw the establishment of the Academy of the Intronati—approximately 'the Dumbfounded'—copied by the 'Lazy' and the 'Anxious' at Bologna, the 'Sleepers' at Genoa, the 'Dullards' at Spoleto, the 'Befogged' at Ancona, the 'Hidden' at Brescia, the 'Insane' at Perugia—which included among its members, under the names of Madman, Ecstatic, Yokel, Mortified, etc., poets as famous as Tasso, Sannazar and Guarini. With less nonsensical titles, there were the 'Olympics' at Vicenza, the 'Philharmonics' at Verona, the 'Humorists' at Rome; the last named, founded in 1603 to cultivate fine language, at the same time as the Academy of the Lincei, devoted to scientific research (with the keen eyes of the 'Lynx'), still exists today and enjoys world-wide fame.

The foundations peculiar to the eighteenth century had a shorter career but similar characteristics. In 1720 Countess Clelia Borromeo founded at her home the Academy of the 'Vigilants' who were solely concerned with the sciences— mathematics, physics, medicine, botany, etc.—while in 1743 Count Guiseppe-Maria Imbonati revived in his own Milanese palace—today the home of the Manzoni Theatre—the Academy of the Trasformati, one of the most famous in the sixteenth century, subsequently declining and disappearing definitively in 1768 on the death of Imbonati. But in the meantime it had as members a number of famous Settecento writers, notably Baretti,

9 Pietro Longhi: a Wedding   Pietro Longhi: the Baptism

Domenico Tiepolo: the Quack.

8 *Overleaf*: Bucentaur in Venice by Francesco Guardi

Pietro Verri, Beccaria and, in his youth, Parini, whose academic pseudonym was Ripano Eupilino.[1] At Venice, the Academy of the Granelleschi, founded in 1745 for the purpose of cultivating satirical poetry, had an even shorter life since it only lasted for sixteen years, not without having fulfilled its purpose brilliantly, mainly through the two brothers Gaspare and Carlo Gozzi. But the most characteristic literary academy of the epoch was 'Arcadia', set up at Rome at the end of the seventeenth century after the death of Queen Christina of Sweden by the habitués of her salon. The academicians adopted names with a pastoral flavour and published a journal (*Giornale Arcadico*), still in existence under the more dignified name of *Atti dell'Accademia degli Arcadi*.

However, the most productive intellectual activity went on outside these closed circles, with their frequently antiquated atmosphere. It principally developed around a few university chairs, such as the chair of political economy held by Father Genovesi at Naples — founded on the initiative and at the expense of a private individual, Bartolomeo Intieri, which is not without significance—that of the expert in canon law Bon at Turin who influenced large numbers of young minds in favour of 'Jurisdictionalism'[2] from 1758 to 1797, and especially those of the teachers at the University of Pavia, an extremely active centre of Jansenism of the regalian persuasion with Tamburini, Zola and Palmieri, and even of advanced democracy with the Barnabite Alpruni. In another direction the Benedictine Dom Rabatta, who had studied theology at the Abbey of Saint Anselm under the future Pius VII, became professor of the physico-chemical sciences[3] at the University of Florence.

French works directly inspired either by the Port-Royal, or by its successors, adepts of the second Jansenism, were introduced into Italy and praised by the librarians of the royal, ducal or grand ducal libraries at Turin (Berta), Parma (Paciaudi), Florence (Lami), and even of the Vatican (Bottari, Foggini), while those inspired by illuminism were even more widely distributed. The writings of Montesquieu, Rousseau, Raynal, Mably and Condillac were in high favour. The *Encyclopaedia* reached Italy in large numbers and three French reprintings of it were made in Italy itself, one at Lucca, the second at Leghorn, which had

H

twelve hundred subscribers, the last at Padua by the presses of the seminary in an extremely handsome form in the last quarter of the century. It went as far as Trieste, Turin and Geneva but could not be finished and stopped with the twenty-first volume owing to the fall of the Most Serene Republic. The whole of Montesquieu's works were similarly reprinted in 1773 with Amsterdam as the false place of publication. The *Lettres persanes* came directly from Paris and Lausanne, together with the *Lettres philosophiques* by Maupertuis and those of Toland, Voltaire's *Candide*, the writings of Helvetius, La Mettrie and Baron Holbach, prohibited but nevertheless familiar to nearly all men of culture, especially in Venetia and Lombardy.

A fairly large number of English and American historical works or books with religious pretensions—Robertson, Wollaston, Barclay and especially Franklin—also circulated, generally in French translation. The law of nations borrowed its principles from Grotius and Pufendorff, regalism from Febronius and the Viennese specialist in canon law Eybel, whose book *Was ist der Papst* appeared anonymously in 1782 and was immediately circulated in the peninsula in Latin, French and Italian.

A public of avid readers also collected in the public libraries. President de Brosses noticed this at the Ambrosian Library, open morning and evening every day, which he found 'always full of people studying, unlike our own'. Later, also at Milan, Grosley confirmed that at all hours of the day he saw 'public and private libraries full of people reading and making extracts . . . They imagine that every Frenchman must know everything and that he does in fact know everything', for the majority of the books consulted were French. At Venice, where a number of patricians owned private libraries with a European reputation, the library of the Pisani was open to the public on Wednesdays and Saturdays every week. At Florence the great *Magliabechiana* library, which by successive extensions became the largest in Italy—the *Nationale*—was inaugurated in January 1747 and at first was only open for three days a week, on Tuesdays, Thursdays and Saturdays; in 1749 the construction of the *Marucelliana* began. At Milan, a private library belonging to Count Pertusati, bought for 240,000 lire by Count Firmian in 1774, administrator of Austrian Lombardy, formed the basis of the *Brera* library, while the *Pinacoteca* was founded in the same palace in 1776 by Father Bianconi.

A more attractive and certainly less tendentious culture than that of the theoreticians of Josephism and illuminism developed in numerous gazettes. It is true that some of them under a harmless but misleading title such as the *Novelle letterarie* of Father Lami at Florence, also served between 1740 and 1770 as a cautious but effective medium for the propagation of the Jansenist and regalian theses, to which the *Annali ecclesiastici* devoted themselves more openly, likewise at Florence, provoking a violent reaction from the Roman organs defending the rights of the Holy See and Catholic orthodoxy, the *Giornale ecclesiastico di Roma, Annali di Roma, Gazzetta di Bologna*, etc. But the eighteenth century saw the simultaneous appearance of periodicals whose prototype was the Milanese *Il Caffè*, founded in 1764 by the Verri brothers in imitation of the London *Spectator*, and which had nothing to do with these polemics, although they were very open to new trends of thought. It only lasted for two years and dealt in a lively fashion with subjects of general interest and the most varied kinds of literature—from vaccine to the growing of flax, from the masques of the Italian theatre to the development of trade—thus creating a didactic tradition closely akin to the spirit of the Encyclopaedia, which earned it the praises of Voltaire and d'Alembert and came to life again at the beginning of the nineteenth century under the title of the *Conciliatore*. The *Caffè* had had a forerunner at Venice in the *Osservatore* of Gaspare Gozzi, which lasted an even shorter time, only during the year 1761, and showed the same serious and yet brilliant qualities of which the model had been given by Addison.

In this Venice which strove to deserve its nickname of the Athens of Italy beneath its apparent frivolity, the eighteenth century saw the birth and death of a multitude of other gazettes which managed to obtain the collaboration of the most eminent men of letters and scholars in the country and to circulate widely, thanks to the support of well-known printers in the Venetian State. For example the *Giornale dei Letterati d'Italia*, founded in 1710 by Apostolo Zeno with the advice of Scipione Maffei, dealt with erudition, history, legislation, mathematics and the sacred sciences. Descartes, Locke, Newton, Vico and Giannone were mentioned in it. Muratori and Manfredi did not disdain to write for it. Foreshadowing our modern digests, important works were summarized in numerous articles which made up a whole of four volumes annually. The fault inherent in these undertakings depending on a single man, or two at the most, who performed other public or intellectual tasks at the same time, was unfortunately always the same: once the original editor left or died, the publication disappeared with him. Summoned to the court of Vienna in 1718, Apostolo Zeno had as successor his brother Pier Caterino, a Benedictine and professor at Venice. But the latter got tired of it in 1727 and disappeared in 1732. On his return from Vienna, Apostolo took over the journal again in 1733, while Maffei, who had quarrelled with his friends, founded on his own at Verona in 1737 the *Osservazioni letterarie* appearing every four months, which disappeared three years later and in which his personal polemics with Muratori took up an excessive amount of space.

In a different form from summaries of outstanding works or full-length translations and reprints, French intellectual influence, owing to the initiative of Albrizzi, an enterprising printer, made itself felt again at Venice after 1723, through the free distribution of small-sized weekly literary sheets containing bibliographical notices of important books published in Europe. In the following year Albrizzi gave extracts in Italian and Latin from the main erudite journals of Europe. Essentially the *Journal des Sçavans* and the *Journal de Trévoux*, but also the *Journal littéraire de La Haye* published by Justus Van Effen, which succeeded to the *Nouvelles de la République des Lettres*, founded by Bayle, as well as from similar periodicals in Germany and England. Another printer, Luigi Pavini, launched the monthly *Mercurio storico e politico* in 1718, in small volumes of about 100 pages, a translation of the Dutch review with the same title which was founded in 1686 and published for nearly a century.[4] In this case the enterprise was lasting because it had a solid commercial basis; it lasted until 1773 and in 1722 Pavini duplicated it with a *Giornale dei Letterati oltremontani*, also made up of translations of learned French journals.

All these publications, in the same way as the *Racolta di*

opuscoli scientifici e letterari which the Camaldolite Angiolo Calogerà, reviser of books at the University of Padua, carried on for thirty years from 1727 to 1757, were purely scholarly and refrained from judging contemporary events for fear of falling foul of a strict censorship.

Another Venetian bookseller, Fr Pitteri (the Most Serene Republic was much more liberal than many of the other states), managed, as from 1737, to publish annual volumes dealing with the events of the preceding year. The undertaking was carried on until 1810.

The second half of the eighteenth century was particularly disturbed in the field we are now dealing with by the gazette of that curious figure Baretti, tireless traveller and polemicist, long established in London but also seen at Parma, Turin, his native town, Milan, Bologna, Leghorn, Genoa and in France, Spain and Portugal. Venice was the town where in 1762 he published his *Frusta letteraria* (The Literary Whip) whose name is sufficient to indicate its character and which earned him a host of enemies. After the suppression of this gazette at Venice in 1765, Baretti went into hiding at Ancona in order to continue it and managed to do so for some time. There was something of Voltaire's caustic wit in this perpetually dissatisfied figure.

Venice also possessed a galaxy of genuine humanists, continuing the glorious traditions of the Renaissance and at the same time open to all the innovations of modern science and criticism. The most eminent was undoubtedly Marco Foscarini, who throughout his career as ambassador, procurator of Saint Mark and doge, managed to remain the official chronicler of the Republic, a man of learning and a Latin poet. He drew up a plan of reform for the University of Padua and 'wore out ten copyists who were following him'.[5] In his villa of Altichiero Angelo Querini, a correspondent of Voltaire's, lived among his books and antique sculptures; busts of Horace, Marcus Aurelius and Bacon showed where his elective affinities lay and dotted about his gardens sphinxes, sarcophagi, columns and obelisks recalled the great epochs of the past which were still living in the minds of those who revered them. Others took on the task of learned and costly editions: e.g. Francesco Foscari, who worked on the thirty-four volumes of the *Thesaurus antiquita-*

tum sacrarum, and Francesco Pesaro, who was responsible for the critical edition of the *Storia* by Cardinal Bembo.

Men of letters of this stature were found here and there in eighteenth-century Italy, especially in Sicily with Prince Biscari, archaeologist, poet and collector, a native of Catania, which he embellished, provided with a theatre and a new mole and whose industry and public works he developed, or Prince Torremuzza, an unpretentious man of learning, who preferred solitude but was of the highest merit. However, except at Venice and Milan these isolated men of talent did not create a genuine circle. The zeal of the reformist ministers of Grand Duke Leopold was misunderstood, the new dynasty was unpopular. At Turin the spiritual ferment secretly kept up among the intellectual élite owing to the proximity of French and Swiss centres of thought emancipated from the old routines had absolutely no influence on the court and the higher civil servants. At the end of the century there were only five printers in Sicily, and only one at Palermo, who had Greek or Arabic type. They only printed scholarly books, works of devotion and almanacs. Any other work was brought out at the author's expense or by subscription. There was not a single library at Trapani, a town of 20,000 inhabitants. The libraries of Messina, apart from works of piety and almanacs, only possessed a few secondhand bound foreign books and knew nothing at all about modern works. French works penetrated in fairly large numbers via the French booksellers in the three main towns, but also, undoubtedly, by direct orders from Paris which the propagandists of the new ideas undertook to fill.

CHAPTER XII

CRIME AND PUNISHMENT

'WHAT ASTONISHES all foreigners and is the talk of the town again today, but only the talk, are the murders, which are an everyday occurrence. Four people have been murdered in our quarter within three weeks. Today a worthy Swiss artist named Schwendimann, a medallist, was attacked just like Winckelmann.[1] The murderer, with whom he grappled, struck him as many as twenty blows with a dagger and as the guard had run up the villain stabbed himself. Incidentally that is not the fashion here; the murderer escapes to a church, and that is an end of the matter.' Thus Goethe described one of the aspects of Roman life in his travel diary for September 24, 1786. And Young counted fifty crosses commemorating murders on the road from Brescia to Verona. According to him, a swarm of robbers infested the country, hence the need to have doors and shutters fitted with iron bars which could not be sawed through.

Perhaps he drew too hasty a conclusion from these hermetically sealed fastenings. Henri Bédarida, noting that doors and windows in the duchy of Parma were closed by clumsy and ugly 'large bolts or heavy iron bars', simply imagined that the people had no idea how to make them more attractive; but his work, which is so precious because of its exhaustive documentation, tells us that in the zone of the Upper Parmiggiano adjoining Tuscany there were parishes enjoying special privileges and immunities, which had become a veritable haunt of deserters, smugglers and malefactors. These zones were even more abundant in the Centre and South and there seems no doubt that night was a dangerous time[2] in the majority of large Italian towns in the eighteenth century. This insecurity was certainly aided by the abusive extension of the right of asylum which guaranteed impunity to a mass of ruffians, although the lower classes, as much as and more than the religious authorities, defended it passionately as a sacred privilege.

At Mantua at the end of the seventeenth century, a French dragoon was very nearly torn to bits by the population because he had made short work of a wretch inside a church. This man, concealed inside the church porch and seeing him pass by with a comrade, had stabbed the latter in the back without the least provocation. The colonel of the troop which occupied the town at that time was forced to imprison the soldier and then give out that he was dead (in actual fact sending him elsewhere by night in great haste) in order to avoid an uprising.[3] President de Brosses also related that during his stay in Rome the Cardinal Chancellor Ottoboni refused to accede to the request of the Governor of Rome that he should be allowed to arrest the porter of the palace of the chancellery, who had accidentally shot and killed a priest passing by in the street when aiming at another individual. Undoubtedly this was not a case of deliberate homicide; nevertheless total impunity was excessive.

The task of the police was complicated by the immunity which foreign embassies and their staffs, the residences of cardinals and, of course, monasteries enjoyed. The luckless policemen were forced to carry a special map of the streets of Rome and the places they could pass through when pursuing a criminal. If they infringed these prohibitions, the staff of an embassy sometimes took it on themselves to give them a thrashing. We can imagine that in such conditions policemen were often disgusted by their profession.

As soon as he entered Italy, Lalande noted that the doors and steps of churches were 'infested with people who come seeking immunity'. It was even known for them to transform them into evil haunts, settling there comfortably with prostitutes and catamites. With good reason the 'philosophers' protested against this scandal, and the 'enlightened despots' of Florence, Milan and Parma managed to bring it to an end, but it persisted in the Papal State and the Two Sicilies. Nevertheless, towards the end of the century, Dupaty, in spite of his critical attitude to Italian morals and in spite of the readiness with which the Romans and Neapolitans reached for their knives, did not seem to be shocked by the four or five murders committed annually in the Kingdom of Naples. 'They send many people to prison, but they very rarely punish,' he observed, 'and hardly ever with the extreme penalty; but people rarely stay in prison for less than four years and three-quarters of the accused die there, because the law requires the guilty person's confession before authorizing a capital sentence, and so long as he has not confessed he is shut up in a dungeon without light and straw. He sleeps on the stone floor and his only food is bread and water.'[4]

Moreover the police of Naples seem to have been better organized than in other Italian States. The policemen responsible for supervising the security of the town at night were distributed in twenty-two squads, seven of which went their rounds each night. Each squad, in addition to ten policemen and a corporal, included a 'captain of justice', a substitute and a commissioner (*scrivano*), who was obliged to take two citizens with him to act as witnesses in case of need. The commissioner of the main squad (*sopraronda*) was responsible for distributing the other six among various quarters without them knowing in advance which quarters they would be. Three times during the night they had to come to give him an account of their actions and every individual arrested was taken in front of the 'regent of the Vicariate', the head of civil and criminal justice, in the morning. Incidentally, Lalande noted that, in spite of its large numbers, the Neapolitan populace was easy to hold in check provided that three things were available: *Farina, Forca, Festini*. So the gallows was added to the *panem et circenses* of the ancient Romans, at least as a latent threat. Alas it was only widely used for so-called political crimes against the moral and intellectual élite of Naples during the repression of the emancipation movement of 1799.

At Lucca, where we know that even the nobility never wore swords, which were only allowed for foreigners, any individual surprised in the possession of arms was liable to the gallows. This small town had forty *sbirri* at its disposal, of which two squads worked at night.

Even at Rome, there were few burglaries: pillage in certain circumstances, but never organized robberies. Comparatively minor crimes such as pocket-picking, tampering with the weights in the market, receiving stolen goods, etc., were normally punished by exposure in the pillory (*berlina*) with a placard around the neck giving the name of the guilty man and the nature of his crime in large letters. Next come the *cavalletto*. The sufferers were tied down flat on their stomachs on a bench, which in turn was placed on a dais, and two administrators of justice rained blows on their spines with a bull's pizzle—fifty was the maximum—to the applause and laughter of the crowd who were insensible to their cries.

At Rome, however, cardinals, ambassadors and other important personages had the privilege of obtaining mercy for them, if their carriages passed by one of these places of public punishment and the condemned man appealed to them. They had only to make a sign to the *barigel*, always present at this type of punishment, and he hastened to obey them. We even find mention of men condemned to death being so freed on the intervention of a cardinal and the fickle crowd, who a minute before were enjoying the spectacle of their sufferings, applauded the liberation of the poor wretches just as loudly. The pillory and the wooden horse lasted until 1825 and were finally abolished by Gregory XVI, but only in public. The use of the *cavalletto* in prisons persisted until 1870. In the Northern States the famous treatise by Marquis Beccaria, *Of Crime and Punishment*, published in 1764, had produced a great impression and excellent results. Quoting Montesquieu as his authority, he advocated a fair relation between crimes and their punishment, the division of these crimes into set categories in order to avoid discretionary sentences by the judge, the elimination of secret grounds for accusation, the suppression of torture and the necessity for prompt application of the sentence pronounced; he fought against the death penalty and right of asylum, and defined the crime of acting as accessory; in a word, he sought to put in order a criminal procedure hitherto dependent in all the States on obsolete rules, pointless cruelty, and even the absence of an imperative and respected code. The book immediately had an equally great success abroad as it had in Italy, but, by an amusing application of Cartesian logic, the translation made by Abbé Morellet at Paris in 1766, without changing a single paragraph, completely altered the book's arrangement in order to improve it and make it more convincing, as he explained in the preface. And Beccaria, delighted, recognized that his translator had increased the value of his book by submitting it to the requirements of the French mind.

In order to appreciate the novelty and worth of Beccaria's book, it is only necessary to compare it with the *bandi* or decrees of Cardinal Valenti, Secretary of State to Benedict XIV, for the repression not only of common law crimes but also crimes of impiety and a series of others which have completely disappeared from the modern penal code. Blasphemy, for example, was punished for the first time by three *tratti di corda* (the torture of the strappado) administered in public, for a second offence by public flogging and for a third by five years in the galleys. Violation of the enclosure of a convent at night could merit death, even if no crime was committed, and also for all the intermediaries or accomplices. To embrace or even try to embrace a respectable woman in public was punishable by a life sentence to the galleys, or even by death, with confiscation of property. For damaging libels or lampoons of any kind, *even if they were true*, the penalties were death, confiscation of property and perpetual disgrace or at the very least a life sentence to the galleys. (These severe penalties never managed to stop lampoons, but we know that they were only stuck on the famous statue of Pasquino during the night, with a thousand precautions.) In the same way, either the galleys for life, or death were awarded for insulting inscriptions or signs put on the doors and walls of houses, even those of publicly known female sinners and *a fortiori* of respectable women. The characteristic common to the punishments of these various categories, which could include death or not, was that they were all accompanied by the phrase *ad arbitrio di Sua Eminenza* (at His Eminence's choice), i.e. the arbitrary nature of the punishment was publicly proclaimed and confirmed.

Baking bad bread or selling it underweight also exposed bakers to severe punishments, although they were less heavy: three *tratti di corda* and a fine of ten écus, half of which went to some pious work and half to the informer. The penalty for keeping weapons (bludgeons, clubs, etc.) was the same, but the fine was increased to twenty-five écus—and double that if the crime was committed at night, whether the weapon was a catapult or a plain stick. The authorities were particularly mistrustful of pistols. It was forbidden to manufacture, sell or keep them under penalty of death and confiscation of property, with the specious clause that if such a weapon was found less than six feet away from anyone, it would be presumed to belong to him and would constitute sufficient grounds for putting him to torture. These *bandi* remained in force until the French occupation of the Roman States and were re-established in 1814.

We might imagine that in a century so given to libertinage and mockery these Draconian measures had every chance of remaining a dead letter, all the more so as they were in flagrant contradiction with the licence of the monasteries, the frequency of murders, the maintenance of the right of asylum, etc. Admittedly, but the ordinance remained in force and from time to time a terrifying example was made of someone. In July 1711 a citizen of Orvieto was hung and burnt before a numerous crowd because he had passed himself off as a priest. On April 26, 1717, a young man aged twenty-two was hung for having stolen a *ferraiolo* (an ecclesiastical mantlet[5]) which he had resold for twenty-five *baiocchi*. The case was dealt with in eight days. On February 3, 1720, another young man of twenty-two, Father Volpini, was beheaded on the Campo Vaccino accused of writing 'malignant and seditious letters'. He had written to Count von Zinzendorf at Vienna that Pope Clement XI (Albani) was keeping up an amorous intrigue with Princess Clementina Sobieski, wife of the pretender to the throne of England, James III, who had shared the papal carriage more than once. Volpini's letter had circulated in manuscript at Vienna; the Nuncio Spinola got to know about it and denounced the fact to the Holy Father. The young and elegant priest died with great courage and joked with the friends whom he met on his way to the block.

Criminal legislation was very much the same at Milan. For example, an edict published in 1749 authorized the imprisonment without trial of receivers of stolen butter, on secret information or the testimony of a single reliable witness. The barbarous custom of the wheel, cutting off the hand of the condemned man before beheading him and dragging him from a horse's tail was still laid down in a regulation of 1762, the executioner's wages including the obligation of supplying the horse! But the trend of opinion unleashed by Beccaria proved strong enough to obtain in 1769 the suppression of the galleys of the Levant and the dungeons of the religious communities, except those of the episcopal Curiae, the reform of the Penal Code in 1785, and in 1789 the abolition of torture.

This belated progress was not confirmed at Naples. As late as

1794, at Caserta, a man was condemned to be dragged from a horse's tail, then to be hung, to have his tongue, hand and head cut off, his body burnt, his property sold and his name cursed with perpetual disgrace for profaning a church. His profanation had consisted in shouting 'Long live Paris! Long live liberty!' three times during a service. Only six hours elapsed between his arrest and his execution. The king agreed to grant that he should not be dragged by the feet. He was bound to a table, with his mouth gagged, in the executioner's cart. It was a case of scaring the liberals at a time when the revolution was being prepared at Naples by the enlightened élite of the capital.

Side by side with these horrors and owing to another form of arbitrary power stigmatized by Beccaria, but this time to pious customs, certain confraternities enjoyed the right to free debtors from prison by paying their debts,[6] or even setting free known criminals once or several times a year after examining their files. A procession went to fetch the lucky man from the prison with great pomp in order to lead him to the church of the confraternity, where he heard high mass with devotion, holding a candle in his hand; afterwards he was encouraged to lead a Christian life and given a little money, sometimes after a banquet.

We may mention a murderer condemned to ten years in the galleys, freed by the Archconfraternity of Prayer and Death on St Michael's Day 1713.[7] At Palermo, in 1787, Goethe saw a condemned man led right to the foot of the gallows by a confraternity. He had to make his devotions in front of the ladder and kiss it. 'He was a handsome lad, with curly hair,' commented Goethe, 'with white hat and clothes. He held his hat in his hand. He only needed a few gaudy ribbons sewing on him to look like a shepherd at a fancy dress ball.'[8]

CHAPTER XIII

THE MILITARY CLASS

T HE ARMIES of the Italian States in the eighteenth century existed mostly for show, except in Piedmont, a country perpetually preoccupied with extending her dominion, which took a great part in the Wars of Spanish, Polish and Austrian Succession. But Venice, Florence, Rome and even Naples hibernated in a long period of peace. Lucca had had no enemies for two hundred years. Its nobility was unaccustomed to the life of the camps and took all their pleasure in the salons, or the academies if they were men of letters. Parini emphasizes this with bitter irony in the reminder of the exploits of his ancestors which he gives the effeminate young hero of *Il Giorno*. Moreover, the troops garrisoned in Italy were nearly all foreign; in any case foreign leaders were most often in command of the armies.

Count von Schulemburg, after having served in turn the sovereigns of Denmark, Poland and Holland, and then under Prince Eugene of Savoy, assumed supreme command at Verona in the first quarter of the century of the Venetian land forces, which were almost entirely made up of mercenary slaves. Prince Eugene himself being at the orders of the Emperor, foreign officers, French (such as the Chevalier de Brissac), Swiss or German, shared the command of the Piedmontese regiments with members of ancient families devoted to the House of Savoy. In 1730 the Grand Marshal of Savoy was an Esthonian Baron, Bernard-Otto Rehbinder, firstly in the service of the Palatine Elector, later, in 1708, in that of Victor-Amadaeus II, who covered him with honours even before his naturalization as a Sardinian subject, his marriage at Turin and conversion to catholicism.

At Florence in 1734, Spanish troops marched past on their way to recapture from the Austrians the Kingdom of Naples assigned to Carlos of Bourbon. This chance contact with real soldiers excited the combative streak which always slumbers in young men's hearts and four or five hundred young Florentines began to drill, to march past in ranks to the sound of drums, with banners flying, carrying wooden sticks and sabres instead of muskets, wearing baldricks and headgear of foliage, setting up 'armament depots' here and there, or even fighting against each other with such fury that many of them had to be treated in hospital. The adults enjoyed watching them manoeuvre, remembering their town's epic past. But the authorities were swift to intervene and forbid any assembly by these young scallywags under penalty of the arrest and imprisonment of their leaders. That was all that was needed to calm their ardours and a few years later an imperial garrison installed itself at Florence on the occasion of the change of dynasty. Four thousand seven hundred Austrian soldiers distributed between Pisa, Leghorn, Portoferraio and Aulla provided the Tuscans with a concrete lesson of the humiliation—which lasted for more than a century—of being nothing but the province of a foreign empire.

When Montesquieu passed through Florence in 1728, he noted that: 'The Grand Duke maintains about 3,000 men and could maintain 7,000 or 8,000 with what he spends . . . These 3,000 men are so many canons. They get four *livournines* [about 9d] a month and, apart from that, they work and have their own trade. So the majority of them are dressed like officers.'

The insignificance of the contingents under arms was an observation common to all French visitors to Italy who took any interest in military affairs. At Genoa, Montesquieu had already remarked that there were only 4,000 to 5,000 rankers in the whole State and said of its governors: 'Their forces consist in their mountains; the country virtually defends itself'. At the end of the century, when the Republic was on the verge of succumbing after having displayed so much heroism in the past, Dupaty observed that there were not even 2,000 soldiers, if the garrisons of forts and the galley-slaves in pressed service with the navy were not counted. 'Public opinion does not exist here. The heart has ceased to obey,' he concluded. At Venice, Lalande was astonished that there were only 5,000 to 6,000 rankers, whereas the Most Serene Republic could easily have made use of 25,000. And Milan, capable of lodging 7,000, only had a garrison of 1,000 men.

As regards outward show, on the other hand, these troops, whether foot soldiers or cavalry, generally cut a fine figure. We know that military dress of the eighteenth century shared in the elegance which characterized the epoch. Uniforms were often white, set off with light colours, with coat-tails turned up in front and very becoming three-cornered hats. For example, those which de Caylus, himself a regular officer, did not fail to describe in each town through which he passed. At Villanova d'Asti four of the Chevalier de Brissac's companies, in white lined with blue, were encamped; at Alexandria, four dashing regiments of guards, who had buttons of white material; at Pavia, an Italian regiment, also in white with blue trimmings. At Cremona, Prince Eugene's dragoons were in red with black trimmings and 'made up of every nation'. Mantua, the principal Austrian stronghold in Italy, had a garrison of 6,000 Imperial Guards divided into three regiments, one of which was wholly Hungarian. At Parma, the governor of the fortress and the guards were all Swiss. At Lucca, the gonfalioner's guard was composed of seventy Swiss, in doublets and breeches with a blue ground striped with red and white. Swiss, dressed in red, trimmed with white braid, also formed the personal guard of the Doge at Genoa, a service they had also carried out for many years for the Pope at Rome.

The quality of the troops responsible for the defence of the pontifical territory in case of war proved to be rather low. On paper they included 80,000 militiamen on foot and 3,500 cavalrymen with eighty pieces of artillery. The largest contingents were quartered at Ferrara and Avignon. Of the arsenals founded by Clement VIII, at the end of the sixteenth century, the main one, established at Ferrara, could arm 25,000 infantrymen, that at Bologna 10,000, and two others, at Ravenna and Ancona, 5,000. The Castle of Sant'Angelo, with a garrison of 200 bombardiers considered as permanently mobilized (and therefore paid all'uso di guerra), could arm 12,000 infantrymen and the actual Vatican Palace 5,000. As we know, these troops lasted no more than a few hours against the French army in Italy under the directoire.

To tell the truth, the only effective military force was in Piedmont. Victor-Amadaeus II, on the death of his father, Charles-Emmanuel II, found the defence of the duchy assured by 6,000 picked militiamen, divided into twelve regiments, and he added five infantry regiments, which formed the first nucleus of

10   G. Godbis: a Wine Cellar

Pietro Longhi: the Toothdrawer

11   Giacomo Ceruti: Soldiers playing Cards.

Giacomo Ceruti: Beggar and Boy   *Photos: Mansell*

a permanent army, plus three cavalry regiments. During the wars he had to sustain in the eighteenth century, he was able to raise the number of his soldiers to 35,000.

But it was quality rather than numbers which gave the Piedmontese army its value. The historian Gallenga shrewdly remarks that as long as it only played the part of an auxiliary, now of France, now of Austria, the two powerful neighbours of his native land, it was difficult for the Piedmontese soldier to be inspired by deep patriotic feelings, periodically snatched away from his work in the fields as he was, often in the service of foreign interests; and the habit of its princes of never becoming too deeply committed to any ally, today's ally possibly being tomorrow's enemy and vice-versa, was well suited to exercise 'a pernicious influence on the people's moral character', from whom emerged only 'warriors lacking passion'. With the elevation of the duchy into a kingdom and the new importance it acquired in Italian politics under Charles-Emmanuel III, a new authentically national feeling began to spread, even among the working classes, which however only had its full effect on the following century. While continuing to employ some mercenary forces, the Piedmontese sovereigns henceforth tended, like Frederick II, to count solely on soldiers deeply devoted to their fatherland for victory in war.

I

Part III

HOLIDAYS and
ENTERTAINMENTS

CHAPTER XIV

CARNIVALS AND PROCESSIONS

T HE NORMALLY austere life of the great majority of
Italians in the eighteenth century was brightened up on
certain fixed dates during the year, particularly at carnival time,
and also provided them with material to satisfy their liking for
show in the interminable stately processions for which the excuse
was the election of a Pope or a Doge, the entry of a new Cardinal
into his episcopal town, the visit of a great personage, the patron
saint's day of the city or guild, and a mass of other religious
anniversaries with which the calendar was filled.

The carnivals of Rome and Venice have often been described;
Goethe especially wrote about the former with great insight and
verve.

At Rome, carnival began eleven days before Ash Wednesday
to the sound of the bell in the Capitol, but it was interrupted on
Friday and Sunday, which left eight days of gaiety.

A previous ceremony took place in the Capitol itself from the
time of the pontificate of Clement IX (1667-1669). Instead of
having the cavalcade surrounding the senator of Rome preceded
by a procession of young and old Jews dressed up in grotesque
cheap finery and running the length of the Corso under the
lazzi, this Pope decreed that the ghetto would simply pay an
annual tribute of three hundred écus earmarked for paying for
the prizes won by the victors in the horse races—the main
attraction of the carnival—and that the grand rabbi and some
other notables would come to pay homage to the conservators
and the senator,[1] who thanked them for it by a simulated kick
in the small of the back. As humiliations go, the second had
little advantage over the first, except that it was less public.
After which the senator, escorted by pages, dressed in a robe of
cloth of gold with a red belt, an ample yellow cloak and wearing
a three-cornered hat, left his Capitoline palace, while the
senators left theirs and passing between two ranks of *capotori*,
civic guards in red uniforms carrying arquebuses, the municipal
magistrates climbed into seven gala carriages and set off in procession along the Corso. There they were rejoined by the
governor of Rome—the highest dignitary in Rome after the

133

Cardinal Secretary of State and the Cardinal nephew[2]—in his own carriage, which was always preceded and followed by a double file of halberdiers in black and violet costumes and accompanied by his chancellors, gentlemen, train-bearers and servants. Thus the ecclesiastical and the lay authorities gave the people official license to enjoy themselves decently. In spite of the familiarities which were almost impossible to avoid among the crowd of maskers, the Roman authorities were concerned with limiting their seriousness. During carnival, the Corso was expressly forbidden to courtesans and the rabble, and also to monks. The last-named were only allowed to see it from windows or adjacent streets.

The Corso, then, was the centre of amusement, with a length of about 1,500 yards between the Piazza del Popolo and the Piazza di Venezia. The houses which lined it were decorated with hangings, foliage and flowers. For lack of wide pavements, narrowed even more by occasional daises and rows of chairs in front of the houses, the crowd of maskers mainly thronged the middle of the street. But it had to keep a lookout for two rows of carriages, one of them coming from the Piazza del Popolo, the other going towards it, and in addition make way for the carriages of the authorities when they appeared—the Governor, the Senator, ambassadors and the pretender to the throne of the Stuarts, Charles Edward, Count of Albany—who, disdaining to take part in the procession, had the privilege of passing through the centre of the Corso. However they only took advantage of it on the first day as a rule, except Charles Edward, who, wrote Goethe, 'comes daily to show off the individual masquerade of his role as pretender to the throne of England in the midst of the general masquerade'.

At the beginning of every afternoon, a troop of guards took up station at intervals along the Corso and kept a semblance of order in the mob which soon gathered there and was a particular hindrance to passing carriages.

Every kind of disguise was allowed except priests, cardinals, monks and nuns. The most common were those of traditional figures in the *Commedia dell'arte* — Harlequin, Pantaloon, Brighella, Truffaldini and most of all Punchinello, all of whom were special favourites with the ladies and in which many of them looked charming, while many of the men adopted a female costume. But there were also sham beggars, Turks, Cossacks, students dressed as English sailors, artists and even priests or gentlemen. People laughed and shouted to their hearts' content among the battles of confetti and the tangles of paper streamers, with which were mixed handfuls of flour thrown by pierrots all dressed in white. Some maskers walked around on stilts, climbed on each other's shoulders or jumped on the running boards of carriages or the stone benches lining the palaces, among the crowds of spectators who were seated there. A very common disguise was the *quacquero*, a type of comic opera buffoon in old style French clothes made of expensive material (but rented cheaply from the second-hand clothes man), a wig with short pigtails, and a small trimmed three-cornered hat. This character was obese and chubby cheeked, skipping about and free with burlesque greetings. A good hundred *quacqueri*, mixed with the punchinellos, were constantly darting about the Corso in every direction. Their favourite amusement was to advance with short quick steps in a straight line taking up the whole width of the street, then they suddenly turned into a side street by a fast ninety-degree turn to right or left and equally suddenly returned by reversing the manoeuvre and finally slipped through an open door.

Every carnival included symbolical floats, decorated with flowers and festoons of greenery, often fitted out at the expense of aristocratic families who did not disdain to ride on them themselves. So the crowd in 1711 saw Prince Pamphili take part in the procession surrounded by hussars and Prince Ruspoli on horseback dressed as a Sultan with a retinue of mamelukes, janissaries and eunuchs. In 1719 the House of Colonna fitted out a series of triumphal floats, a different one every day for the duration of the carnival. In 1721, after the diplomatic victories over Spain won by the Empire owing to the Quadruple Alliance and the disgrace of Alberoni, the crowd at Rome saw a grand masquerade of German horsemen symbolizing the Germanic successes with mythological emblems. In 1735, the pupils of the French Academy organized a Chinese Cavalcade and Prince Rospigliosi appeared on a float dressed as a Polish magnate surrounded by a crowd of attendants. In 1747 a tournament was

organised in the courtyard of the Barberini Palace, since the
Corso was not suitable for it. In the following year the young
students of the French Academy again had the idea of putting on
a pilgrimage by the Grand Seignior to Mecca; the Sultan threw
his handkerchief to the most beautiful odalisk, Marchioness
Gabrielli, who at the time had the reputation of being the most
beautiful woman in Rome.

In 1763 one float excited intense curiosity: it represented a
mountain covered with trees and pierced with caves, from which
charming nymphs emerged, although it was impossible to see
how it moved; it was the float of Diana the Huntress, the
Duchess of Gravina Orsini. In order to represent a sacrifice to
Indian gods by Hindu priests and priestesses the Borghese
family joined company with the Boncompagnis, the Spadas and
the Barberinis, the men in turbans, the women with their heads
veiled but their arms and shoulders bare, with necklaces and
bracelets of diamonds, emeralds and rubies, dresses of pink or
blue silk trimmed with magnificent lace. The group was not
particularly oriental, but the effect was so magnificent that when
the float passed the crowd stopped throwing confetti so as not to
spoil the sumptuous garments and the charming décolletés.
Humbler Hindus went ahead of them on foot with carriages full
of musicians in long blue robes. In the same year the Colonnas
decorated a float in which eight men and eight women, in the
costumes of figures in Italian comedy, represented the various
towns in Italy which had created and made them popular: e.g.
Harlequin for Venice, Pantaloon for Bologna, Stenterello for
Florence, etc.; standing next to them, the young and witty
Father Benedetti, an intimate friend of Prince Colonna, addressed
acquaintances encountered during the procession in verse.

The horses drawing the floats had harnesses of red leather
tinkling with silver bells, embroidered blankets and heads
adorned with plumes as was the custom of the epoch. Elegant
women also passed through the Corso towards the end of the
carnival, either masked or unmasked, in large open carriages
with six high seats facing each other, so that they could easily
be seen; often a beautiful white poodle, adorned with pink
ribbons, was seated between the coachman's feet and the horses
decorated with flowers shook the mass of tiny bells attached to

their harness. And lastly, on a high dais, 'in the proximity of the Ruspoli Palace, the most beautiful ladies of the middle classes disguised with wonderful taste and surrounded by their friends, show themselves to the eager gaze of the passers by', wrote Goethe. 'Everyone was keen to make out, possibly in a handsome officer, the object of his passion',[3] for we know that transvestitism was common during carnival, and the Ruspoli Palace, situated approximately in the middle of the Corso between two enlargements of the road, was particularly suited for this exhibition. In addition comedies were put on throughout the town, in private houses and seminaries and monasteries alike. In 1711 there were ninety of these spectacles in private houses alone.

The daily race between *barberi*, Barbary horses — originally from the Berber countries, belonging to various Roman noblemen—eclipsed all the other attractions at the end of the afternoon. These races were the real highlights of the Roman carnival. The animals were trained for the race they were going to run. Covered with a tight-fitting caparison of white cloth for these preliminary exercises, they were led in front of the obelisk in the Piazza del Popolo, which was the starting point; their trainers got them used to turning their heads towards the Corso, which they were led through at a walk after standing motionless for some time, and in front of the Palace of Venice they were given some oats. This was repeated with some fifteen horses accompanied by a group of street urchins whose shouts prepared them for the uproar of the actual race. When the race took place, the caparison and bridle were removed, but along the horses' backs were laid cords ending in balls covered with sharp points, a sort of dangling spur against which they were protected with leather until the start. At that moment they became unmanageable and jumped over the barriers, and the grooms had the greatest difficulty in holding them back. In the meantime, a picket of dragoons had ridden from one end to the other of the Corso—the paving stones of which were covered with fine sand to prevent the horses from slipping—in order to see that all the carriages moved off into the side streets. The crowd was plastered against the houses. A party of conservators sat in boxes decorated with drapes in the Piazza del Popolo at one end of the course, and another group, together with the Senator and the Governor, did likewise at the other end, next to the Palace of Venice. Once the Corso was completely cleared, eight dragoons rode through it at full tilt from north to south to inform the authorities and the *barberi*, trembling with impatience, were finally released in the Piazza del Popolo. Then followed a frenzied gallop along the narrow thoroughfare amid stamping of feet and the shouts of the crowd straining their necks to see the competitors arriving in a flurry. In the Piazza di Venezia, which was much less open than it is today, men threw themselves at the horses' heads to stop them at the entrance to a *vicolo* which has since disappeared. This was the *ripresa* and the owner of the winning animal received from the hands of the senator, with his congratulations, a considerable sum of money and a *palio* of gold brocade, a sort of banner fixed to a gaudily coloured pole and bearing the figure of a galloping horse embroidered on its lower part.

Once the race was over the gay scrimmage was resumed on the Corso, to which the carriages returned, and when night fell the *moccoli* were lit, the candle ends which everyone carried while trying to blow out those of his neighbours with the mock-aggressive cry of 'Sia ammazzato chi non regge il moccolo!'[4]

The carnival at Venice lasted for a whole season, namely all the end of the winter, since it began at Vespers on Twelfth Night. In the perpetual holiday, of which life in eighteenth-century Venice seemed to foreigners to consist, and which it was in fact, at least for the nobility, carnival with its masquerades, its spectacles, its booths, its jugglers and its stories in song was a success without equal in the rest of Italy.

The mask became a uniform: a black velvet mask only covering the middle of the face (*moreta*) or a white waxed mask, generally in company with the *bauta* and already rather caricatural. The distorting mask (*gnaga*) only went well with grotesque fancy dress and was only worn by the *popolani*. But the white or black mask gave a person the right of entry everywhere, even to the Ridotto, the famous gambling house in the Via San Mose, closed in 1774 by a decision of the Grand Council, where long rows of tables were occupied by patricians ready to act as banker against any chance arrival provided that he was noble or masked;

it even enabled the wearer to be present at the beginning of the sumptuous banquet offered by the Doge on the Feast of the Ascension—la Sensa—to the highest authorities in one of the biggest halls in his palace.

In addition to the amusement of the mask, 'the finest convenience in the world', says one of Goldoni's characters, facilitating all kinds of intrigues and audacities, enabling everyone to split his personality as it were and appear to be someone else while remaining himself, there was a whole whirlwind of amusements at Venice made for the enjoyment of the crowd rather than the squeamish.

The feasts were a means of government, and the noblemen intended to amuse their people, and still included among the favourite spectacles were bullfights, boxing matches and the 'labours of Hercules',⁵ human pyramids such as are still seen in circuses today. The Seigniory and the ambassadors were present when the people indulged in boisterous follies: they cut off the head of a bull after having set mastiffs onto cows; on Shrove Tuesday a firework display took place in broad daylight, companies of butchers walked in procession in bizarre costumes and an agile woman tightrope walker walked from the top of the campanile to the loggia of the palace.

All the attractions of a travelling fair were assembled daily on the Mole, with wild beast tamers, clowns, acrobats, fortune tellers who pronounced their oracles through a long tube to which the questioner put his ear, and men and women from other countries who excited the crowd's curiosity, while the traditional characters of Italian comedy in the costumes of Scaramouch, Brighella, Zerbinetta or Columbine carried on and capered about in a fantastic saraband.

The brushes of minor Venetian masters of the Settecento painted the various aspects of carnival to the life, as they did for the ceremonial official processions and the gallant free-and-easiness of the Ridotto and the convent parlours. Domenico Tiepolo provides examples in two valuable pictures in the Louvre. One shows two dancers in the open air who perform their steps without touching each other, as if in a minuet, before an inattentive circle of seated and standing ladies in silk dresses, some chatting to each other, the others wearing the *moreta* and listening to gallant remarks made by the people in grotesque false noses and the women selling biscuits. Hand on hip, making a leg, and wearing a plumed toque, the man, in a red costume with a short cloak turned up on one sleeve with elegant stripes, gives an impression of strength and subtleness; the young woman, holding her long dress with hoop petticoats of yellow silk in the tips of her fingers, a beauty spot in the corner of one eye but no mask, a narrow band of fur round her neck falling to the waist and shod in dainty shoes, is all charm and youthful beauty. This sort of salon in the open air was a very Venetian feature with its mixture of different classes all enjoying the same spectacle without a trace of envy.[6]

The other picture illustrates quite a different carnival scene: a quack dentist at work, mounted on a trestle and showing the object in his pliers. In the foreground there are noblemen wearing the *tabarro* and *bauta*, three-cornered hats and white masks, gloves and large fur muffs; to the right there is a man dressed as a Turk and others dressed like Scapin.

Carnival at Milan included a very special type of Masquerade in which the protagonists were members of one of the innumerable academies which thrived in Italy, the *Facchini* of the Blenio valley—in the Ticino dialect *doi Fechin dol Lagh Mejo*—composed of artists and gentlemen who had nothing to do with the profession from which they had taken the title. As the inhabitants of the Blenio valley came down from the mountains to Milan in great numbers to work as porters there, the *Facchini* made a point of writing in the Ticino dialect and under a borrowed name like the Arcadians. They took part in the masquerade in a costume of grey wool, with a grey hat with a rich plume, and tied to their belts an apron embroidered with gold and silver, decorated with the emblems peculiar to each category of porter. A sack on the shoulder and a grotesque mask completed their costume.

Apart from carnival this entertainment (*Facchinada*) was also given on the occasion of certain public rejoicings, for example for the marriage of Archduke Ferdinand of Austria to Maria-Beatrice of Este in 1771. The procession from the Ticinese Gate, which was the entrance to Milan for anyone coming from Lake Maggiore, made its way to the ducal palace as a tribute to the government and afterwards made the rounds of the town before disbanding.

For the feast of St John the Baptist, the patron saint of Florence, horse races were held in the city as at Rome but over a longer course, from the *al Prato* gate to the *alla Croce* gate, i.e. the whole length of the right bank of the Arno. There too, the horses were left to themselves between two rows of carriages and windows thronged with countless interested spectators, before being stopped at the end of the course by a large taut cloth. The race lasted for four minutes as against two and a half at Rome and the distance was about 9,000 feet. The prize was a piece of velvet embossed with gold estimated at 2,240 livres.

Apart from this highly popular interlude the feast of the patron saint of Florence had preserved a character of purely religious solemnity of a high standard until the middle of the century. The Austro-Lorrainese regime thought it would please the population by authorizing masquerades from the vigil of St John (June 23rd) until the evening of St Peter and St Paul (June 29th), but this innovation was not bound up with any republican or Medicean tradition: the Florentines were shocked by them and took no part; the only people who wore masks were a few policemen and the lowest of the lower classes.

On the other hand, the re-establishment by the Prince de Craon, at his own expense, in 1744 of chariot races round the square of Santa Maria Novella, which the last of the Medicis had suppressed for reasons of economy, excited keen enthusiasm. In 1766, after the death of the Emperor Francis, they were held with great show in spite of the court being in mourning, on the night before St John's Day, in the presence of the new sovereigns, the Grand Duke Peter-Leopold and his bride, for whom a tribune of honour ornamented with cream velvet had been erected. Before the race, Sienese horsemen had given a display of *haute école* and in the evening the customary firework display took place from the illuminated tower of the Old Palace. On the actual day of the feast, a sumptuous military and civilian procession, starting from the Villa of Poggio Imperiale, traversed the whole town, the Grand Duke on horseback, in a costume of cloth of gold with his sceptre in his hand, the Grand Duchess Maria-Louisa in a gala carriage drawn by eight horses surrounded by pages and noble guards on horseback. A throne had been built under the Loggia dei Lanzi, where the sovereign received the homage of the representatives of all the cities, lands and fortresses in the Grand Duchy; then he went on foot to the Baptistry of St John to offer his personal reverence to the patron saint of his capital. The public was then admitted to the 'grandiose sight of the banquet',[7] served in the Pitti Palace to their Imperial and Royal Highnesses and their court, who had stopped wearing mourning for the occasion. The afternoon was devoted to the *barberi* race and in the evening the same brilliant procession returned to Poggio Imperiale after a spectacle performed at the Pergola Theatre.

Let us move on to the extreme south of Italy and see how in Sicily the cult of patron saints, carried to the point of fanaticism, the love of tinkling decoration and illuminations, and the need to waste time felt by a largely idle population, combined to give an extraordinary vivacity to the feasts of St Rosalia at Palermo, which lasted five days, St Agatha at Catania, the Virgin of the Assumption at Messina, St Barba at Paterno, and Corpus Christi at Syracuse (seven days), contrasting strangely with the dull passivity of a country which was poor and abandoned for the rest of the year. There too, as at Rome and Venice, the feasts did away with social differences in a momentary equality between monks and people, and children and old men. And when, as at Syracuse, two rival confraternities each competed in putting on a pantomime around an edifice of wood and cardboard, their efforts to outdo each other added still more to the enthusiasm of the two groups.

Even if the feast of Santa Rosalia remained the most ambitious because of the size of its floats and the scale of its decorations, Corpus Christi at Syracuse was undoubtedly the most original. Houël, the engraver, witnessed it and has left us a lively description. The two confraternities of St Philip and the Holy Ghost both built their 'masterpiece' in front of the cathedral. On that particular year the Holy Ghost's effort represented a fort with towers and drawbridges, defended by batteries of cannons on two storeys, while St Philip's represented Troy and the wooden horse. The day of Corpus Christi was devoted to parishional processions and the churches themselves were given a decoration evoking palaces, ruins and rocks. The popular feasts began the next day and included two series of three *marches* left to the imagination of each confraternity.[8]

The main interest of the feast of Santa Rosalia, also spread over several days, was divided between the interior of the cathedral of Palermo, decorated on this occasion in a most unliturgical fashion but satisfying the Sicilian taste, the gigantic float on which the patron saint sat, the horse races, similar to those at Rome, and the decoration of the town itself.

During the feast, the people of Palermo transformed their magnificent cathedral, which was normally dark, with the beauty of its stone as the only decoration, into a palace from the Thousand and One Nights. The arches and the walls were entirely covered with fragments of multi-coloured mirrors set at different angles and interspersed with gold and silver paper. As for light, it was dispensed by a thousand chandeliers each with six candles and hung so that three or four were attached to the same cord. In addition nine thousand candles and lanterns were burning in the cathedral. Houël and other travellers were apparently greatly taken with this decoration; he remarked, 'One would be tempted to imagine oneself in a ballroom prepared to receive all the kings in the world if at the same time one did not hear the sonorous voices of a hundred priests coming from the choir'. We can easily believe it.

As for the floats, that of 1770 seen by the Englishman Brydone was seventy feet long by thirty wide and more than eighty feet high; it was drawn by fifty-six mules in double file, mounted by twenty-eight postilions in garments trimmed with gold and silver, with ostrich plumes in their hats. That of 1776, described by Houël, was only forty feet long and twenty wide, but still eighty feet high; it only needed forty mules and twenty postilions, the latter wearing long red robes in the Spanish fashion. The traditional shape of this float was that of a conch (or a Roman galley) with raised prow, while the stern expanded into an oval amphitheatre to hold a large orchestra surrounding either a dome supported by six Corinthian columns, decorated with figures of the saints and crowned with a gigantic silver statue of Santa Rosalia, or a triumphal arch in the rococo style which sheltered the saint's image between its pilasters, dressed in magnificent garments and borne as if on a cloud, surrounded by a halo. In spite of this assured position in an ultra-terrestrial empyrean, soldiers were posted nearby as if to defend her.

This enormous float was built on the beach and moved off on the first evening at five o'clock to the sound of the cannon, then took the Cassaro—now the Corso Vittorio Emanuele—arriving in front of the vice-regal palace at nightfall, preceded by a company of dragoons with trumpets and kettledrums. A master of ceremonies on horseback, draped in a large black cloak and wearing a broad Spanish-style hat trimmed with white plumes, began the march and controlled it with a little bell which he held in his hand. The dense crowd separated unwillingly to make way for the float in the streets thronged by the *popolino*, while ladies in sumptuous toilettes watched the procession from balconies. When night came, the Cassaro was lighted by lanterns which everyone carried with them, and a firework display was set off in front of the royal palace. On the morrow, after the races, the float returned to the Cassaro to the strains of special music played by its orchestra, stopping *en route* in front of the houses of the principal notables.

During the races on the second and fourth days, the horses, unlike those in the Roman races, were mounted by tiny jockeys about twelve years old, who rode bareback without spurs. The Cassaro, where they took place, was about a mile long and even more crowded than the Corso at Rome. The ringing of a bell by a senator gave the crowd fair warning that the race was nearly ready to start and the firing of a cannon that it had begun, but the people only left a narrow passage for the horses and accidents were frequent. For this reason the jockeys were suppressed in 1783 and, as at Rome, the horses raced without riders, with a flurry of ribbons round their necks. The prize was also a cloth banner embossed with gold and the honour of having taken part in the test was sufficient satisfaction for the owners. No bets were ever made.

On the third day the crowd watched a regatta and a firework display on piles; on the fourth, after the races, the Viceroy followed by the nobility went to the cathedral in procession to see its illuminations; and the fifth was devoted to the final procession which began one hour after sunset and in which crowds of children dressed as monks or saints took part. Complicated altars, each one honouring a male or female saint, were erected in the square in front of the cathedral. The great silver reliquary of Santa Rosalia carried by thirty-six important citizens concluded the procession. It finished in front of the palace of the Praetor,[9] where there was a fountain which spouted flames for the occasion.

For the feast of St Agatha at Catania, horse races also took place, in the presence of all the nobility on horseback arranged in a semi-circle around the finishing post. On the last day at dawn, an interminable procession took place on leaving the cathedral, which was blazing with lights. In it figured the bishop, the nobles, the Senate, all on horseback, preceding the silver bust and the reliquary containing the relics of the saint, the bara,[10] 'a dome supported by six Corinthian columns lit by a dozen hanging lamps—all of silver—and placed on an enormous stretcher which a hundred men, dressed in the white robe of penitents, carried on their shoulders'.[11]

At Messina, the bara was a veritable piece of machinery with horizontal and vertical wheels, and a central shaft rising sixty feet from the ground, all worked by men hidden inside a vast square box mounted on broad iron runners which served as its base. It had neither statues nor musicians, but several storeys of living cherubs and a young woman representing the Virgin. When she descended from the lofty summit where this pious ceremonial placed her, a tight cordon of troops was needed to protect her from the veneration of the devout crowd, who would have literally torn out her hair to keep as a precious relic.

The many foreign witnesses of these feasts have all emphasized at the same time as the enthusiasm they excited among the Sicilians the character of calm happiness they produced, tending to a feeling of universal goodwill, so that there were never any riots or disorders. These two sentiments seem to be contradictory. However, protestants and freethinkers as well as Catholics bore witness to it: 'Everyone rejoices in good faith and his thoughts are wholly taken up by the sweet emotion he feels . . . The soul is so full that it wants nothing more; it seems to have attained supreme happiness.' (Houël.)

We can understand that the plan of the viceroy Caracciolo,

K

the philosopher, to lop two days off the festivities of Santa Rosalia must have met with fierce and unanimous opposition.

Together with the carnivals and religious feasts, coupled with profane rejoicing, processions afforded the Italians of the eighteenth century another visual pleasure. All the corporate bodies took part in them in gala dress, the clergy, the pious associations, the guilds, various military forces and numerous domestic servants. We have already described their importance in connection with the funerals of high dignitaries in the State of Venice. When a new archbishop entered his residential town, especially if he was also a cardinal, a whole establishment accompanied him, mules carrying his baggage, a servant with his red hat and three or four carriages each with six horses. The new pastor himself was often mounted on a white mule and gentlemen walked by its side, one of them holding the animal's bit. Triumphal arches were erected at selected spots, but in any case at the entrance to the town. Halberdiers and guards on horseback flanked the highest authorities taking part in the procession which sometimes extended for as much as five-eighths of a mile.

When a procession took place, it was rare for the members of the political assemblies and the head of the State himself not to take part, and the members of the communal assemblies always appeared in them, even in the small towns. In his correspondence, Giovanni Lami described a procession he saw at Genoa in 1727—the procession of Corpus Christi by the sound of it—and which had this particularity in that after 'an innumerable quantity' of priests came a mass of guilds—'almost all those existing in the world' — which, instead of banners, carried enormous candles decorated with insignia directly relating to the professional activities of each guild. Thus to the candle of the watchmakers were attached keys for winding them up and small chains; to that of the sailors, miniature vessels, masts and rigging; to that of the butchers bits of meat covered with gold; the poultry-sellers' candle was surrounded with cages, pigeons, capons, quails and live hares with their feet tied; that of the market gardeners with cabbages, lettuce and fennel. In addition to these symbols, which must have greatly increased the weight and made them unwieldy, certain candles were adorned with marionettes whose strings were pulled by the bearer so that the farmer was digging, the smith beating his anvil, the carpenter planing wood, etc. After the guilds came the officers, then the nobility, the chapter of the cathedral, followed by a choir of musicians and a group of adolescents representing angels. Then the Blessed Sacrament appeared, in a gold monstrance placed on a chased silver base carried by sixteen priests in stoles and surplices, beneath a canopy held up by noblemen. The Doge and the Senate closed the procession, from which only the archbishop was missing. 'He had quarrelled about precedence with the prince.'[12]

In spite of the decline of the guilds in the eighteenth century, their dignitaries continue to appear in the majority of important processions in gala dress, long robes with very full sleeves and tall headgear shaped like round mitres ornamented with plumes and various decorations. In front or by the side of the representatives of the most notable guilds, such as the *Arte della Lana*, marched *donzelli* or servants, similar to the pages of the nobility, wearing short cloaks.

In 1739 President de Brosses saw a solemn procession at Venice on the occasion of the feast of St John, 'one of the five days in the year when the Doge has permission to leave his house and go to mass in state'. There were no guilds or priests this time, but a large and brilliant guard of honour:

'Grenadiers in tall caps marched in front, followed by the Swiss guards in breeches, ruffs, etc. [. . .]; then the Doge's pages, magnificently dressed in doublets of red velvet, with green breeches and stockings, red cloaks lined with green satin and red toques; the whole absolutely plastered with gold both inside and out. Then a part of the body of noblemen in short wigs and cloaks. Next came a senator, accompanied by two mace-bearers, carrying the inordinately long sword of the Republic on his shoulder in a vermilion sheath. The general-at-arms in palace dress and wearing a sword marched immediately ahead of the Doge, clad in a long robe of red damask over a vest of the same colour and wearing a positively enormous square wig. . . . After the Doge the senators, two by two, concealed beneath colossal wigs and large robes of black damask heaped up on their shoulders so that they appeared quite hunchbacked . . . '

When the Doge of Venice left his house to go to church, in a cloak covered with gold and precious stones, a similar ceremonial was observed. A number of standards, the cushion and gilded chair on which he would sit were carried ahead of him. Six large silver trumpets, so long that children had to hold up their ends, sounded in unison among a group of musicians and the whole ducal suite in hierarchical order surrounded the head of the State.

On Ascension Day (*Sensa*), the religious feast was united with the profane ceremony of marrying the sea and no pomp was spared to make it more solemn. The whole length of the canal which led from St Mark to the channel of the Lido, where the *Sposalizio* took place, was lined with the merchant ships and battle-fleet of the Republic, dressed with hundreds of flags. Three or four thousand gondolas, the *peote* of Murano and other nearby islands, followed the *Bucentaur*, the famous vessel reserved for the Doge, which was sumptuously beflagged, as were all the palaces; and even in front of the humblest shops small daises painted in bright colours witnessed in their own way to the pride of the Venetian people, while the cannons roared, all the bells pealed and shouts went up as the gilded *Bucentaur* went past.

However, as regards solemn ecclesiastical ceremonies, Rome still surpassed all the other Italian capitals, owing to the profusion of offices in the pontifical court, the luxury which was displayed in it, the background provided by the town itself, the wealth of its aristocracy and the constant presence of foreign notables. The procession which traversed the streets of Rome when the newly crowned Pope left the Quirinal to take possession of St John Lateran, *mater ecclesiarum et caput mundi*, renewed several times in each century a display of pomp which bedazzled the crowd of spectators and . . . shocked some of them. This cavalcade has often been described and we shall not linger over it again. We prefer to dwell on another one, which was equally traditional and equally sumptuous, but which was celebrated with particular brilliance in 1776 and came close to being the last occasion: the presentation of the 'palfrey' on the eve of the feast of the Apostles St Peter and St Paul, i.e. the tribute of vassalage paid by the King of Naples in the form of a white mule and a large sum of money to the Sovereign Pontiff, by which he recognized a sort of temporal sovereignty over his actual kingdom.

The custom was of ancient date. Pope Urban IV had called in Charles of Anjou to fight the impious Manfred, a descendant of the Hohenstaufen, in Southern Italy, and had conferred on him the investiture of the Kingdom of Naples. After him, Rome had continually reclaimed this suzerainty from all the dynasties which succeeded each other in the Two Sicilies and the majority of them had admitted it. But enlightened despotism, which spread at Naples as elsewhere, supported with growing impatience, in the third quarter of the eighteenth century, the Roman claims to maintain a purely theoretical right to States freed from the ecclesiastical guardianship; the conflict began to appear in 1776 on futile pretexts before ending in 1787 in the suppression of the tribute.

The essential feature of the ceremony was the handing over to the Holy Father beneath the porch of the Vatican Basilica of a casket containing 7,000 gold écus loaded on the richly harnessed 'palfrey', which was only handed back in exchange for an additional 800 écus. The procession of patricians, prelates, ambassadors and cardinals, feudatories of the King of Naples, assembled in the Colonna Palace in the square of the Holy Apostles, because Prince Colonna was High Constable of the kingdom. Detachments of papal troops on foot and on horseback, pages, the drummers of the Capitol and the captain of the Swiss Guards opened the march.

Then came the Ambassador of Naples surrounded by lancers and followed by the Swiss Guard in the famous costume designed by Michaelangelo, which we still see today, and after them the pages of the House of Colonna, the Pope's Master of Horse and lastly the constable on horseback, wearing purple and cloth of gold.

Other seigniors of high rank accompanied him, his gentleman of honour, the (Neapolitan) Prince of Cimitile, the Spanish ambassador Duke Grimaldi, for the Bourbons of Naples were of Spanish stock; the governor of Rome, Mons. Cornaro, a patrician of Venice, each one with his retinue of pages and valets. A quarrel over precedence as to who should take the lead threatened to turn the affair into a tragedy. Prince Colonna settled it by the wise advice 'to ride anyway they liked', which was immediately adopted.

The ambassador's grooms led the palfrey by the hand. The bishops native to the Neapolitan provinces, a company of Swiss Guards and four gala carriages closed the procession.

Custom had it that on the occasion of the payment of tribute to the Holy Father by the most powerful of his vassals, the other feudatories and grantees of the Holy See, towns, monasteries and baronies also paid tribute, each according to its importance. The cardinal camerlingo received these gifts in a hall in the Vatican. Several of them only had a symbolical value—for example the two pheasants or a dog offered by the owners of poor land—but the principle was maintained.

During this time Pius VI came down from his apartments and, born in the *sedia gestatoria*, stopped at the entrance to St Peter's. The constable knelt before him and taking the precious casket from the mule handed it to him at the same time pronouncing a few words of homage in Latin. The Pope thanked him briefly and reaffirmed his suzerainty by saying: 'We receive the quit-rent due to the Roman Pontiff for the domain exercised over our kingdom of the Two Sicilies, on this side and the other side of the Faro'.

In the evening, the Square of the Blessed Apostles and the cupola of St Peter were illuminated, which was always a grandiose sight. And the next evening Prince Colonna opened his wonderful palace to the whole of Roman society, especially the great columned salon built a few years previously, as well as his marvellous terraced gardens at the foot of the Quirinal Hill. The following is the sight which one can still see today with only minor changes, for the ceremonial of Roman receptions, together with that of the English court, is undoubtedly the one which has varied least for two centuries: the cardinals in the *cappa magna* of purple silk carried by a train bearer, received at the foot of the great staircase by six servants carrying a *torchère* — or a candelabra — the profusion of light — electric lamps instead of wax torches—the rows of gilded chairs, the ceremonial major domos, the procession before the prince and princess and the large silver platters piled with refreshments and cakes handed round by valets in livery. But there are no longer, as there were in 1776, Berber slaves dressed in striking colours waiting at the top of the monumental staircases, gentlemen of honour all dressed in black with a small collar of Flanders lace, ballets danced in an open-air theatre by Arab and Negro dancers, or the cantata performed in honour of the Colonna family.

And there is no longer a palfrey. After the incident over precedence, the Prince of Cimitile told Cardinal Pallavicini, the Secretary of State, that henceforth the payment of tribute would be made without ceremonial. Pius VI would not hear of it. Cardinal de Bernis intervened in vain. The argument continued for twelve years without any modification of the ceremonial. Then a tribute was no longer paid. In the face of the protest raised by the Pope in Rome, the property of the Bourbons of Naples, the Farnese Palace, the Farnesina and even the Neapolitans' own church in the via Giulia, were very nearly devastated by the people, furious at being deprived of a beautiful spectacle in the future. The police and the Corsican Guard had to intervene. A few years later it fell to much more daring innovators than Ferdinand IV—the agents of the Directoire wearing tricoloured cockades—to arouse popular fury and violence.

CHAPTER XV

OPEN-AIR AND PARLOUR GAMES

OPEN-AIR GAMES did not have the same importance in the eighteenth century as in the fifteenth, for example, when tourneys were in great favour and were sometimes celebrated with great brilliance, especially in the Florence of the Medicis. The *Canti per la giostra* by Angelo Poliziano were written for a joust in which Juliano di Medici wore the colours of the beautiful Simonetta Vespucci, his beloved.

There was a reason for this decline. In the eighteenth century the life of the salons was all the rage. Civilized behaviour had spread to new classes and women of high birth in particular were freed from a mass of restrictions. It was pleasant being with them and young men frequently preferred their company to sporting pastimes. Parlour games and especially gambling, which could be played under the candelabra of the palaces, won over everyone who was lost to open-air games.

However, they still lingered on, mainly among the lower classes. On his arrival in Italy in the autumn of 1786, Goethe described a ball game which he saw at Verona between four young noblemen, wearing a short white close-fitting garment, and four natives of Vicenza. The game was played with wooden racquets on a sloping floor two hours before nightfall and was watched by four or five thousand spectators, all men. It was probably a game of court tennis, which was the forerunner of our modern tennis and ping-pong championships.

A football game was played at Milan in the Piazza Borromeo —roughly rectangular and not particularly large. The square was closed by a row of benches across the four streets which led into it and lining the Borromeo and Molinari Palaces. The two opposing teams were called *battitori* and *postieri* and wore simple armbands to distinguish them.

At Venice, target practice had a great vogue either in the *campi* of the town or at the Lido. The *calcio* was played at San Bonaventura between noblemen, but with less solemnity than at Florence, where it involved fifty-four young gentlemen forming two companies distinguished by their colours — elegant Renaissance costumes—and their standard, each one commanded by a captain (*alfiere*) followed by pages and marching in great state. Once they reached the field to the sound of musical instruments—generally a magnificently decorated square in the town —the two teams marched round it to show off their charm and litheness, then each one gathered around its flag. Afterwards the match began and the game was not unlike football, with the difference that in order to win the ball had to be driven from the territory of the opposite team instead of shot into the narrow present-day goal. Once they had achieved this and the match was won, the players struggled with each other to occupy the enemy camp with skill and agility, using feints rather than brutality.

The game of *calcio* dated back to the beginning of the sixteenth century and had been popular for a very long time, but it lost its popularity because, being a privilege of the nobility, it could not be played by the *popolani* under the rules and during the years the young noblemen, growing more effeminate, no longer enjoyed it. However the municipality of Florence was anxious to organize a match in January 1739 for the entry into his capital of the new Grand Duke, François II of Lorraine, accompanied by the Empress Maria Theresa, his wife. They had to call on the experience of old gentlemen who had played the *calcio* in the past and have several rehearsals, for, writes a chronicler of the epoch, 'the young noblemen had abandoned themselves completely to farniente, cicisbeism and having a good time, in short to effeminacy, and avoid exercizing their minds and bodies to the best of their ability: the result is that the majority of them are ignorant . . . and also of sickly appearance, having entirely given up the pastimes which would make them strong and robust'. Nevertheless the game, put on as a show, was a great success. Tribunes surrounded the Piazza Santa Croce where it was to be played; that of the Grand Duke hung with gold embroidered damask with a roof, windows and window panes. The two captains were the youthful Marquis Bernardino Riccardi, whose team was victorious, and Folco Rinuccini. Such was the success that the imperial couple asked for a second match during their stay in Florence.

There was still another one in 1744, on the occasion of the feasts given by Andrea Gerini. But henceforth the fashion for it was over. The Florentines had become attached to another football game also of very ancient origin but available to everyone and which could be played anywhere. More and more out of the way scraps of land were reserved for it and notices on the walls threatened with fines and *tratti di corda* the players who disturbed the quiet of hospitals, monasteries and churches with their shouts.

Unlike the *calcio*, the game of *ponte*, long traditional in Pisa and still played in the eighteenth century on the bridge over the Arno joining the two parts of the town, was a working class game with rough and vigorous tussles. Originally it was held from Christmas to carnival on the Piazza dei Cavalieri and was then called *Mazzascudo* because the players carried a mace (*mazza*) and a buckler (*scudo*), as well as a breast-plate, a helmet, cuisses, etc. After the defeat of Pisa in 1406, its submission to the Florentines and its decadence as a maritime republic, even the sticks used in the game were taken away from the Pisans, but Lorenzo the Magnificent treated them less harshly and gave them back their taste for this game, which was resumed on the central bridge after 1490 with the same equipment as before.

It included 480 combatants divided into two factions, the Boreal and the Austral, each with six squads with their own colours and a large silk oriflamme. The officers—those of the Boreal in scarlet uniforms with white trimmings, those of the Austral in green uniforms also with white trimmings—were elected by councils of war and comprised all the ranks of a regular army: captains, lieutenants, sergeant-majors, corporals, standard-bearers, etc., who studied the plans of battle and carried challenges. On the day of the fight, the bridge and the two squares which gave access to it (*di Ponte* and *di Banchi*) were cleared and surrounded by railings. At the sound of the bell in the clock tower they were opened, the two teams marched around them and took up position diagonally opposite each other on the bridge.

The defensive weapons comprised a morion, beneath which a beret full of cotton was worn; beneath the cuirass, a leather and cloth jerkin, also stuffed with horsehair. The rest of the mediaeval-style armour, covering the limbs, also had an additional inside protection of thick cardboard or cotton waste. Over everything they wore tunics of linen or silk falling to the knees, of the same colour as the banner of the squad. The offensive weapon was a *targone* or shield of thick wood, about the length of a man's arm and a half, and wider at the base than at the top, which was held by two grips on the inside through which the hand and the forearm were inserted. The player used the rounded base as a shield and the almost pointed top to repulse his adversaries. In short, rather than striking blows it was a question of making a thrust which would disorganize the enemy ranks, make it possible to breach them and take up a position in the opposite camp's terrain. It was a test of muscular strength without brutality. However, by grabbing the *targa* in both hands at the narrow end and using it as a mace, it was possible to stun and dismay an opponent.

Players wearing a helmet without crest or visor, four to six in number per squad, led away those prisoners who had fallen to the ground. To do so, they had the right to open the ranks of the two teams drawn up for battle. The commanders stood on the parapets of the bridge where they could take in the whole of the battlefield. At the signal for the end of the game, if the combatants had kept their position, peace was proclaimed and when one of the sides had given way, the conquered team sent one of its members to beat a drum in the middle of the bridge shortly after its defeat and issue a challenge to the other group who replied in the same way.

After the game, a triumphal chariot passed through the town, but the captains did not ride in it. It was laden with weapons and standards taken from the enemy, decorated with mottoes, surrounded by musicians and an allegorical figure was placed in it, Merit, Renown, Victory, and even Peace. The game lasted until 1807.

We may compare it with the popular Sienese feast of the *Palio*, still celebrated annually on July 2nd and August 16th, which assumes the double character of a horse race with jockeys and a colourful procession of representatives of the seventeen *contrade* (or quarters) of the city, designated by the name and emblem of an animal: the Goose, the Hedgehog, the Sheep, the Snail, the Silkworm and also the Tower, the Forest, etc.

This race engendered very keen but not bitter rivalry between the quarters of Siena. Each one possessed an oratory or church of the *contrada*, in front of which the animal was blessed before the race and where it entered afterwards if it was the winner. The course consisted of galloping twice round the famous square in the shape of a shell sloping slightly towards the centre— which in the eighteenth century was sometimes filled with water from the Gaia fountain, the sculptural masterpiece of Jacopo della Quercia, forming an artificial lake around which the carriages drove. The race was preceded by a slow procession, in which heralds in mediaeval costumes skilfully twirled above their heads the large shimmering flags of the *contrade*. A banquet in the victorious *contrada* ended the day.

At Florence and Venice, jousts on the water were also very popular, and from Easter to the end of September a race between three or four hundred gondolas, called the *fresco*, took place towards the close of day from the Church of St Jeremiah, then Santa Lucia, on the Grand Canal—near the present-day station —to the della Croce bridge. Patrician ladies, often accompanied by their chambermaids, entered the gondolas and smiled graciously at the gentlemen who were taking part in the competition in other gondolas.

The passion for games of chance was very ancient in Italy, especially at Venice. We know that basset was introduced into France by the ambassador Giustiniani about 1675. It was all the rage in the eighteenth century, together with faro, biribi, the ancestor of roulette, and the *minchiate*, of which President de Brosses wrote at length, which were played without excessively high stakes. But at Venice gambling seemed to be a sort of public institution which brought the Republic some 100,000 écus in taxes annually from the hall of the Ridotto alone. The demoralization and ruin brought on some families by permitting games of chance nevertheless reached such proportions that in 1774 the Grand Council decided (by 720 votes to 21 with 22 abstentions) to close the Ridotto, as we have already mentioned. But it continued more or less clandestinely in the *casini*, those small meeting halls dotted about the town, especially in the neighbourhood of St Mark's Square. The noblemen preferred them to their palaces and Mme du Bocage tells us that a husband and wife each had their own, or even more than one, and went there 'with gondoliers as their only retinue' for the purpose of conversation. 'The key of the little house is in the pocket; a nun's lantern lit on the staircase of the middle class house leads to the *casin* which is a part of it. You go in, take your ease, in company or *tête-à-tête* as you wish, without anyone scandalmongering about it. I have seen several of these family retreats and told the ladies that they have infinitely more freedom than we do.'

Apart from the *casini*, there were also the gambling dens for the men of the people and in 1782 the State Inquisitors were actually warned that valets, their wives and other people of the like station had opened a casino 'behind the hotel Salvadego with regulations, arrangements, ballotting for offices, in absolute imitation of and on the same footing as those of the nobility . . . , where they gambled and lived in a luxury quite out of proportion to their status'. The tribunal ordered it to be closed immediately.[1] In his *Bottega del Caffè*, Goldoni introduces an inveterate gambler, the willing victim of a card-sharper. He had the models before his eyes.

The majority of elegant theatres, as we shall see, included a gambling room for those who were bored by operas or plays. And even those who liked them could not resist the temptation to play, as is the case at Monte Carlo today. Mme du Bocage further tells us that when she asked the organizer of the superb ballets put on at Reggio in the Duchy of Modena how such a little town could meet the expense of so many actors and such decorations, he replied: 'The contractors lose sixty thousand pounds and more in six weeks on the opera and get back a hundred thousand from the gamblers attracted by the magnificence of the spectacle'.

At Milan, the lottery of the *seminario* of Genoa—wagers on the names of the five senators renewable ten times a year among the ninety members of the council—had been authorized in 1644 as a privately run concern. The privilege was given to a convent of Spanish nuns and half the profits made on the gamblers had to be paid into a local bank. This form of lottery was maintained throughout the eighteenth century and became national in 1789 with branch offices at Bergamo, Brescia and Mantua where the draw was made in alternation every ten days. Biribi was introduced into the ducal theatre in 1679 and was even played in the public square in a large tent divided into thirty-six compartments, although it was forbidden by edicts which remained a dead letter.

Parini could not fail to allude to gambling, the favourite evening occupation of the nobility, in his portrayal of them in *Il Giorno*. He also recalls with charming fancy the origin of trick-track or backgammon. Despairing of eluding the supervision of a jealous husband who watched his glances and slightest word, a lover implored the aid of Mercury to find a way of getting a young beauty to listen to him and the god inspired him to make up the rules of backgammon which can only be played by two players seated opposite each other. The tedious husband sat down close by and even looked under the table from time to time to see whether their feet were touching. But the noise of the dice in the shakers and on the wood deafened him. Soon he could not stand it any longer, squirmed, got up and put his fingers in his ears. Then the lover was able to declare his love in a few rapidly understood words. That happened in 'the iron age', of necessity. But today the noise has become superfluous: 'The table and the inside of the gaping shakers were covered with soft cloth; then the importunate din was stifled, but the game retains its name which still recalls the racket of the past'.[2]

CHAPTER XVI
THE THEATRE AND MUSIC

THE NATURAL gifts of the Italian people for music found their full flowering in the eighteenth century. The abundance of great composers and virtuosos, wealth showered by princes and patrons on the theatre, which was essentially operatic theatre, the precocious training in music of the children of the people who sometimes formed choirs (particularly at Venice), admired by the whole of Europe, the development of religious music with Marcello, Porpora and Scarlatti—all these favourable elements simultaneously served the spontaneous penchant of the sons and daughters of Italy to translate the emotions of their soul by singing or instrumental concerts. 'You already find a marked taste for music in the first towns you come across in Lombardy,' observed Grosley. 'Everyone plays the violin; even the service in village churches sounds much like a concert, each person singing his part according to the range of his voice and the organ forming the bass for all the parts with full sustained sounds. The further you advance into Italy the livelier this taste seems to grow, so that . . . Italy can be compared to a diapason of which Naples plays the octave.'[1]

Father Coyer used almost identical terms. 'Hardly has one crossed the Alps . . . before music appears quite spontaneously. The violin, the harp and singing stop you in the streets. In the public squares you hear a shoemaker, a blacksmith, a carpenter and other folk of the kind singing an *aria* with several parts with an accuracy and taste they owe to nature and the habit of listening to harmonists formed by art. It is quite a different matter if you go at random into any house of importance. There you find concerts which elsewhere would call for a good deal of preparation, refinement and planning, while remaining much inferior. The further one advances into Italy the closer to perfection the music. Naples is its zenith.'[2]

However, society life and the pleasure of conversation used the theatre more as a background than a source of stimulation. Noblemen went to the performances more to see and be seen, to gamble and pay court to the ladies than to thrill on hearing what was often exquisite music. There was not a single foreigner

159

really taken by *bel canto* who did not complain about the fact, even if he was a mere amateur and not a genuine artist. Jean-Jacques Rousseau was very upset about it during his stay in Venice as secretary to Comte de Montaigu, who, with five boxes at his disposal, abandoned those he did not occupy to the staff of his embassy. 'When I listened to barcarolles I felt that I had never heard singing until then, and soon I was so infatuated with opera, that bored with the chattering, eating and gambling in the boxes, whenever I wanted to listen, I often left the company to go to another part! There, shut in my box, I gave myself up to the pleasure of enjoying the show to the end and at my ease, in spite of its length.'

At Rome, as soon as the opera season began—from November, or at the latest Christmas, to Lent—the assemblies ceased in the aristocratic salons, the ladies held their *conversazione* in their boxes, where people called on them. The seats were not arranged as in France, in rows of stalls one behind the other, but formed a circle as large as each box permitted, sometimes with a card table in the middle.

At Turin, the royal box, which occupied the middle of the hall on the second storey, was closed at the back by doors made of mirrors in which the spectacle was reflected for the gamblers with their backs to the stage. The presence of the King himself did not even stop the excessive noise, for no one listened to the recitatives which were normally very long. At Milan, Grosley, too, saw lighted boxes walled with mirrors and surrounded by sofas, which could even be closed in front 'so that the show interfered less with the conversation'. At Venice and Padua the boxes were also closed by shutters and a *ridotto* or gambling room preceded the halls. The Pergola Theatre, the most elegant in Florence, built in 1755, had about fifteen of them in the eighteenth century.

However, Italy owed the appearance of her genuine theatres to a few noble families. In 1637, at Venice, came the San Cassiano, owned by the Tron, where Francesco Manelli's *Andromeda* formed the first operatic performance in Italy. In 1639 the theatres of St John and St Paul, and San Mosé, the latter inaugurated with Monteverdi's *Arianna*, were built by the Giustiniani. Later the Grimani became the great patrons of dramatic art in their town, where a total of sixteen theatres were opened between 1637 and 1699, most of them bearing the name of the patron saint of the parish. In the middle of the eighteenth century the dramas of Metastasio were performed in the hall of St John Chrysostom. In Goldoni's time, the hall of St Benedict held pride of place; there were two theatres for opera, two for comic opera and three for the drama.

At Genoa the Adorno, owners of the *del Falcone* Theatre which had replaced the mediocre annex of an inn with the same name, putting on variety shows without artistic merit, became from 1646 onwards such pioneers of the operatic stage that they were able to present Monteverdi's *Orfeo* there in the same year. Five years later the Falcone was entirely renovated by the Milanese architect of the same name, who also built the luxurious Durazzo Palace, into which family's hands the theatre passed in 1679. A fire destroyed it in 1702. They immediately commissioned Carlo Fontana to rebuild it. He finished it in 1705. It was in the latter guise that the eighteenth century knew 'this delightful theatre which had many famous admirers: from Goldoni to President de Brosses, from Casanova to Rousseau, from Burney to Roland'[3]. In 1702 it was duplicated by the Sant'Agostino Theatre, also commissioned by the Durazzo family.

The Falcone was a theatre of five tiers, with boxes, plus a pit where the spectators stood. In other cases, as at Turin, there were six tiers of boxes, and the pit was equipped with benches, the most usual arrangement. The pit at Padua even included 250 independent seats which could be padlocked, but seated or standing the pit 'was almost solely filled with the rabble'— Charles, Comte de Brosses *dixit* — on whom the Venetian patricians felt quite free to spit or rain candle ends. Even the front row of boxes, corresponding to the French ground-floor boxes, were given over to 'women of doubtful virtue as being too near the pit'. In fact, in some theatres a sort of gallery, the *ringhiera*, was arranged below the first boxes, extending for their whole length. There sat the men who could converse with the ladies seated slightly above them by standing up during the intervals. People of quality rented the second, third or even sometimes the fourth tier of boxes. The servants occupied the

L

amphitheatre. When their masters wished to leave, they sig-
nalled to them below. Then the valets lit lanterns in full view
of the audience and conducted them to the waiting carriages.

Although the halls were oval or semi-circular like our own,
boxes in the same row were often built projecting slightly
beyond each other the further they were from the stage, so that
a better view could be had. This was so at Padua and Verona,
for example, with twenty-nine and twenty-seven boxes per tier
respectively. Lastly, the San Carlo Theatre at Naples, the most
magnificent of all and belonging to the royal family, contained
six tiers with only twenty-four boxes each, in which ten to
twelve persons could easily fit[4]; seventy of the boxes belonged
to the main Neapolitan families who had bought them and
could not give them up without the King's permission. The
prices varied from 770 ducats for the first two tiers, plus an
annual rent of 230 ducats, to 580 for the fourth tier, plus an
annual rent of 180 ducats. A ticket for the pit cost three
carlins. Valets in livery were denied admittance.

At San Carlo it was forbidden to clap and call for encores;
that was a royal privilege. On an average three operas were put
on annually, each with twelve or fourteen performances. The
staircases, entrances and exits were resplendent, and the stage,
almost as deep as that of the Garnier Palace, allowed of the most
spacious decorations.

It was opened on November 4, 1737, with Metastasio's *Achille
in Sciro*, with music by Porpora. The décor, by the famous
designer Pietro Righini, represented a grandiose temple surrounded by porticoes forming a vast square. Between the colonnades could be seen the sacred wood on one side and the beach
of Skyros on the other. Next came the *Olympiad*, which contemporaries considered divine, also with music by Porpora, and
Artaxerxes.

During the next few years, Metastasio and the opera were all
the rage. In 1738, on the occasion of the royal marriage, his
Demetrius, with music by Leo, was given; then *La Clemenzia di
Titus, Themistocles, Semiramis, Parthenope, Adrian in Syria,
The Triumph of Camilla, Zenobia*, etc., in collaboration with
the best musical directors of the epoch, mainly Porpora and
Vinci, who was the director of the Pergolese Theatre. Only one

comic opera found a place among these operas, with occasional one-act farces, but they were abandoned definitively in 1741. On the other hand, several composers sometimes wrote different scores for a single work by Metastasio. For example, Leo for *Achilles at Skyros* in 1740 and Gluck for *La Clemenzia di Titus* in 1752.

Milan's La Scala was the last of the great opera houses to be built in eighteenth-century Italy. It replaced the ducal theatre, which was built of wood and had burned down twice, in 1708 and 1776, and was opened on August 3, 1778. Piermarini, the architect, took the greatest pains to protect from fire the master-piece, which shed lustre on his name. A hydraulic machine of recent invention was connected with three large reservoirs full of water situated under the arches above the stage. The cost of construction was shouldered by the owners of boxes under the authority of the 'associated knights', a sort of promotion and administrative committee formed of four members of the Milanese nobility rich enough to underwrite any possible losses. In fact, the undertaking went through a difficult time in its early years and from 1778 to 1788 the 'associated knights' had to meet a deficit of 24,000 sequins. Subsequently they handed it over to various companies.

No expense was spared with regard to the building's external splendour and interior decoration. Like San Carlo it had six tiers of boxes, and these formed a sort of annex to the aristo-cratic palaces in which the nobility received their friends, gambled, ate—a back box could be used for cooking—and slept, if they felt like it. They were vast, hung with silks and Viennese linen, similar to French Jouy cloth, with ceilings which were either painted, or flashing with mirrors, or made of carved and gilded wood. They contained a varied collection of seats and divans. Applied ornaments of chased bronze were interspersed between Venetian mirrors; alternating panels of stucco or country landscapes completed these rich apartments.

The pit included 600 seats divided between chairs and sofas covered with yellow bombasine. The sumptuous lobby (*Ridotto*) and its lateral halls, with vast marble fireplaces and arches decorated with garlands of flowers, enclosed, as was the custom, a quantity of English-style gaming tables and carved armchairs.

In the artists' dressing rooms there were tapestries from Flanders decorated with foliage and birds. In keeping with the neo-classical style of the building, Piermarini strove to keep the hall itself, which had perfect acoustics, as austere as possible. The fronts of the boxes were only decorated with the blazons (or the initials) of the owners and these emblems disappeared themselves in 1798 when the French Republican government exported Revolutionary equality. The orchestra was seated on a large plat-form which could be lowered hydraulically below the level of the pit. The stage, which was very deep, was at first only lit by the traditional oil lamps, but as from 1788 it was replaced by the Argand lamp, recently introduced in London and Paris.

However, musical art did not have such ancient and deep roots at Milan as in Naples and Venice. As we have said, the first years of La Scala were rather disappointing. Two years elapsed between the inaugural spectacle and the resumption of opera in 1780. In the interval and afterwards, frequent dramatic pieces, farces and even marionette shows alternated with music during the various seasons of the year, especially the one known as l'autunnino in August. The theatre put on shows with equilibrists, acrobats and jugglers, and even, in the spring of 1786, tightrope walkers. But it was also available for veglioni, balls, especially masked balls, as well as comic operas. However, several works by Cimarosa were given their première there between 1780 and 1783; and the last work written by Cherubini, before his departure for France, Iphigenia in Aulis, was also put on there for the first time in 1788.

Italian opera in the eighteenth century was a veritable tragedy, usually in three acts, which were in turn divided into several tableaux forming an excuse for changes of scenery, and included interminable recitatives, which were capable of justify-ing the lack of attention of part of the public. The scenes ended with a sung aria; then the spectators' interest reawoke, all the more so as certain singers enjoyed immense and generally well-deserved popularity. As a rule men played all the parts in these operas, since women were not allowed on the stage, at least in Naples and Rome, such was the fear that their attractiveness would cause trouble among families. But there were a few exceptions. There were some great female opera singers in the

Settecento. Sometimes, even, a woman played a man's part, but the contrary was the rule. Hence the abundance of *castrati*.

Castration, largely practised on poor children with a disconcerting mixture of lack of feeling and hypocrisy, for the young boys had to request it themselves at an age when they could not foresee its consequences, i.e. at about seven or eight years, supplied not only the papal chapels, but also the operas with *soprani* and *contralti*. The operation was prohibited in the conservatories, but candidates for a possible musical career first had to be found a place in them in order to ascertain their natural aptitudes. Then the parents took their children back home for a period and returned them to the conservatory after the surgical operation. Some *castrati* earned fortunes — one thing compensating for another. Caffarello became rich enough to buy the domain of San Donato, with which went the title of duke. According to contemporary chronicles, he was arrogant, impertinent and indispensable.

Another pupil of Porpora, Farinello, after having charmed Italy, Germany and England with his voice, was summoned to the court of Spain, where he enchanted Philip V in his old age, accumulated honours and, on returning to his fatherland, put his great wealth to good use until an advanced age. President de Brosses quotes among the numerous *castrati* who charmed him, too, the Sienese Senesino, the Milanese Appianino, Monticelli and Salimbeni, all pupils of Porpora at Naples, and the one who was known as Porporino, 'as pretty as a pretty girl'. At Rome, Montesquieu also heard two *castrati*, Mariotto and Chiostra, who performed dressed as women, 'the most beautiful creatures I have seen in my life,' he wrote, 'who would have inspired people who had the least depraved taste in this respect with a liking for Gomorrha'. But these successes could by no means be guaranteed and often the voices of these unfortunate children changed when they came to puberty so that they could not exploit them, or they lost them altogether. Lalande claimed that barely one case in a hundred was a complete success, which seems exaggerated. Of course, there were also excellent tenors among the Italian singers of the Settecento; however, *soprani* seemed to have been the most sought after.

King Charles was bored by opera and really only appreciated

the ballets, but he liked comedy. While he was still only Duke of Parma, he had in his service a company of eleven actors working in a small court theatre which he took with him to Naples in 1735. They put on rather coarse farces which finally wearied him and the scandals caused by some of the actresses definitively compromised the impresario. The company was disbanded in 1744. A better behaved troup directed by a popular but prolix playwright, Baron di Liveri, replaced it and played before the court until the eve of Charles III's departure for Spain. It only put on one play a year, with scrupulous attention to detail and daily rehearsals. It was not unknown for a sigh to be repeated thirty-two times![5]

In addition to the gambling and gossip in the boxes, and the boredom induced by the recitatives, a further reason hindered music lovers from enjoying what was often beautiful music as they would have desired: the noise made in the pit by admirers of famous artists, often divided into rival factions. They were applauded and acclaimed all the time they were singing and no one listened to them. Sometimes the working-class public in the pit carried long sticks with which they thumped the benches as a sign of admiration, while from the fifth-tier boxes others threw handfuls of printed sonnets into the hall, in praise of a particular virtuoso or diva. People leant out of their boxes to catch them and scuffled in the pit to pick them up. All this produced a fantastic racket which the singers received with a smile, used as they were to these delirious tributes.

Nevertheless comparative silence was the rule in the opera houses, especially when the King of Naples, the King of Sardinia or, at La Scala, the representative of the Emperor was present. But Italian exuberance could not be restrained at the theatre. Used for many years to the traditional themes of the commedia dell'arte, based on beatings, misunderstandings and coarse jokes of which only the most delicate have passed into the farces of Molière, the majority of the public in the peninsula would have had to be completely re-educated for them to be able to enjoy genuine character comedies. Goldoni himself failed in his native town, although his observation was sometimes superficial and he did his best to make himself intelligible to as many people as possible. His plays in the Venetian dialect, which incidentally are among the best, because he wrote badly in Italian, were the only ones which were really appreciated. The reason he agreed to come and direct the Théâtre Italien at Paris in 1762, which he was never to leave, was that he felt that he was too controversial in Venice.

Comedy theatres were numerous but sketchily equipped. An hour before the curtain rose, 'two wretched candle ends, stuck into two wooden sconces, were lit and they had to serve to illuminate the stage until the performance began'. The hall remained in complete darkness, except for a little light in the largest boxes on the tiers of the nobility and a few evil smelling tallow candles lighting up the orchestra. The front-row stalls in the pit, in demand by ardent lovers of the theatre, were often occupied in advance by servants when a large audience was expected. Only men and a few working-class women occupied them. These stalls were of heavy wood, like those in churches, and in between two acts the theatre porter, carrying a wax taper, passed from row to row collecting the money for the seats, which varied little and was very reasonable, normally one *paolo* (about 5d) in the theatre and two and a half *paoli* for a seat in the pit in opera houses.

The best boxes also had owners, but the latter did not sell the seats; they lent them to their friends if they were not using them themselves. There was no service keeping order in the hall; one or two plain-clothes policemen only appeared in case of need, no matter how great the din. No one thought there was anything wrong in this. 'In the Venetian theatres, the public clapped or whistled to show their opinion; one could hear endless bursts of laughter, low voices and piercing voices, women whispering to each other, spectators imitating cats miaowing, cocks crowing, sneezes and coughs, and yawns and exclamations of every kind.'[6] Goldoni had an absurd rival, who, however, was appreciated by a large public, in a certain Father Chiari. For years the two camps argued over their merits, not only inside the theatre, but outside, through the medium of epigrams, satires and sonnets.

In the other capitals things were very much the same. At Rome, where Neapolitan masques were all the rage, the public was so crude that they preferred Punchinello to good comedy and the pit was full of priests, who often not only whistled but also harangued the interpreters of Goldoni.' Addison wrote that he had seen a performance at Bologna of a translation of El Cid into which the masques of Italian comedy had been introduced! 'It would never have pleased the public if a place had not been found in it for these buffoons.'

On the other hand, sentimental domestic drama or middle-class tragedy experienced its greatest popularity in eighteenth-century Italy as in France, without however producing a single work worth remembering. Italy had no Diderot or even a La Chaussée in this field. But a taste for tears, emotion over the domestic virtues, or the virtues of the noble savage, provided an unconscious alibi for the libertinage of the aristocracy and the spread of the callousness which accompanied the revolution in the middle classes.

To get back to music. Luckily there were other places besides the theatre where really sublime music could be heard in silence: they were mainly the conservatories maintained at state expense in the four hospitals of Venice: *Pietà, Incurabili, Derelitti* and *Mendicanti.* Orphan girls and girls born out of wedlock were trained in vocal and instrumental music by famous choir masters (among them Monteverdi, Cavalli and Lotti) and the results, in the unanimous opinion of everyone who heard them, could satisfy the taste of the most difficult to please. King Frederick IV of Denmark, Emperor Joseph II in 1769, Pope Pius VI in 1782, Grand Duke Paul of Russia and the Grand Duchess Sophia, his wife, and King Gustavus Adolphus of Sweden in 1784, listened to these artistes in the hospitals. The government felt that it could not offer its illustrious guests a more refined pleasure.

The best performers among these very young girls, cloistered like nuns who could only be glimpsed behind their grilles, were known at Venice by their Christian names, la Zabetta, la Margarita, la Chiaretta, etc., and were the subject of general popular fervour, rather like a cult. President de Brosses did not spare his praise for the 'transcendent music', the 'adorably light voices' and 'the perfection of the symphonies' which he heard at the *Pietà.* Rousseau was equally enthusiastic in his *Confessions.* He never missed Sunday vespers at the Mendicanti because of the motets 'with a large choir and orchestra' which were performed there. 'I can imagine nothing as voluptuous and as touching as this music,' he wrote, ' . . . everything in these delightful concerts combines to produce an impression . . . which I feel no human heart could be unmoved by.' In 1784 Goethe was just as fascinated. He heard an oratorio at the *Mendicanti*: 'a soprano was singing the part of Saul, the protagonist in the drama. For my part, I have never heard such a voice: in some parts the music was indescribably beautiful.'

As for the choreography, which subsequently was to confirm the fame of the dancers at La Scala, it was eclipsed by the music in the eighteenth century. Admittedly, the pleasure of dancing was familiar to all classes of society—at Milan there was perhaps never so much dancing in the salons—and there were always a few professional dancers at the theatre; but ballet was far from being as important as it was on the French stage from Lulli to Rameau. The actual arrangement of Italian opera, with its interminable recitatives, did not lend itself to ballet. So it was only towards the end of the century that the celebrated French choreographer Jean-Georges Noverre produced one of his compositions on the stage of the Ducal Theatre at Milan in 1774, of which town a writer was able to say that it was 'chock-full of Francomania'.[8] It was a triumphant success, and from then onwards ballet was gradually introduced into opera, although more or less artificially. There were seven at La Scala in 1779, nine in 1780 and twelve in 1782, especially in the form of ballet known as 'semi-character' ballet, a mixture of the comic and the sentimental, of fact and fiction. Noverre's ballet, *Jason and Medea*, was received with enthusiasm in 1788. Certain families then began to produce every type of dancer of both sexes and, like the violin-makers, the goldsmiths and the typographers of the past, established choreographic primacy in Italy, with whole dynasties of stars.

Part IV

ECONOMIC LIFE

CHAPTER XVII
INDUSTRY AND COMMERCE

THE EIGHTEENTH century in Italy, especially at Milan, marked the beginning of industrial activity of a capitalist nature, which took the place of the family and corporative workshops existing hitherto. According to certain historians, similar establishments using paid manpower existed as early as the sixteenth century, but they were short-lived undertakings which could not survive an economic crisis.

Successive governments were much in favour of these enterprises and helped them in many ways. The first example which we know in Milan dates from 1703. Franz Tieffen, a German, sought permission to set up a large factory for weaving wool, which could produce fine cloths in the English and Dutch style. He obtained the following privileges: the exclusive right for twenty years for carding, spinning and weaving wool *all'uso anglolandese*; exemption from military service and from the obligation of belonging to a guild for all his workers.

Naturally, these favours excited fierce opposition from the local manufacturers, who were thus prevented from improving their own processes. Nevertheless, Philip V confirmed the privileges granted on June 9, 1704. Undoubtedly Tieffen had completely won the confidence of the authorities and he showed that he was worthy of it. He engaged excellent workmen from England, Holland and France and models of machinery and supplementary plant which he speedily had built on a large scale in Milan, using a capital of 300,000 lire. The first cloths woven seemed to be even better than the samples. But Tieffen finally had to give up some of his advantages and accept that every manufacturer properly registered with the guild had the right to spin in the English way merchandise whose importation was forbidden because it was foreign; if these prohibitions were violated, he would keep his privilege. In spite of the competition thus authorized, his factory was still flourishing in 1720. But at this time other similar factories were established on Italian initiative.

In 1746, Felice Clerici, a very Milanese name, set up an undertaking of considerable size for the period, which treated goat and camel hair, and added a dye-works to it. Clerici was granted similar advantages to Tieffen's: exemption from customs dues on merchandise imported for twenty years; from communal taxes for eighteen people for twelve years; from service in the urban militia for all his workers. In 1752 he doubled his production. In this year he employed forty-seven workers of both sexes and five 'cadres'. The lists of personnel witness to a continuous increase until 1759. In 1763 he added to the weaving of camel hair in the Franco-Anglo-Dutch style the manufacture of Amiens velvet and wool velvet, both new to Milan at the time. He had thirty-eight looms and 265 workers, in addition to the directors and the clerical staff. The exemptions were extended to twenty-four years and he obtained a government subsidy of 100,000 lire on condition that he increased the number of his looms to sixty within two years. Which he did.

In 1755-6, the brothers Rho established two factories on even wider bases, one for bleaching and printing calico, the other for spinning cotton and weaving raw linen. The henceforth normal exemptions and privileges, as well as a subsidy of 80,000 lire, were granted by royal decree in 1757. In addition to weavers brought from abroad, the Rho brothers interested themselves in a 'pious work' for training young female workers on the spot.

In 1762 the house was growing rapidly. It had a large staff, partly Alsatian, Swiss and Austrian, and produced 10,000 pieces a year. The haberdashers' guild opposed its being allowed to sell retail, as they had in the case of Tieffen. An agreement was reached which recognized the factory's right to sell a whole piece to a private individual with a rebate to the haberdashers, up to a maximum of three pieces. In spite of everything they continued to exhibit hostility to the development of large-scale industry which was, nevertheless, favoured by the government. Moreover there was no lack of obstacles, and after a bankruptcy in 1768, followed by a long period of misfortune, the Rho factory only resumed its normal production in 1785 under new management which trained a large number of local peasants to spin in order to give them work in the winter.

It was in the manufacture of silk, once so flourishing at Milan, but fallen into complete decay during the Spanish regime, that the great Lombardic town asserted its supremacy, especially in the eighteenth century.

In 1765 an important local company (Pensa-Lorla) set up a factory making silk cloth *all'uso di Francia*, including a section with cloths 'in the Persian style', then absolutely new to Milan. At the end of the year, it already had fifty-four looms and 238 workers, including ninety-one foreigners. Together with exemption from civic dues and royal taxes, it was granted a subsidy of 150,000 lire out of a special business fund set up by the Austrian government. In 1772 the company, operating eighty-seven looms, manufactured self-embossed velvet *all'uso di Francia*, Genoese velvet, brocades, satins and handkerchiefs damasked on both sides—those silk handkerchiefs of which Grosley wrote that Milan used 'a prodigious quantity' and that the Italians 'regard them as a tried specific against the throat infections which the humidity of the air makes very common in Lombardy and the Romagna'. He adds that 'these handkerchiefs form part of the wardrobe of princes and lords; the middle classes and the working classes never take them off at home or when travelling'. They were worn loosely over the shoulders in summer and tied round the neck at nightfall.

The house of Pensa-Lorla made an innovation by extending apprenticeship. It, too, had foreign foremen and workers (forty-one), weavers recruited on the spot (229, of whom fifty-two worked at home), and fifty-three winders, but it also housed forty boarding pupils in the factory whose primary and religious instruction it looked after, at the same time as teaching them the trade. There were also twelve day pupils. The government granted it a subsidy of 4,500 lire a year for this apprenticeship department, with 1,500 lire for the teacher and an equal amount for the head designer. The factory provided work for local industry which was unable to meet the large imperial orders for silk materials; thus the guilds, which were stagnating, no longer opposed the innovators.

Before Milanese industry could be independent of foreign countries, it needed the lustring process. In 1774, François Poid, a native of Lyons, proposed to set up an establishment for calendering with a golden tone and watering both sides of Paris-style ribbons. He only asked for a minimal subsidy, but on condition that he kept his secrets, and he agreed to train pupils. An agreement was reached on these lines and lustring was henceforth practised on a large scale at Milan.

The development of new industries brought about a large influx of population into the Lombardic capital and its environs. In 1785 there were twenty-nine firms making silk on 1,384 looms. About half of them made silk piece goods, the others voiles, gauzes, braid and trimmings, as well as stockings and jersey. An almost equal number of looms were distributed among the outlying centres, Cremona and especially Como.

Towards the end of the century the government had put a brake on the concession of industrial privileges. Beccaria—who was a member of the Royal Commission on trade—observed that universally applicable measures of a general nature contributed far more to the prosperity of the manufacturers than subsidies and individual assistance. In effect only a minority profited by them on the one hand, while on the other they encouraged luxury and sometimes unnecessary expenditure by the manufacturers. In 1786 the authorities decided not to grant any more subsidies for new construction and not to make loans before a precise evaluation of the advantages to be gained from them; and also to reserve the privileges exclusively for consumer goods in great demand, especially those using the country's raw materials.

Thus the eighteenth century saw the return to its place of origin of the textile industry which had gradually passed from Lombardy into France, where Henry IV and Colbert had developed it, and other European States, but it returned enriched by wider and better informed experience and less subject to regulations and excessive controls. At the time when guilds were being suppressed in France, they were also considerably weakened in Lombardy. After 1703 and the advantageous conditions granted to Tieffen's capitalist enterprise, there was a 'continuous downfall'.[1] In 1703 there were still five manufacturers of woollen cloth registered with the *Arte della lane*; they were reduced to two in 1714 and their entire production was limited to sixty-six pieces every six months. In 1757 there were no more than *six weavers* working for them.

Together with Lombardy, Piedmont and Venice were the

2 *Right*: Domenico
Tiepolo: The
Mountebanks

Below: Carnival
at Venice
(engraving
by Leonardis
after Tiepolo)
        Photo: Hachette

13 Francesco Guardi: Gala Night at S. Benedetto Theatre

main centres of the textile industry, principally the silk industry.

In 1702 there were 432 looms running in Turin, operated by some 450 foremen and workers, including 318 Piedmontese and 119 Frenchmen, and twenty-nine silk merchants. They produced damasks for clothes and furniture, moires, velvets, satins, satinettes, etc. Before Victor Amadeus II, silk, worked in great quantities, was only put through the first two processing operations — spinning and twisting — before being exported semi-finished and subsequently reimported from abroad in the form of cloth. The first textile factories date from his reign. At first small spinning centres were set up, but sometimes a large factory appeared with a fairly high number of tanks[2] and workers, for example at Caraglio, Ceva, Cherasco and especially Mondovi. In the province of Acqui only thirty-nine parishes out of eighty-three did not practise reeling and spinning at home. They converted 80,000 pounds of raw silk into organzine.

In 1738, at the end of the Polish War of Succession, which enlarged Piedmont in particular in an eastward direction, the spinning mills numbered 220. There were 1,510 looms for weaving silk, nearly all concentrated at Turin and Mondovi, 1,434 looms producing woollen cloth, divided between Biella (with more than half), Nice, Saluzzo, Ivrea, Susa, and Coni, and 10,334 looms for weaving linen, of which all the provinces in the State had a comparatively large number, the highest being around Turin, at Biella again and Casale Monferrato. One thousand two hundred and sixty merchants distributed these manufactures inside and outside the country. In 1787 spinning mills in Piedmont had increased to 272, with more than 16,000 workers.

At Venice, whose cloths were so prized during the Renaissance, the woollen industry, in competition with the factories erected in the provinces on *terra firma*, as well as at Milan, not to mention the fabrics coming from abroad, encouraged by a brisk smuggling trade, was declining badly. From 28,000 pieces of woollen cloth produced annually towards the middle of the fifteenth century there was a drop to an average of 700; fourteen factories for manufacturing cloth 'in the Dutch and English manner', immediately highly popular, were set up at Schio, two others at Thiene and Verona, three at Treviso, Bassano and

M

Soligo on the Piave. Silk-weaving mills fared better. In the middle of the century there were still 12,000 workers operating 800 looms in Venice alone. But there, too, the competition of the workshops on the mainland was felt. As early as 1739 President de Brosses noted that trade at Verona was mainly kept going by its manufactures of velvet and silk cloths. Other factories appeared at Vicenza and Bergamo. For this reason there were no more than 374 looms operating at Venice in 1779. There was a certain improvement in the 'eighties, then a new decline. In 1791 there were still nearly 300 looms idle out of a total of 752.

Fairly large numbers of glass works in the town and especially on the island of Murano kept up one of the industrial marvels peculiar to Venice throughout the century, but the trade required skilled manpower more than numbers and that solely male. Lastly, Venice kept its traditional supremacy in the field of printing.

In the Duchy of Parma and Piacenza, the local industry also consisted mainly of spinning mills, before the arrival of that energetic innovator du Tillot. Cotton goods and *calencars* popularized by the India Company were made there. The encouragement lavished by the Minister on French industrialists to induce them to establish themselves in the country had only temporary results on the whole, either owing to a certain hostility on the part of the local merchants, who were already used to buying stocks from abroad, or lack of capital and over-production in relation to internal demand, at an epoch when free trade was still opposed by antiquated decrees forbidding the passage of both raw materials — cocoons and raw silk, for example — and finished goods. However du Tillot's fillip to Parmesan listlessness was effective enough to make Father Coyer write in 1775: 'When Don Felipe came to reign at Parma everything came from abroad. . . . Today factories are going up on all sides. Here skins are treated with oil. There the linens of Dantzic, Silesia and Moravia are imitated, now that they have improved the cultivation of flax. I have seen faience which could compete with Strasbourg ware. A building is nearing completion in which imitation Bohemian glassware will be made . . . The mulberry-tree plantations have at least tripled . . . Spinning in the Piedmontese way has been established. The fabrics, damasks, taffetas and velvets are improving every day.'³

Apart from weaving, which was also practised in Central Italy, industry was rather underdeveloped in the eighteenth century. Here and there there were a few well-known factories, such as the china firm belonging to Marquis Ginori near Florence. In the Papal State another noble family had the monopoly of manufacturing pins; anyone who procured them from another source incurred heavy fines. The coral taken from the coasts of Sardinia, Corsica and Tunisia was processed industrially at Leghorn. Bologna, which from the fourteenth century threw silk by a sort of hydraulic tower of local invention, also manufactured such excellent cards for combing that they were even ordered from France. Bologna also produced fine quality paper and playing cards, toilet soap and artificial flowers. Phosphorus and rock crystal were found there; walnut furniture was manufactured. However, it was mainly owing to her trade that she earned her nickname of 'rich' (commemorated in the following century by Carducci in one of his most famous sonnets). Cervelas, mortadella, macaroni, quince preserves (*cotognate*) and other jams, rossolis, olives, melons and, towards Ravenna, what were undoubtedly the finest fruits in the whole of Italy, made the lower plain of the Reno a veritable land of milk and honey. Lastly they also reared very fine dogs there.

Spoleto possessed prosperous soap and hatting industries. Matelica and Pergola, two small towns in the Marches, had mills weaving coarse cloth ('good for making livery,' it was said) but manufactured a bare 500 pieces per year: this could not compare with the industrial development in the north.

The poor industrial progress of the whole of Southern Italy was essentially the result of obsolete regulations, the multiplicity of inter-State Customs and the lack of liquid capital. A strange affair of semi-clandestine traffic between Scilla, a modest city on the Tyrrhenian coast of Calabria, and Venice provides evidence of this. Towards the middle of the century some inhabitants of Scilla decided to send a felucca loaded with fustian, a cloth peculiar to the handicraft industry of Southern Italy, to Venice, which was still basking in its ancient glory. It was necessary to collect a capital of some 25,000 Neapolitan ducats; 149 people were engaged in the enterprise with individual shares of twenty-five to 1,800 ducats. Apart from a few subscribers from Messina and Matera, all the others lived at Scilla and were of very humble condition; a priest, some captains and skippers were the only ones to provide large sums. Interest of twelve per cent was forecast. The expedition successfully avoided the corsairs infesting the Mediterranean and the cargo was so well received at Venice that Venetian manufacturers applied to the Senate to stop 'a trade which threatened them'.

The main Italian item of export, as we know, together with woollen goods and raw silk, was olive oil, principally produced in the Kingdom of Naples, where it represented about two-thirds of the country's turnover. The greatest trade was done with England; traffic between Naples and France often passed through Genoa, from where the oil was re-exported to Marseilles. The eighteenth century, incidentally, was a period of tension as regards Franco-Neapolitan commercial relations, owing to the preferential tariff granted to Great Britain. Instead of the 1,500 bales of woollen cloth imported annually into Naples by France about 1700, in 1716 she only imported 100 bales of 'drapery, serge goods and rope of various kinds', i.e. fabrics of every category.

Sugar was the only French export to Naples which remained active. It was carried on by merchants who travelled directly to the fairs of Aversa and Salerno, from where the sugar was redistributed throughout the kingdom. Nevertheless many items of merchandise entered Naples as contrabrand; smuggling was to some extent officially accepted: so much so that a whole zone of the *Molo Piccolo* was considered as belonging to smugglers of salt and tobacco; it was not unknown for it to be surrounded by cordons of police who tried to catch them in the act, but the collusion of the inhabitants of the quarter with the smugglers was so obvious that the policemen sometimes had to withdraw, even when assisted by a strong contingent of foot soldiers and cavalry. The court turned a blind eye to all this.[4]

CHAPTER XVIII

SALARIES AND WAGES

IN ORDER to evaluate salaries and wages in the eighteenth century, it is first essential to understand the relative value in relation to the French livre minted at Tours (the *livre tournois*)* of the numerous coins in circulation in the peninsula, which were different at Rome, Naples, Venice, Milan and elsewhere. The rate of exchange of these coins, moreover, varied quite considerably between the beginning and end of the century: thus the gold louis, which towards 1710 was worth 33½ *paoli*, the monetary unit of the Roman State, was worth 44½ in 1765. The same gold louis, which corresponded to 24 livres in France, was only worth 20 at Turin, but 29 at Genoa or Milan and 95 at Parma. We must try to find our way through this jungle of different currencies.

Comparison with the *livre tournois* is the only one which is in any way accurate. Any comparison with present-day fiduciary coins cannot even be qualified as approximate. In fact, during the revolution, an equivalence was established, as we know, between the *livre tournois* and the so-called Germinal franc, which was remarkably stable in France until the 1914 war.

The monetary system of the Papal State was fairly simple and was already based on the decimal system. The Roman *scudo* contained 10 *paoli* and the *paoli* 10 *bajocchi*; the *bajocco* was itself subdivided into 5 *quattrini*, corresponding approximately to centimes which are not normally mentioned. On the basis of the value of the gold louis towards the middle of the century, the *paolo* was worth 10 sous 8 deniers (a little more than 5d), and the Roman *scudo* 5 livres 6 sous (about 4s 5d). A stronger unit, the Roman sequin, was worth 10 livres (about 8s 6d).

In Florence they also reckoned in *paoli*, *scudi* and sequins, but the *paolo* represented 11½ sous (about 6d), the *scudo* 5 French livres 12 sous (about 4s 8d), the sequin 20 *paoli* or 11 livres 10 sous (nearly 10s). The smallest coin, the *crazia*, was worth 7 centimes (about ¾d).

---

* Roughly the equivalent of the franc established in 1789 and worth 10d in English currency. Thus the louis, which equalled 24 French livres, was worth approximately £1 sterling.

Leaving out the smallest coins (*cavalli, quattrini, tornese, pubblica*, etc.), the basic unit at Naples was the *carlin*, corresponding to 8½ sous (about 4¼d). In 1765 56 carlins were given for one louis (or £1); 26 carlins made one sequin (9s 3d) and 30 carlins (10s 8d) a coin of three ducats or *uncia d'oro*, which was widely used. The Neapolitan ducat was worth 4 livres 6 sous (3s 7d).

The value of the Venetian silver ducat in relation to gold was roughly equal, i.e. 4·368 livres (3s 7d), and corresponded to 8 Venetian lire of 0·546; the lira itself was made up of 20 sous of 0·027 and the sou divided into 12 *bagattini*. But there was also a ducat of account in more common use representing 6 lire 4 sous (about 5s 2d). The Venetian *scudo* was worth 12 lire 8 sous (10s 4d) and the gold sequin 22 lire (18s 4d).

There were several sorts of *scudi* at Turin: the small *scudo* worth 3 lire (2s 6d) and the silver *scudo* minted in 1755 worth 6 Piedmontese lire (5s). We know that there were two kinds of silver écus in France, one worth 3 livres, the other 6 livres, for which the institution of the decimal system substituted the single five franc piece in circulation in the nineteenth century. In Piedmont there were also the following gold coins: the *scudo d'oro* of 6 lire (6s), the *doppia* of 12 lire (12s), and the most common, the *doppia* of 24 lire (24s) minted in 1774. To reckon their value in French livres it is necessary to add one-fifth, since the louis of 24 livres was only worth 20 at Turin. The largest gold coin, the gold *carlin*, was worth about 6 louis (£6).

To sum up, the unit of money in current use for small expenditure in several Italian States in the eighteenth century was roughly comparable to half a *livre tournois* (or 5d), a little more at Florence and Rome (*paolo*) a little less at Naples (*carlin*). The *lira*, already introduced in Northern Italy, was worth more at Venice, Milan and especially Turin than half a *livre tournois*, but nowhere was there a coin equal to the Germinal franc, which subsequently became the basis for monetary exchange throughout the Latin Union. Big payments were usually reckoned in large silver or gold units: *scudi*, sequins (*zecchini*), ducats, *doppie* and also *louis*, especially by French travellers, whose gold coins were at a premium everywhere.

Since the majority of court appointments and political offices were confined to members of the aristocracy who were presumed to be rich, they were never matched by large salaries. Montesquieu was struck by this as soon as he had collected information on the subject on his arrival in Piedmont. He found the nobility by no means wealthy and court appointments very modestly paid: 'There is no office worth more than 500 Spanish pistoles (the eighteenth-century pistole, a simple coin of account, was worth about 10 livres (or 8s 4d). The army is slightly better paid; General Rehbinder may well receive about 40,000 livres £1,650).'

Going into more detail because he was less of an aristocrat, Lalande gives us extremely accurate figures. Secretaries of State at Turin received 13,000 livres (£550), and expenditure for all the offices under them amounted to no more than 97,000 livres (£4,000). The Marquis of Ormea, who held the Secretaryships of State at the Foreign Office and the Exchequer as well as the Grand Chancellery of the Order of the Annonciade, was only paid 11,500 livres (£500). The first President of the Senate had a salary of 5,000 livres (£210) and the Chancellor of the Exchequer 6,000 (£250). The total salaries of the 21 Piedmontese Senators only amounted to 13,000 livres (£550), 12,000 (£500) for the Senate of Savoy and 26,000 (£1,100) for the Senate of the County of Nice. The body of financial officials cost 168,000 livres (£7,000). Administrators of provinces received from 1,500 to 3,000 livres (£62 10s to £125). Ambassadors received different salaries according to the size of the capital cities; the best paid, the ambassador to France, received 48,000 livres (£2,000), to Spain, 40,000 (£1,670), to England 38,000 (£1,610), to Vienna 30,000 (£1,250), to Naples 24,000 (£1,000) and to Rome 20,000 (£835). At the same epoch, the French ambassador in England had a salary of 150,000 livres (£6,250), plus 50,000 (£2,100) entertainment allowance.

A cavalry colonel's pay was 4,000 livres (£165), a lieutenant-colonel's 3,000 (£125), a major's 2,700 (£112), a captain's 2,023 (£85) and a lieutenant's 1,368 (£57). In the infantry, the pay was less than half as much for a lieutenant, less than a quarter or a sixth as much for the higher ranks and only higher for colonels. The university cost the King 52,000 livres (£2,200) and the total of the special pensions paid by him 54,000 (£2,250). The largest expenditure was the maintenance of his troops, which exceeded 8,000,000 livres (£333,000).

Modest as these payments were, they seem quite large in comparison with the salary of the Doge, which was 1,500 livres (£62 10s) at Genoa and insignificant at Venice in relation to the costs for entertainment which he had to shoulder. As for the Senators and members of the Council of Ten, they received no payment at all. An enormous private fortune was indispensable for all of them, if they were to maintain their rank.

At Parma, du Tillot, the Prime Minister, received 64,000 livres (£675) a year, reduced by 20,000 livres (£210) when he gave up the office of Administrator-General, which he had held conjointly; the Parma livre, as we know, was only worth a quarter of the *livre tournois*. Du Tillot was primarily compensated for his devotion to the Bourbon dynasty by the gift of property making up the Marquisate of Felino. Although Condillac, the tutor of the hereditary prince, received 32,000 livres (£335) because he was French, Father Paciaudi, the ducal librarian, was paid only 14,900 (£157) and the chief official in the Secretariat of State 12,000 (£126). But at Florence the officials from Lorraine were also better paid than the local officials, and the *paoli* and *zecchini* had not depreciated as much as at Parma. Count de Vaxoncourt, the new administrator of finance, received 12,000 (£500) livres per annum and an apartment. Two other representatives of the Grand Duke in the department of finance, Grobert and Gavard, were paid 14,000 lire (£583), Digny, Director of Accounts, 10,000 (£416), 'largely wasted', comments a contemporary document, 'because he was only a petty accountant and a much more capable Florentine would have held this office for a maximum of 4,200 lire per annum'.

At Pavia, university professors were paid from 1,500 to 1,800 lire (£62 to £75), including a lodging allowance. The *congrua* for priests was 1,200 lire (£50) at Milan for a parish with eight priests in charge of chapels of ease and much the same in the other Northern States.

At Rome, many administrative offices were venal and sometimes transferable. So much so that they were called negotiable (*vacabili*), not only as regards the principal, but also as regards the income, which was generally considerable because the official figure of the emoluments could be doubled, tripled and even multiplied tenfold, by the gratuities which were practically inseparable from it. The offices of secretaries of papal briefs, numbering eighty-four, were bought for 9,000 *scudi* (£2,000) and brought in 700 to 800 *scudi* (£154 to £176) per year (taking about 750 *scudi* (£165) as an average); they were the officials who issued dispensations from matrimonial barriers, for age, from abstinence from eating meat and conferred the right to have a chaplain, a private chapel, to bear a noble title, etc. The secretaries of briefs for princes were paid a double salary (1,500 *scudi* = £330) and received valuable presents from them. The offices of major domo, chamberlain to the Supreme Pontiff and secretaries of congregations, themselves needed lay secretaries who were well paid and sometimes succeeded each other from father to son or uncle to nephew. On the death of a cardinal, a custom guaranteed the two masters of ceremonies, known as participants, 50 ducats from his heirs and 112 from every new cardinal, in addition to their salary; the two masters of ceremonies known as supernumeraries only received 12 *scudi* from new cardinals.

Employments of secondary importance, extended nevertheless to the secret participant or honorary chamberlains, the secret treasurer paying out alms, the 'harbinger major', an office reserved for the Sacchettis, the keeping of the wardrobe, the papal equipages, etc., received 1,000 *scudi* (£220) per annum and the 'secret assistant chamberlains', all gentlemen, 500 *scudi* (£110), together with never-ending *mancié*. After them came the *bussolanti*, servants inside the apostolical palaces, the servants for service *extra muros*, the stablemen, under the orders of the *cavallerizo maggiore*, a hereditary office of the family of Marquis Serlupi, the under-harbingers, who looked after the harness, the coachmen—strangely named *scopatori* (sweepers) *segreti e pubblici*—twelve mace-bearers and twelve ushers for ceremonies, and lastly an endless number of lower offices: real sweepers, kitchen assistants, porters, grooms, muleteers, *sediari* (bearers of the *sedia gestatoria*), baggage porters, etc., who received wages on a descending scale.

There remained the papal army. The pay of the General of the Guards, who was lodged in the palace—a guard composed of

Swiss, light cavalry, cuirassiers and lancers—was 200 *scudi* (£44) per month and a lieutenant's 80 *scudi*. The artillery and cavalry generals were paid 100 *scudi*, the 'commissioners' and 'camp masters' 50, colonels 30, captains 20 plus numerous gifts. The highest paid officer was the 'General of the Holy Church', or generalissimo of the papal forces, who received 1,000 *scudi* (£220) a month in peacetime and 3,000 (£600) in wartime. He was the man who granted commissions to junior officers, chose the governors of coastal and frontier fortresses, etc. None of the soldiers was paid in peacetime but the troops enjoyed a flock of privileges.

A statement of payments made in 1736 by Clement XII, a pope with relatively simple tastes, although of a princely family (Corsini), shows that the upkeep of the staff, the Palatine Guard and the papal buildings cost 295,921 Roman *scudi* (about £65,000). In the same way as the Venetian nobility, which was terribly in debt and partially ruined when the Republic fell, the popes often lived above their means. Thus Benedict XIV was forced to authorize Charles III of Spain in 1753 to purchase the rights of advowson over ecclesiastical benefices in its kingdom for a lump sum of 6,746,648 lire which went to swell the papal treasure kept in the Castello Sant' Angelo.[1]

The wages of manual workers were generally very low, which partly explains the custom of begging in and out of season of which Montesquieu and President de Brosses complained so bitterly during their stay in Italy. The highest wages were found at Venice where 300 lire was estimated as the minimum wage payable to a worker without a family; but a married worker, father of a family, generally received at least 100 ducats, or 640 lire.

At Padua masons received 60 ducats and foremen 80. However the wages of many labourers and agricultural workers were often as low as 14 sous per working day without food or compensation for holidays, which were numerous, as we know. When the Republic ended, there were still eighty-five holidays in spite of numerous reductions, and a further fifty rainy or snowy days had to be deducted. All in all there were barely 230 paid days, amounting to 161 lire, on which workers had to live and keep a family for 365 days. Seven sous a day were indispensable for food, which consisted almost almost exclusively of corn. There remained only 33 lire 5 sous for rent in the outhouses of monasteries,[2] heating, clothes, medical care, the upkeep of house-hold utensils, taxes and unforeseen expenses. Hence all sorts of expedients to combat poverty: thefts of unripe fruit and vege-tables in the fields, and wood from fellings in the forests; in periods of famine, such as the winter of 1782, assaults on the granaries of financiers and bishops, and finally leaving the land.[3]

Extremely accurate contemporary studies dealing specifically with Lombardy and Piedmont, as well as Tuscany, where the vast enquiry ordered by Grand Duke Leopold supplies the most accurate bases for appreciation, enable us today to make a scientific check of the often precise but fragmentary data left by travellers who visited Italy during the eighteenth century. For the convenience of the reader, the wages and prices in these works, particularly by the books by Messrs. Pugliese and Dal Pane, have been unified with reference to the Italian lira of the first decade of the twentieth century which was as stable as the Germinal franc and had very much the same value.[4]

The general conclusions of these economists are that even in the very fertile zones, such as the wine-growing region of Vercelli, the situation of agricultural workers very often under-went progressive deterioration from the beginning to the end of the eighteenth century; that this deterioration was particularly noticeable for labourers paid by the day in cash, and that the remuneration paid them as from about 1760 was not enough to keep them properly fed.

Mr Pugliese estimates that the maintenance of an adult peasant between 1900 and 1910 cost 363.75 lire (just over £15). But the purchasing power of the lira in the eighteenth century enabled a cowherd, for example, paid by the year and for the most part in kind, either to economize a part of his earnings, rising to as much as forty-five per cent between 1700 and 1794, or to feed himself and his family better than the general mass of peasants. In fact, a Piedmontese cowherd received only 80 to 85 Italian lire a year in cash (about 67s to 71s), but six sacks of rye or millett, four *emine* (a measure equivalent to twenty-three litres) of dried vegetables, one *rubbo* (a little less than three hectolitres) of butter, one of walnut oil, one of salt, one of salt pork and two *rubbi* of curds in kind. On this basis his total earnings work out at about 300 lire (£12 10s) and 190 to 215 lire were enough for him to live on. He was therefore able either to save from 80 to 100 lire, or to buy fresh meat, wheaten bread and wine from time to time.

But the situation of agricultural labourers and hands paid by the day was quite different. In Piedmont, from 1701 to 1793, the former received about 0.85 per day (8½d), the latter 0.76 (7½d). There, as everywhere else in Italy, non-working days were very numerous and as from 1760 the inadequacy of earnings, even for a workman employed all the year round except on Sundays and legal holidays, was from five to twenty per cent of the bare minimum. The difference could only be met by spending too little on food. Things grew still worse under the French regime when it had been estimated that an Italian worker earned two times less than his French equivalent, in view of the considerable rise in the cost of living which was not matched by an increase in wages.

Industrial workers were no better off and when they lived in a town their situation was even worse than if they lived in the country. In the woollen manufacturing zone of Biella, skilled workers only earned 12 sous (6d) per day and women spinners 2 to 3 sous (1d to 1½d). The same wages were paid at Saluzzo in a cloth factory after four years' apprenticeship; pay increased to 15 and 18 sous (2½d to 9d) after five and ten years' regular work, but still without food. On an average, a weaver earned 200 lire (£8 7s), or 13.4 sous (less than 7d) per day, for 300 working days. During the winter at Coni, after the chestnut harvest, the unfortunate women from the neighbouring valleys, forced to crowd five and six together in one room, came to work as spinners for a wretched wage in order to increase the family resources by a minute sum.[5] At Turin only a few privileged workers, for example the *calzettari* (weavers of stockings and socks), managed to earn 30 Savoy sous (1.80 Italian lire or 1s 6d). This wage was not even attained by the deep miners in the State mines of the Val Sesia: they only earned about 17 sous (8½d) and the other workers connected with the mine 15 (7½d). In the service of the Sardinian States turners received 12 sous (6d), blacksmiths 18 sous (9d) and master carpenters 20 sous (10d), but the level was lower in private industry.

In Tuscany, the 1766 enquiry gives an average wage of 1·13 lire (11½d) for reapers, harvesters and threshers. An agricultural labourer employed on digging or weeding only made 1·6 lire (1s 4d) and a woman not more than 13½ sous (6¾d). Generally speaking and especially for agricultural tasks, the winter wage was different from the summer wage which was always higher. It also differed according as the worker was fed or not, but the deduction for food was minimal. A detailed statement of the wages paid in a mountainous district of the Apennines gives 2 lire (1s 8d) in summer and 33 sous (1s 5d) in winter, without food, for a mason; if fed, he received 26 sous (1s 1d) in summer and 1 lire (10d) in winter. Workmen received 1 lira in winter and summer without food, and 13 sous (6½d) in summer and 10 (5d) in winter if fed. The maximum daily wage paid to a mason came to 2 lire 13 sous (2s 2d) in the zone of Grosseto and fell to 36 sous (1s 6d) in the immediate neighbourhood of Florence. Wood cutters and stone cutters had approximately the same wage, but women were scandalously exploited: a girl working in the straw hat industry earned a maximum of 4 sous (2d) per day; again the contractor would often pay her in kind, putting a higher price than normal on the hats.

In the Ginori china factory, workmen earned from 22 to 33 sous (11d to 1s 5d), and decorators up to 2½ lire (2s 1d). In the silk industry, which had to be reeled by hand, men got 1·70 lire (1s 5d) and a fifteen-year-old girl 11 sous (5½d). At Modena, masons and carpenters received 1·10 lire (11d) and printers in the duchy of Parma 1·70 lire (1s 5d).

Craftsmen, although they were often self-employed workers, did not manage to earn very much more. A net profit of 2 lire per day (1s 8d) for a blacksmith, a cutler or a carpenter appears to have been the maximum. If the craftsman was in the service of an employer and worked for 260 days per year—an average rarely exceeded—for a wage of 2 lire, he still only made 520 Tuscan lire, or 443·52 Italian lire (£18 10s 11d). He did not starve but he could only save very small amounts.

In Emilia and Romagna the papal coinage was current. In Bologna an agricultural labourer received 10 *bajocchi* (about 5d) in winter and 12 plus two flasks of wine in summer; harvesters received up to 20 *bajocchi*. Manufacturing workers earned from 5 to 20 *bajocchi* and hemp spinners only 3 or 4 *bajocchi*.

For servants paid by the month, a footman in livery at Bologna was paid 50 *paoli*, a cook from 20 to 40 *zecchini*, or an average of 22s 6d. We have already seen (chap. XVI) that a coachman in a noble house could earn 6 *scudi* per month. This was a summit in the hierarchy of domestic staff, a summit which could also be reached by a good chef. Sometimes the latter was French, for the fashion had been introduced among the Venetian and Milanese aristocracy who were more concerned about the quality of their meals than their counterparts at Turin or Florence.

Obviously the wages paid to the French staff of the child Duke of Parma were quite exceptionally high for Italy. Chefs were paid 12,000 livres (£125) per year, their assistants 4,000 and the scullions 2,600, almost as much as a major in the royal Piedmontese army, on condition that the wages were spent on the spot and not converted into livres minted at Tours.[7]

At Naples and in Southern Italy it was estimated that a craftsman, his wife and four children could live 'reasonably' on 4 ducats or less than 15s per month.[8] This was considerably lower than the northern average, and it barely exceeds the resources of present-day African workers. This clearly shows how it is almost impossible to establish a valid relationship between epochs so different as the eighteenth century and our own, in which so many new necessities have been included in even very low Western standards of living.

CHAPTER XIX

THE COST OF LIVING AND DYING

LET US imagine a foreigner arriving at Milan in the middle of the eighteenth century, coming from England, France or Germany via Switzerland. If he was alone and had hired a saddle-horse at the frontier, the postmaster would have charged him 3·10 lire per stage of two leagues, or 2 livres 4 sous (1s 9d). If he preferred a poste-chaise with two horses and had luggage weighing less than sixty-six pounds, it would cost him 10·10 lire (5s 9d) for each two leagues or fraction of two leagues, for every stretch which has started had to be paid in full and in advance. If he had one or two companions and wanted a four-wheeled carriage with three seats, including one in front, with three horses, each stage would have come to 14·10 lire (8s). Lastly, if he had wanted a carriage drawn by four horses for three or four people whose luggage did not weigh more than 132 pounds, he would have had to pay 21 lire per stage (nearly 12s). This assumes that the postmaster was honest and stuck to the official tariffs, for experience would have taught him that the latter varied not only from State to State—Piedmont and Lombardy being the dearest—but also with the postmasters, expert in exploiting foreigners' ignorance of local practice, shortening the stages at will by once or four times their length or even more, and skilfully faking the accounts to meet the apparent wealth of the client. A knowing traveller, especially if he carried letters of recommendation, used what were known as 'letters of *cambiature*', which forced the postmasters to apply a tariff which was less than half the normal tariff (for example in Piedmont, 4·10 lire—2s 4d—for two good horses), but they obeyed with the greatest reluctance and instead of using a smart trot ordered the postilions to go at a walk. In order to go at a faster speed it was necessary to haggle and pay a supplement.

At Milan and Turin, an innkeeper asked 6 Milanese lire, or 1 *scudo* per day (4s 6d), for a room, dinner and supper, but at Venice a foreigner would only have paid 8 *paoli*, i.e. 4·20 lire (or 3s 4d) if he had changed English money) for an excellent bed and very good food. Several dishes at each meal and two bottles of an average wine, which was neither very good nor very bad.

Breakfast would have cost him 10 *soldi* and at Venice he could have hired the services of a gondolier for 6 *paoli* per day. If he wanted a seat at the theatre in the evening, he would have paid 3 *paoli* for it. Adding up all these expenses, we see that room, board, servant, gondola and entertainment (the theatre) represented an average daily expenditure of 7s 6d or 9.75 lire. (A carriage for hire by the day, however, would have cost twice as much as a gondola at Milan or Bologna. In 1789 Arthur Young came to the conclusion that one could live better in Italy on an income of £100 sterling than on £500 in London, although the difference in price for essential items was insignificant and a liking for luxury inclined people in Italy to the superfluous rather than the indispensable: sobriety, for example, was the rule there in all classes of society with a few rare exceptions.

If one set up house there, as so many English and a few French did until 1914, it was possible to live the life of the local nobility, to have a carriage and valets, to play faro and allow oneself every pleasure, as happened to the small group of Burgundian friends who accompanied President de Brosses to Rome in the eighteenth century and have not left us any of their accounts. But one could also lead a comfortable life without luxury and in such a case a well-to-do middle-class man from the northern countries cut a better figure in Italy than in his home country. Canon Clement, the future constitutional bishop of Versailles, on arriving in Rome in 1758, found 'a decent apartment' for 8 sequins a month (less than £4) in a good hotel in the Piazza di Spagna, on condition that he kept it for six months; but shortly afterwards a friend arranged for him to rent an apartment pleasantly situated on the Farnese Square for half as much with a few supplementary local charges.[1] A certain Mr Taylor, a friend of Young, had made an arrangement at Bologna with a caterer who supplied him with an abundant mid-day meal for nine masters and their five servants for 20 *paoli* a day (less than 10s): he would not have found the equivalent in France and certainly not in England.

More than one foreigner, attracted by the country, was tempted to settle there for a time at least. He found it quite easy to do so in town or country. There was no lack of the excellent masons which Italy has always produced to restore an old resi-

14　Ball in the S. Carlo Theatre (Naples) (engraving by de Lorrain after Vincenzo)

Photo: Hachette

15 Two views of
    Naples in 1765
    (engravings by
    Cardon after
    Gabriele Ricciardelli).
         Photo : Hachette

dence according to the taste of a new master or to build a brand
new one. One thousand bricks cost 22 livres at Turin and 30 at
Milan. Domestic staff were abundantly available, cheerful, docile
and as obliging as could be wished. And if the food in the
majority of Italian homes was mediocre, it was because the
family income was used for other purposes and not because it
was impossible to find excellent provisions.

Meat at Rome was of the highest quality and very cleanly
served: we can believe Father Labat who emerges as a great
gourmet in his travel books.[2] The average price of beef was from
13 to 14 sous (1 sou = approx. ½d) a pound in Northern Italy,
of veal 16 sous, of mutton 4 to 13 sous and of pork 18 sous.
When beef rose from 14 to 16 sous a pound in Venetia towards
the end of the century, the people stopped eating it; it was
already an inaccessible luxury for the majority of wage earners.
In Tuscany and Papal State, meat was cheaper.

Poultry did not vary much in price from one district to
another, if we take into account the differences in the relative
value of the coinage. Chickens were 15 sous a pound from the
Alps to the Adriatic, ducks and geese 25 sous and pigeons 10 or
12 sous each. A four-pound turkey was worth 3½ paoli at
Bologna, or about 36 sous, and 30 sous at Turin where the
monetary unit was stronger; on the other hand the bird cost
11 sous a pound at Milan where the lira had depreciated considerably in relation to Piedmont. A dozen eggs cost 8 sous at
Turin and 26 at Milan: here Lombardy appears to be at a considerable disadvantage; the price of 1 bajocco per egg at Bologna
comes between the two, but is closer to Turin.

A good deal of fish was also consumed in Southern Italy, even
salt fish, mainly coming from England and also at Venice the
salted sardines of the Adriatic. At Milan salt cod was sold for
6 sous the pound of 12 ounces, pickled eel 11 sous, raw tunny
fish and anchovies 16 sous, and cooked tunny fish 18 sous. Fresh
water fish cost no more, even pike which was worth 12 to 15
bajocchi a pound at Bologna; tench and eels were even cheaper
(10 to 14 bajocchi).

Like the different currencies, weights and measures in Italy
were variable and complicated with all sorts of traditional divi-
sions instead of the beautiful simplicity of the metric system

N

which could only have been the child of a Cartesian brain. In Lombardy and Venetia there were two different ways of weighing merchandise. The pound of twenty-eight ounces, or *peso grosso*, was used for heavy or coarse articles: soap, candles and sometimes meat, butter and cheese. The pound of twelve ounces, or *peso sottile*, was used for weighing sugar, bread, rice, coffee and the precious chocolate which was the basis of everybody's breakfast and the evening *rinfreschi*. In Venice it was sold for 3½ or 4 lire the *peso sottile* pound, about the same as coffee, sugar for 25 to 35 sous, butter for 30 sous (35 at Milan), cheese for 32—but as much as 44 for *lodigiano*—and ham also for 44. All these prices were a little lower in the Papal States: sugar and coffee only cost about 22 *bajocchi* a pound. A bottle of table wine cost from 3 to 5 *bajocchi*.

The people's basic food was bread, but rarely made of pure wheat. In Piedmont and Lombardy, where it was made of a mixture of rye and millett, it cost from 1½ sous to 1 sou 8 deniers a pound. In Venetia maize took the place of wheat, also mixed with rye, and often with bran and *sorgo rosso* in the mountainous districts. Farmers were only just beginning to experiment with growing potatoes, which did not compete with maize until after the first quarter of the nineteenth century, and their consumption was delayed in Venetia because of the disastrous results of trying to mix it with other flours to make bread. The latter were generally bought among the working classes by the bushel (or *moggio*) of 146 *peso grosso* pounds—or about 222 present-day pounds—which in 1770 cost 24 Milanese lire and enabled them to bake their bread at home. The flour for making pasta, also widely used, as was rice, cost only a little more than 21 lire a *moggio*. These essential provisions had cost about half as much at the beginning of the century but after 1770 their price never stopped rising until it reached three times the normal average in 1795. Haricot beans constituted another popular food which was greatly appreciated in Venetia and Tuscany.[3] The most commonly used oil among the peasants in the north was rape oil, which was also used for lighting and making black soap. The finer walnut oil was worth one lira a pound (of twenty-eight ounces) at Milan. Olive oil was only in current use in the south.

Candles also provide proof of a considerable difference in prices between the centre and the north: from eight *bajocchi* a pound at Bologna, they rose to nine or ten sous at Turin, where the currency in addition was stronger. Coal, delivered by sea, was rarely used outside Venice, where it cost 4.50 lire per 100 pounds. At Rome and in the south we know that heating was practically non-existent. Cooking was done with charcoal, which cost three lire per 100 pounds (of twenty-eight ounces) at Milan and from five to eight lire at Venice.

Wood for heating was sold in various forms of cubage. In Venetia the *carro* of 108 cubic feet corresponded closely to the old French *corde* of about 4 steres and cost 22 lire.

As for the cost of housing, it remained one of the lowest items in Italy for the working classes, both because of the abundant manpower and the minimal requirements of the working class. Towards 1750, a rent of 20 lire per annum was already considered high in the country, nor did it increase much subsequently. Obviously it was more expensive in the large towns. At Milan it had reached 40 lire per room at the end of the century and a normal family had to have at least two rooms. However, the estimates of economists who have studied the problem and who put the annual expenditure on rent for the working classes in the country at 50 lire between 1900 and 1910 only reckon it at a little more than 25 lire between 1700 and 1802. The slow increase in the population meant that there was never any shortage of housing in the peninsula in the eighteenth century. However, we should add that in Southern Italy a large part of the people was (and still is) housed in a way which is unfitting for human beings.

There were no private clinics in the Italy of those days, but the hospitals in the large towns could provide medical care for patients of every social class, in the same way as we tend to conceive of them today in England. Their principal fault was their shortage of accommodation: the *ospedale maggiore* of a large town such as Milan only had room for 650 men and 310 women, which sometimes meant that two or even three indigent patients had to sleep in the same bed. Hospitalisation was free for them. Apart from them there were three classes of paying patients. The first class were entitled, for 3 lire a day, to a private room, to bring a servant with them and choose their doctor or surgeon. Patients in the second class, who paid 30 sous a day, were treated in rooms with from four to six beds. The third class, who paid 12 sous, were housed in wards.

In case of death at Milan, there were three classes of funerary tariffs and only the first included a coffin (at 3·50 lire), as we have already mentioned in a preceding chapter. Paupers were buried without covering. The expenses for tolling the bells (6 and 4 lire) and transport to the cemetery including digging the grave (3 lire) were very much the same for all three classes. The major differences concerned the number of priests officiating at the service (24 for the first two classes at 2 lire per head, 12 for the third at 1·50) and the number of candles around the deceased's body. They were less strictly limited than at Florence, while being far from the lavish illumination current at Venice and Palermo, and entailed an expenditure of 58 lire for the first class, 18 for the second and 12 for the third. The fees of the priest celebrating the funeral varied from 2 to 5 or even 7 lire. Altogether, with a few supplementary expenses, the total bill for the three classes varied from 47 to 302 lire, about six times as much.

CONCLUSION

I F THE essential points of the detailed contents of this book had to be summed up in a brief synthesis, we should say that at no time and to no country could Talleyrand's phrase about '*la douceur de vie*' before the Revolution have been so fittingly applied as to eighteenth-century Italy, at least as regards the upper classes.

No great interests at stake involving the whole people, no deadly wars, no colonies to defend, since the country did not possess any, no bitter religious quarrels—at the most a few disputes between theological schools—no widely distributed wealth, but also very few needs and no envy felt by the less privileged for the élite.

Admittedly, a large number of reforms appeared desirable to the intellectual élite and they preached the need for them, but without the mordant irony of Voltaire or the acrimony of Jean-Jacques Rousseau. The Encyclopaedists had a following in Italy among the better minds, who were closer to the humanists of the Renaissance than to French revolutionary orators and members of the National Convention.

There were no great men among the sovereigns and even, at Florence, some miserable specimens of humanity in the shape of the last members of the Medici family or Ferdinand IV at Naples; but there were also some princes well worthy of esteem —Charles III of Bourbon, Charles Emmanuel III and especially Leopold Hapsburg-Lorraine, with Benedict XIV among the popes. Among the nobility a few good public servants and great men of letters stood out against the mediocrity of a class which had exhausted its high virtues and maintained antiquated traditions more out of pride of class than out of a rational conviction of its excellence. Consequently these traditions were seen to fall without resistance when the *fin de siècle* storm blew.

In a growing middle class of businessmen and officials, considerably fewer and poorer than in the old monarchies north of the Alps, there was an assiduous devotion to work, simple tastes and an exemplary family life in which the father's authority was not disputed, and the behaviour of the wife, devoted to her household duties, was generally irreproachable.

Among the poor inhabitants of town and country there was

an astonishing moderation, which did not stop workers on the land and the workmen of a people of builders from having great resistance to fatigue, gentle manners sometimes shot through with flashes of violence in certain provinces where the blood was hotter or passions stronger, extremely affable but often superficial greetings cleverly shaded to capture the benevolence of the 'lord' on whom they lavished honorary titles.

From top to bottom of the social scale the great preoccupation was still love, but in association with religion. It was by no means condemned by the church and not necessarily illicit. Love and religion satisfied the impulses of the heart, the one turned towards the earth, the other towards the sky, between which there could be no opposition, since this life is only a journey. Dogma was not disputed, which does not mean to say that it was properly understood, and the fervour of the simple people was generally based on superstition. Non-believers were rare in eighteenth-century Italy and never dared to proclaim themselves as such; in any case they only belonged to a small intellectual minority; although widespread, scepticism was never aggressive.

Always rich in artistic talent, Italian genius in the *Settecento* blossomed forth in music of every kind, composed and spontaneous, religious and profane. The great painting tradition was almost exhausted and only survived among the Venetian decorators and landscape artists, but Italian architects were still numbered among the best in the world, and the minor arts, including cabinet-making, still produced some charming creations. Parallel with this, an interest in scientific culture developed among a still restricted élite and erudition in the schools of Muratori, Eustachio Manfredi, Genovesi and other less famous investigators of the treasury of human knowledge, prepared the way for the galaxy of scholars, historians and economists of the next age, of which Italy could be rightly proud when she took her place among the great powers after acquiring national independence.

The men who were preoccupied by this high destiny were still rare. The mass of the people was satisfied with more modest ambitions. Strongly attached to their local customs, they returned to them as soon as a reformist prince had given up legislation aimed at suppressing them, as Spaniards, Austrians and Frenchmen all tried to do. Proud of its Latin ancestry, of the

Italian nationality of the Sovereign Pontiffs and of the glories which had made it famous during the centuries, but not boastful to foreigners who inspired in it a sympathetic curiosity, the Italian people, then, appear at the beginning of the contemporary epoch as essentially easy going and better constituted for the happiness to which its luminous sky seemed to destine it than for long ordeals.

NOTES

INTRODUCTION

1. A doctrine explained in his works by the Rhenish theologian Jean-Nicolas de Hontheim (1701-90), who wrote under the pseudonym of *Justinus Febronius*. This doctrine aimed at restricting the Rights of Rome in favour of those of the temporal sovereigns and therefore encouraged Josephism.

CHAPTER I

1. A scrupulously accurate census of the inhabitants of Rome carried out by M de Saint-Seine in 1709 gave a figure of 138,568 Christian inhabitants composing 32,442 families, plus 8,000 to 10,000 Jews. In this number were included 2,646 priests, 3,556 monks and friars and 1,814 nuns. In 1790 the total population had only risen to 162,982 inhabitants.
2. Abbé Coyer, who had experienced it and commented on it in his *Voyages d'Italie et de Hollande*, Paris, 1775 (vol. I, p. 80), credited this theatre with 15,000 seats, but this was an obvious exaggeration. In 1714-5 the Comte de Caylus made the same observations about the excellent acoustics of the Farnese Theatre.
3. On the left bank of the Arno, in the Via dei Bardi, in Florence, there is another Capponi Palace, built in the fifteenth century for Niccoló da Uzzano, the statesman whose bronze bust by Donatello is one of the masterpieces to be seen in the Bargello Museum. The family is one of the most ancient in Florence.
4. Mainly known for his *Nouveau Voyage aux Isles de l'Amérique*, Father Labat showed that he was also a very acute observer of Spain and Italy.
5. Like the majority of his contemporaries, Caylus understood nothing of the art of the Middle Ages and the early Renaissance. At Padua, he did not even look at the frescoes by Giotto or at the works of the Sienese primitives at Siena. He only devoted four trivial lines to the Olympic Theatre at Vicenza. He felt that Ravenna was uninteresting; he was bored and only spent a few hours there. The only thing he found to praise at St Vital was a painting by Baroche!
6. Mme du Bocage confirmed that Ferrara was 'deserted and badly paved'.
7. 'Anywhere you like.' Similar contempt for the proprieties and elementary hygiene has continued in the Italian countryside and even in some of the small southern towns until a recent

date. In his novel *Bread and Wine* Ignazio Silone recalls the amusing distinction which was made in a market town in the Abruzzi between the latrines of the *cafoni* (poor peasants) and those of the local lower middle classes. At the beginning of the twentieth century they still had not advanced to the stage of individual w.c's, even of a primitive type.

CHAPTER II

1. It took two days to cross the lands of the Count of Gira. Certain landowners, such as the Duke of Assinara or the Duke of Santa Piera, had an income of 160,000 to 300,000 livres (£6,600 to £12,500): so the means were certainly not lacking for them to prove themselves good administrators of their wealth.

2. These gardens show that the opinion of President de Brosses that French gardens were better than Italian ones cannot be accepted (with the possible exception of Versailles). Some Frenchmen blamed the Italians for their self-conceit in making excessive use of the word 'palace' where French would say more simply 'hotel' or 'house', but this was balanced by their preference for the unpretentious term 'villa' for their country houses, instead of the usual French 'château', even to designate the suburban residences of the Roman, Milanese or Venetian nobility, with much simpler lines than the châteaux of the Loire, for example, but also containing vast and rich apartments.

CHAPTER III

1. Some less sumptuous palaces had floors made of pulverized brick mixed with mortar and then rubbed with oil, which produced a smooth and brilliant red surface. The walls might also be hung with gilded leather.

2. Cf. P. Molmenti: *Private Life in Venice*, Venice, Ongania, 1882, pp. 397-8.

3. An excellent example of these brilliant costumes is furnished by the full-length portrait of Count Valletti by Vittore Ghislandi in the Venetian Academy of Fine Arts. In it he appears in a rich dressing gown of green and gold brocade lined with grey-pink silk, open over a *camisiola* of red flowered brocade. Black stockings and toque.

4. The women of the people covered their heads and shoulders with vast scarves which only left their eyes showing.

5. That indefatigable traveller and wit the Venetian Francesco Algarotti has written some verses about this craze in an amusing vein:

> Quella di cui tanto aspettar s'è fatto
> La bella di Parigi alma fantoccia
> Che d'ogni villa feo levare a stormo
> Donne gentili devote d'amore,
> Tu le vedresti a lei dinnanzi in frotte
> L'Andrienne, la cuffia, le nastriere
> L'immenso guardinfante a parte a parte
> Notomizzare, e sino addentro e sotto
> Spinger gli avidi sguardi al gonnellino.

The following is a free prose translation: 'In front of her who has aroused such expectations, the superb and respected Parisian dummy, who has brought so many charming enthusiastic ladies running from their houses, you will see them in troops minutely dissecting the *andrienne*, the hairstyle, the ribbons and the enormous hoops, and plunging their hungry looks inside, even under the first petticoat.'

Gasparo Gozzi has also commented wittily on the fact in his journal *l'Osservatore veneto* in 1767: 'While looking at them (the window display of Paris fashions), they fall in love with them, can never get enough of looking at them and come and go several times after having asked first this merchant, then that, here the price of one thing, there of another and made the men accompanying them very impatient.'

6. Pronounced like the French *toupet*.

7. 'All the women at Rome wear wigs,' wrote Dupaty about the same epoch. 'It is a sacrifice which their coquetry makes to their indolence.' In fact since they slept in the middle of the day, after lunch, the effort of doing their hair twice would have been too much for them.

8. At Milan, the fashion was also determined by the *pupattola di Parigi*, a large dummy.

At Rome, a certain Madame Souquet, 'French fashion merchant', had the best name in town (Lalande). President de Brosses wrote of the women of Bologna: 'every day they are sent large dolls dressed in the latest fashion from head to foot and they never wear nick-nacks which they have not had sent from Paris'.

CHAPTER IV

1. Good hotels of this name still existed at Bologna in the first quarter of the twentieth century.

2. Cf. Hélène Tuzet: *La Sicile au XVIIIe siècle, vue par les*

voyageurs étrangeurs, Strasbourg, 1955, p. 221, from an account in the *Deutsche Merkur*.

3. Quoted by Pompeo Molmenti, in *Private Life at Venice*, after Longo, Memorie, V, chap. XXV, Venice, 1820.

CHAPTER V

1. Lalande quotes the case of a nobleman who held a magistrature in the Highways Department and wanted to emphasize his integrity by showing much larger incomings than were customary, so proving to the government that his predecessors had filled their own pockets shamelessly. Far from being grateful to him, the government considered it an unwelcome lesson and a condemnation of ancient customs, and subsequently he was only given a village to administrate.

2. The dramatic fate of Antonio Foscarini has inspired poets more than once, in particular in the nineteenth century a tragedy by Niccolini, which nevertheless has no historical foundation and grafts a moving story of crossed love onto a purely political plot. Foscarini was a man of keen intelligence but 'restless, bizarre, boastful and with depraved morals', who had already aroused suspicions as to his indiscretion during his ambassadorship in London. At the home of the Countess of Arundel, whom he saw a lot of in Venice and who was supposed to be his mistress, he certainly saw foreign diplomats. The preoccupation with justice which made the Venetian government continue its inquiry even after an over-hasty execution and proceed to immediate rehabilitation, having admitted its error, does honour to this government which is too often accused—as is Lucretia Borgia on another level — of imaginary crimes and whose severity was always tempered by a keen awareness of its duties. Cf. Pompeo Molmenti: *La Relazioni tra patrizi veneti e diplomatici stranieri*, in *Nuova Antologia*, March 1, 1917.

3. Cf. Jérome de Lalande: *Voyage d'un Français en Italie*, vol. VIII, p. 165.

4. Literal translation of the Italian *mercadanti*: merchants .

5. Two similar lotteries existed in the eighteenth century at Rome and Paris (Ecole Militaire), considerably more advantageous for the betters.

6. The context seems to indicate that the Duc de Richelieu would have thought them too sumptuous even for him.

7. The Grandeeship of Spain was granted to Count Carlo Borromeo

in 1708, to Duke Gabrio Serbelloni in 1710 and to Count Giorgio Clerici in 1716, as well as to the town of Milan itself.

8. French ambassador to Turin at the time of Montesquieu's journey, after having served in the diplomatic service at Brussels and Vienna. Husband of the famous Marquise de Prie, mistress of the Duc de Bourbon.

CHAPTER VI

1. Lalande informs us that a celebrated preacher who came to preach during Lent in Venice in 1760 'brought with him his mistress, who was very well dressed and very pretty'. A Benedictine from the monastery of San Martino admitted to Bartels, a future mayor of Hamburg, who visited Sicily in 1786: 'every time I leave the monastery, I leave my vows of chastity behind; they would be an embarrassment outside the cloister'. Such morals were frequent. The case of monastic corruption which created the greatest stir was the famous affair of the Dominican nuns of Pistoia, which in 1781 motivated the measures taken against them and their Dominican confessors by Scipione de Ricci when he was enthroned as bishop of that diocese. The resentment of the Holy See towards him seems to have been caused less by the actual facts, which my pen refuses to describe, for they were already known or at least suspected by Ricci's predecessors, than by the case brought against the guilty persons with the agreement of Grand Duke Leopold. Not only were they condemned as a result, but the Dominicans of Florence were also deprived of all jurisdiction over the monasteries of their order and had to hand it over to the diocesan bishops. It was an enormous scandal. With a wealth of unnecessary detail, to say the least, the Belgian writer, Louis de Potter, has referred to them, after the official reports of the interrogations to which the case gave rise, in his *Vie de Scipion de Ricci*, Brussels, 1825, 3 vol. Octavo.

2. One of them, the Genoese Dominican Tommaso Vignoli, an exemplary monk and stricter than Bousset in his moral austerity, preached from the pulpit that it was a mortal sin to attend a theatrical performance. The Archbishop of Genoa, Lercari, who did not like the Jansenists, deprived him of the right to preach and even to confess.

3. The Benedictine Fathers of San Martino, all members of the biggest Sicilian families, spent whole months with their families in the country during the summer or on the fiefs of the monas-

tery. They received from their father or elder brother the pension generally paid to the junior members of noble houses and in addition a salary for those who held offices in the monastery, which they could leave at will. All that was required of them was 'a brief hour of prayer from time to time' and they spent the rest of the day reading, playing cards and billiards, the lay brothers keeping the score. Their table was excellent. The abbot, elected every three years, did not have to belong to the monastery and the monks usually chose him for his reputation in the world of learning. He was a baron of the Empire and sat in the ecclesiastical benches in parliament. The monks showed themselves very charitable to the poor and extremely hospitable to foreigners.

Of the Benedictine monastery at Catania, in which lived sixty monks served by a numerous domestic staff, Roland wrote that it possessed 'a façade almost equal to that of Versailles, a flight of white marble steps (the fathers chartered ships to fetch the marble from Carrara) and everything which proclaims royal magnificence'. The cells were princely. Cf. Hélène Tuzet: *La Sicile au XVIIIᵉ siècle, vue par les voyageurs étrangers*, pp. 497-502.

4. Cf. J. Leflon: *Pie VII*, Paris, Plon, 1958, vol. I, p. 205—Lalande quotes a clergyman who was a theatre manager and another a fencing master.

5. Cf. Franco Valsecchi: *Gli stati dell'Italia centrale e meridionale nel periodo anteriore alle Riforme* (1715-48), Milan and Niccolo Rodolico: *La Reggenza lorenese in Toscana* (1737-65), Prato, 1908.

6. *Tonnara*, a part of the shore on which the catch of tunny fish was laid out.

7. Abbé Coyer, of the Academies of Nancy, Rome and London: *Voyages d'Italie et de Hollande*, Paris, 1775, vol. II, p. 187.

8. Dupaty: *Lettres sur l'Italie en 1785*, p. 163. This must be taken *cum grano salis*, for if Dupaty was a close observer, he was also very anti-clerical. But such titles as 'devout member of the parish' and 'protector of the monastery' could in reality apply to all the members of Roman high society.

CHAPTER VII

1. President de Brosses wrote of Venice: 'The number of gondolas is infinite, and it is reckoned that no less than sixty thousand people live by the oar, either gondoliers or others'. This was a

O

considerable exaggeration, for in this way about half the people of Venice would have been 'living by the oar'. The census of 1766 listed 3,700 *barcaioli*.

2. The name alone, which means something like 'squabble-catcher', was a happy invention, but it has a more ludicrous flavour in Italian.

3. 'The tip for the customs officer.'

4. At Venice the guilds enjoyed the greatest freedom from internal regulation and, held in high esteem by the government which never took decisions about industrial matters without their advice, they were rich enough in the fifteenth to sixteenth centuries, owing to the contributions, gifts and legacies they received, not only to turn their head offices into such magnificent artistic treasures of the *Scuole* of *San Rollo* (tradesmen), *San Marco* (silk manufacturers and goldsmiths) and *San Giovanni Evangelista* (officials)—far surpassing even the delightful 'guild houses' in the Grand'Place at Brussels — but also to advance money to the State and place its loans with their clientele. On the accession of a new Doge, each guild went to the Palace to congratulate the successful candidate with standards, reliquaries, band playing and wearing gala dress, and the guilds were allowed to walk in procession beside the principal government dignitaries on the occasion of all official ceremonies, especially St Mark, Corpus Christi and Good Friday. Cf. René Guerdan, *Vie, Grandeurs et Misères de Venise*, Paris, 1959, pp. 195-9 ('*Des républiques en miniature*').

CHAPTER VIII

1. Ortolani, relying on the evidence of the Abbés Coyer and Richard, who were by no means naïve, and on a sound knowledge of every aspect of Venetian life, goes so far as to write: 'Contrary to the general opinion I firmly believe that political and moral customs in the middle of the eighteenth century had improved in relation to the preceding century'. (*Voci e visioni del Settecento veneziano*, p. 78.)

2. 'There is little cicisbeism at Naples, women of quality go about more or less indifferently with anyone . . . It is by no means against normal usage for women to visit bachelors in their homes.' (Lalande, vol. VI, p. 339.)

3. Montesquieu also makes an inaccurate assertion when writing about Venice: 'It is no longer shameful to marry one's courtesan, even for those who have been honoured with the

highest offices'. On the contrary, the Venetian government was quite implacable about this. The *Notes of the State Inquisitors* for May 5, 1765 state that: 'A certain Carlina, a ballerina, who had brought a young man belonging to a notable patrician family to the monstrous decision of marrying her, was expelled for ever'. (*Arch. di Stato, anni* 1763-9.) Lalande, who was better informed, mentions that: 'It is very rare for the marriage of a Venetian nobleman to a townswoman to be approved by the Grand Council, and there is not a single example in the highest families'. Therefore, *a fortiori*, with a courtesan.

4. Cf. Benedetto Croce: *I Teatri di Napoli*, pp. 208 and 261.

CHAPTER IX

1. Pompeo Molmenti, pp. 452-4.
2. The *Avogadori di Commune* played a similar part in the Venetian constitution to that of the tribunes of the plebs in Ancient Rome.
3. Abbé Richard: *Description historique et critique de l'Italie*, vol. II, p. 181.
4. We have seen in Chap. III that at Milan Maria-Theresa had forbidden the dressing of servants in mourning and using death as an excuse for an unseemly display of luxury.
5. Casotti: *Lettere da Venezia 1713*, Prato, 1866, p. 22 et seq.
6. Texts quoted by Hélène Tuzet, p. 385.
7. Grosley, vol. I, p. 93.
8. Quoted by Hélène Tuzet, pp. 355-6.
9. In the records of the confraternity for 1701 we find the appointment as *Capo di Guardia of Cardinal Francesco-Maria de' Medici*, founder of the academy of the *Cemento*; for 1707, that of Ferdinand de' Medici, hereditary prince; for 1723, that of Giovanni-Gaston, last Grand Duke of the Medici family, and for 1726, that of Cardinal Lorenzo Corsini, who became Pope Clement XII.
10. At Milan, burial in churches was permitted until 1778. The hospital had its own cemetery to which the bodies were carried. The nobles generally arranged to be buried in their fiefs.

CHAPTER X

1. The *Educazione*, taken from the edition of *Satire e poesie minori* established by Giosuè Carducci, Florence, Barbera, 1858, Sat. VI, p. 39.
2. We may recall here that Parini, together with Alfieri the

greatest Italian poet of the eighteenth century, had to leave the Serbelloni household for having taken the part of a servant unjustly slapped by the Duchess. A famous episode in the *Giorno*, inspired by similar feelings, relates the case of an old servant ruthlessly dismissed after twenty years of faithful service, for having kicked his mistress's favourite lap-dog, which had bitten his wrist. An aggravating circumstance: the Duchess's rancour, spreading the story of the misdeed among the nobility, would prevent the guilty person from finding other employment! The passion for lapdogs was just as keen at Venice in the eighteenth century.

3. Born in Corfu in 1760, married in spite of her repugnance at sixteen to an old and learned patrician, Isabella Teotochi managed to get this union annulled and in 1786 married Guiseppe Albrizzi. She led a most worthy life and had a lofty mind; she lived until 1836, continually in the centre of Venetian high society.

CHAPTER XI

1. Ripano, an almost complete anagram of Parini, Eupilino from the name of the poet's native village, Bosisio, on the small lake of Pusiano, in Brianza, called Eupili by Pliny in the past.

2. 'Jurisdictionalism' was the name given to the tendency to submit to the jurisdiction of the State a host of mixed questions which also concerned the Church, but which the latter felt that she alone had the right to resolve.

3. Cf. J. Leflon: *Pie VII*, Paris, 1958, p. 148.

4. The famous compiler Sandras de Courtilz, founder of the *Mercure* at The Hague, had Jean Rousset de Missy as his successor. Cf. Eugene Hatin: *Les Gazettes de Hollande et la Presse clandestine aux XVIIe et XVIIIe siècles*, Paris, 1865.

5. Cf. Philippe Monnier: *Venise au XVIIIe siècle*, p. 17.

CHAPTER XII

1. The great archaeologist Winckelmann, chairman of the commission on Roman antiquities, was assassinated at Trieste in 1768, on his return from a journey in Germany, by a habitual criminal called Archangeli.

2. In the Roman countryside and the Sabine mountains there were wolves into the bargain. About 100 were killed yearly.

3. This fact is related by Father Labat: vol. IV, p. 21.

4. Dupaty: pp. 411-2.
5. Part of the dress of clergymen of fairly high rank, usually of pleated silk or broadcloth, which was attached to the shoulders behind and fell to the ground.
6. According to a report by the Austrian legation a man condemned to ten years in the galleys could be freed for forty *scudi*, on an average.
7. David Silvagni: *La Corte e la società romana nei secoli* XVIII *e* XIX, vol. II, pp. 95 et seq.
8. Wolfgang Goethe: *Italienische Reise*—Stuttgart and Tübingen, 1827-42.

CHAPTER XIV

1. The funcion of senator of Rome was practically equivalent to that of mayor as regards entertainment, but with less extensive effective powers, especially in police matters, which came under the governor, who was always a prelate. The conservators were roughly the same as town councillors.
2. Every pontiff, with very rare exceptions, entrusted a cardinal of his household, generally a nephew, with a sort of delegated power over the temporal administration of the Papal State, which he was unable to undertake himself. He was the official known as the cardinal *padrone*. The most influential in the eighteenth century were the cardinals Alexandre Albani, Neri Corsini and Braschi, nephews of Clement XI, Clement XII and Pius VI respectively.
3. Goethe: *Italienische Reise*.
4. 'May he who does not carry a candle be knocked senseless.'
5. Pompeo Molmenti: p. 512.
6. Only a few years ago a sumptuous ball in the Beistegui, formerly the Labia, Palace moved out into the middle of the street under the very eyes of the astonished *popolani* who were not in the least jealous by a display of wealth which was so far removed from their own situation.
7. The clumsily flattering expression is taken from the official minutes of the day given by the *Gazzetta Patria*.
8. Hélène Tuzet: pp. 375-6, after Houël's account.
9. The praetor at Palermo, an office filled by a member of the high nobility, was the equivalent of the senator of Rome, i.e. the mayor.
10. The *bara* was the stretcher used for transporting invalids or dying people, but also the support for the reliquaries of saints.

11. Hélène Tuzet: p. 364.
12. Cf. Maurice Vaussard: *Les Lettres viennoises de Giovanni Lami* in the *Revue des Etudes italiennes*, 1955, nos. 3-4, pp. 159-60.

CHAPTER XV
1. Pompeo Molmenti: p. 518.
2. Parini: *Le Jour*, Paris, Editions Montaigne, 1931, pp. 171-2.

CHAPTER XVI
1. Grosley: vol. II, p. 102.
2. Abbé Coyer: p. 209.
3. Remo Giazotto: *La Musica a Genova*, p. 196. The new Falcone was destroyed in 1942 by the Anglo-American bombardments of Genoa, as well as five other theatres. It was in the courtyard of the Falcone Theatre that Goldoni met Nicoletta Conio who became his wife.
4. The Paris Opéra has thirty-five boxes with six seats per storey, not including the stage-boxes, and the salle Richelieu of the Comédie-Française twenty-nine with four to seven seats on the only storey which does not have separate stalls, the second.
5. Benedetto Groce: *I Teatri di Napoli*, passim.
6. P. Molmenti, p. 506.
7. P. Goldoni: *Mémoires pour servir à l'histoire de sa vie et de son théâtre*. Paris, 1787, part one, chap. XXXVIII.
8. G. Morazzoni, *La Scala*.

CHAPTER XVII
1. Ettore Verga: *Le Corporazioni delle industrie tessili in Milano. Loro raporti e conflitti nei secoli XVI-XVIII*, in the *Archivio storico lombardo*, 1903, No. 19, p. 23. We are considerably indebted to this scholar's excellent study.
2. The 'tanks' in silk spinning are receptacles containing almost boiling soapy water which make it possible to find, with the help of brooms, the end of the thread emerging from the cocoon and roll it up. The assembly of eight to twelve or even more of these natural threads produces the silk thread which is used in industry. Today these operations are carried out automatically with a mechanical broom and factories are described as having 80, 100 or 120 tanks. Originally craftsmen often performed this work at home with primitive equipment.
3. Abbé Coyer: *op. cit.*, vol. I, p. 78.

4. Cf. Ruggiero Romano: *Le Commerce du royaume de Naples avec la France et les pays de l'Adriatique au XVIIIe siècle*, Paris, 1951.

CHAPTER XVIII

1. Cf. Umberto Silvagni in his valuable book, *La Corte e la società romana nei secoli XVIII e XIX*, largely based on the daily notes taken during the second half of the eighteenth century by Father Benedetti, a family friend of the Colonna's.
2. In the budget of monasteries in Padua, these rents were normally reckoned at 30 lire per annum.
3. Marino Berengo: *La Società veneta alla fine del Settecento*, pp. 106-9.
4. The decimal system and the establishment of the Lira at five grams of silver with a standard of 900 thousandths, by assimilation to the franc, were introduced into the Kingdom of Italy under the Napoleonic regime and extended to united Italy in 1862.
5. Luigi dal Pane: *Storia del lavoro in Italia dagli inizi del secolo XVIII al 1815*, p. 217.
6. Luigi dal Pane: *op. cit.*, p. 211.
7. Henri Bedarida: *Parme et la France de 1748 à 1789*, pp. 82 and 143.
8. Lalande: vol. VI, p. 391.

1. *Journal de correspondances et voyages d'Italie et d'Espagne pour la paix de l'Eglise en 1758, 1768 et 1769*, Paris, 1802, vol. I, p. 52.
2. We must thank him for the information that at Rome on Maunday Thursday, the pope served the cardinals he invited to dinner with fresh cherries from the Kingdom of Naples from trees which were forced by the lavish use of manure and watering with hot water.

   During the week the Dominicans of St Jerome at Messina were served at mealtimes with five or six kinds of fish cooked with saffron; excellent fruit and melons; iced wine in large wooden pitchers with bands of red copper which were changed from time to time to put them back in the snow which replaced ice in Sicily; chocolate and coffee. On Sundays, the meal with meat, when the monk who acted as cook surpassed himself, included: 'as an entrée two fairly large white onions with a saffron sauce. I opened one,' commented Father Labat, 'and I found it stuffed with minced meat, pine kernels, raisins from Corinth, coriander and glacéd lemon peel. It seemed to me an exceptional dish. It was a delicately flavoured excellently seasoned pâté which only had as crust three layers of white onions. After this dish, we were served a minestrone with vermicelli covered with beaten cinnamon; next came a quarter of larded breast of beef which was tender and cooked to a turn . . . ' Together with melon and cheese this was the normal fare of the community. For Father Labat and his companion they added 'a piece of roast veal which would have been enough for four men with good appetites'.

3. A popular saying at Florence made fun of the passion for this vegetable as follows:

> Fiorentin mangia fagiuoli
> Lecca piatti e tovaglioli.
> (The Florentine eats haricot beans,
> Licks the dishes and the napkins.)

BIBLIOGRAPHY

Addison (Joseph): *Remarks on several parts of Italy in the years 1701-1703*, London, 1705.
Remarques sur divers endroits d'Italie par Mr Addison pour servir de supplément au voyage de Mr Misson, Paris, 1722.

Bailly (Auguste): *La Sérénissime République de Venise*, Paris, 1946.

Barthelemy (Abbé J.-J.): *Voyage en Italie*. Letters to Comte de Caylus. Published by A. Serieys, Paris, 1801.

Beccaria (Cesare): *Traité des Délits et des Peines*, translated from the Italian from the 3rd edition (by André Morellet), with additions by the author, Lausanne, 1766.

Bedarida (Henri): *Parme et la France de 1748 à 1789*, Paris, 1928.

Beltrami (Daniele): *Storia della popolazione di Venezia dalla fine del secolo XVI alla caduta della Repubblica*, Padua, 1954.

Berengo (Marino): *La Società veneta alla fine del Settecento*, Florence, 1956.

Bernis (François-Joachim de Pierres de): *Lettres et Mémoires du cardinal de Bernis*, published by Fr Masson, 2 vols., Paris, 1878.

Bertarelli (A.) and Monti (A.): *Tre secoli di vita milanese (1630-1875)*, Milan, 1927.

Bocage (Mme du): *Lettres sur l'Italie*, vol. III of the 'Recueil des Œuvres', Lyons, 1762.

Bottari (S.), Cocchiara (G.), Giunta (F.), Raffiotta (G.), Santangelo (G.): *Storia, arte, letteratura, economia, problemi sociali e tradizioni popolari della Sicilia dal secolo XII ai nostri giorni*, Palermo, 1951.

Bouvier (René) and Laffargue (André): *La Vie napolitaine au XVIIIe siècle*, Paris 1956.

Brosses (Charles de): *Lettres familières sur l'Italie*, published by Yvonne Bézard, 2 vols., Paris, 1931.

Brydone (Patrick): *A tour through Sicily and Malta*, 2 vols., London, 1773.

Cambiaso (Domenico): *l'anno ecclesiastico e le feste dei Santi a Genova nel loro svolgimento storico* in Atti della Società Ligure di Storia patria, vol. XLVIII, Genoa, 1917.

Caylus (Comte de): *Voyage d'Italie 1714-1715*, published by Amilda A. Pons, Paris, 1914.

Cochin (C.-N.): *Voyage pittoresque d'Italie*, Paris, 1751.

Comisso (Giovanni): *Les Agents secrets de Venise au XVIIIe siècle*. Translation by Lucien Leluc, Paris, 1944.

Concari (Tullo): *Il Settecento*, Milan, no date.

Conti (Giuseppe): *Firenze dopo i Medici*, Florence, 1921.

Coyer (Abbé Gabriel-François): *Voyages d'Italie et de Hollande*, 2 vols., Paris, 1775.

Croce (Benedetto): *I teatri di Napoli dal Rinascimento alla fine del secolo decimottavo*, Bari, 1916.
La vita religiosa a Napoli nel 1700 in Uomini e cose della vecchia Italia, vol. II, Bari, 1927.

Dal Pane (Luigi): *Il Tramonto delle corporazioni in Italia*, Milan, 1940. *Storia del lavoro in Italia dagli inizi del secolo XVIII al 1815*, 2nd edition, Milan, 1958.

Denon (Vivant): *Voyage en Sicile*, Paris, 1788.

Dolcetti (Giovanni): *Le Bischeo il Giucco d'azzardo a Venezia*, Venice, 1903.

Dupaty (J.-B.): *Lettres sur l'Italie en 1785*, Paris, 1786 (published anonymously).

Fattorello (F.): *Il giornalismo veneto nel Settecento*, 2 vols., Udine, 1933.

Gallenga (Antonio): *Storia del Piemonte dai primi tempi alla pace di Parigi del 30 marzo 1856*, Turin, 1856.

Giazotto (Remo): *La Musica a Genova*, Genoa, 1951.

Goethe (Wolfgang): *Italienische Reise*—vols. XXVIII and XXIX of *Goethes Werke*, Stuttgart and Tübingen, 1827-42.

Goldoni (Carlo): *Mémoires pour servir à l'histoire de sa vie et à celle de son théâtre*, Paris, 1787.
Opere teatrali, 44 vols., Venice, 1788-95.

Gorani (Joseph): *Mémoires secrets et curieux des cours, des gouvernements et des moeurs des principaux Etats de l'Italie*, 3 vols., Paris, 1793. *Mémoires*, first French edition established by Alexandre Casati, annotated by Raoul Girardet, Paris, 1945.

Grosley (P.-J.): *Observations on Italy and the Italians made in 1764 by two Swedish gentlemen*, 2 vols., London, 1770.

Hamy, S. J. (Alfred): *Documents pour servir à l'histoire des domiciles de la Compagnie de Jésus de 1540 à 1773*, Paris, no date.

Hayward (Fernand): *Le Dernier Siècle de la Rome pontificale, 1769-1870*, 2 vols., Paris, 1927.

Houel (Jean): *Voyage pittoresque des isles de Sicile, de Lipari et de Malte*, 4 vols., Paris, 1782-7.

Kovalevsky (Maxime): *La Fin d'une Aristocratie*, Turin, 1901. Translated from the Russian by Casimir de Kranz.

Labat, O. P. (J.B.): *Voyages en Espagne et en Italie*, 8 vols., Paris, 1730.

Lalande (Jérôme Lefrançais de): *Voyage d'un Français en Italie fait dans les années 1765 et 1766*, 8 vols., Paris, 1768. Published anonymously.

Leflon (J.): *Pie VII. Des abbayes bénédictines à la Papauté*, vol. I, Paris, 1958.

Lensi (Alfredo): *Il gioco del calcio fiorentino*, Florence, 1931.

Longo (Antonio): *Memorie della vita de Antonio Longo veneziano scritte e pubblicate da lui medesimo per umiltà*, 4 vols., Venice, 1820.

Malamani (Vittorio): *Isabella Teotochi-Albrizzi, i suoi amici, il suo tempo*, Turin, 1883.

Il Settecento a Venezia, 2 vols., Turin, 1891-2.

Misson (Maximilien): *Voyage d'Italie*, 4 vols., The Hague, 1724.

Molmenti (Pompeo): *La Vie privée à Venise depuis les premiers temps jusqu'à la chute de la République*, Venice, 1882.

La Dogaressa, Turin, 1887.

Il decadimento politico ed economico della Repubblica veneta, in *Nuova Antologia*, February 16, 1907.

Epistolari veneziani del secolo XVIII, Palermo, no date.

Monnier (Philippe): *Venise au XVIIIe siècle*, Paris, 1907.

Montesquieu: *Voyages*, published by Baron Albert de Montesquieu, Bordeaux, 1894.

Morazzoni (Giuseppe): *La Moda a Venezia nel secolo XVIII*, Milan, 1931.

La Scala, Milan, 1946.

Morena (Abele): *Le riforme e le dottrine economiche in Toscana*, in *Rassegna Nazionale*, 1886.

Morpurgo (Emilio): *Marco Foscarini e la Venezia del secolo XVIII*, Florence, 1880.

Occioni-Bonaffous (G.): *La Republica di Venezia alla vigilia della Rivoluzione francese*, in *Rivista storca italiana*, 1889.

Ortolani (Giuseppe): *Voci e visioni del Settecento veneziano*, Bologna, 1926.

Parini (Giuseppe): *Le Jour (Il Giorno)*, translated by Sébastien Camugli, Paris, 1931. Bilingual collection of foreign classics.

Prato (Giuseppe): *La vita economica in Piemonte a mezzo del secolo XVIII*, Turin, 1908.

Pugliese (S.): *Condizioni economiche e finanziarie della Lombardia nella prima metà del secolo XVIII*, Turin, 1924.

Rabany (Charles): *Charles Goldoni, le théâtre et la vie en Italie au XVIIIe siècle*, Paris, 1896.

Renier-Michiel (Giustina): *La Festa del fresco*, published by V. Busetto, Venice, 1845.

Ricci (Corrado): *L'Architecture baroque en Italie*, Paris, no date [1932].

Richard (Abbé J.): *Description historique et critique de l'Italie*, 6 vols., Paris, 1766.

Roland de la Platière (Jean-Marie): *Lettres écrites de Sicile et de Malte, par M . . . , Avocat en Parlement*, 6 vols., Amsterdam, 1780.

Rolland (Romain): *La Musique en Italie au XVIIIᵉ siècle*, in the *Revue de Paris*, August 15, 1905.

Romanin (Samuele): *Storia documentata della Repubblica de Venezia*, 10 vols., Venice, 1853-61.

Romano (Ruggiero): *Le Commerce du royaume de Naples avec la France et les pays de l'Adriatique au XVIIIᵉ siècle*, Paris, 1951.

Rota (Ettore): *Le origini del Risorgimento 1700-1800*, first revised and corrected reprinting, 2 vols., Milan, 1948.

Rousseau (J.-J.): *Confessions*, books VI and VII.

Saint-Beuve: *Mémoires de Casanova de Seingalt*, in the *Premiers Lundis*, Paris, 1875, vol. II.

Saint-Non (Abbé Richard de): *Voyage pittoresque de Naples et de Sicile*, 4 vols., Paris, 1781-6.

Salvestrini (Virgilio): *Il gioco del Ponte di Pisa*, Pisa, 1933.

Silvagni (Davide): *La Corte e la Società romana nei secoli XVIII e XIX*, 3 vols., Rome, 1883.

Swinburne (Henry): *Travels in the two Sicilies*, 2 vols., London, 1783.

Tuzet (Hélène): *La Sicile au XVIIIᵉ siècle vu par les voyageurs étrangers*, Strasbourg, 1955.

Valsecchi (Franco): *Gli Stati del l'Italia centrale e meridionale nel periodo anteriore alle Riforme (1715-1748)*, Milan, 1954.

Verga (Ettore): *Le Corporazioni delle industrie tessili in Milano*, in the *Archivio Storico Lombardo*, 1903, section XXXVII.

Vianello (C. A.): *Il Settecento milanese*, Milan, 1934.

Visconti (Alessandro): *Le Condizioni degli operai agli albori dell' industria libera in Lombardia nel secolo XVIII*, Milan, 1923.

Young (Arthur): *Voyages en Espagne et Italie pendant les années 1787 et 1789*, translated by Lesage, Paris, 1860.

INDEX